BROKEN GIRL FLY

Overcoming the Trauma of Childhood Sexual Abuse With the Love of Jesus

MELISSA KAY OLSON

Paper Wings Publications LLC

Scripture quotations marked NIV are taken from The Holy Bible, New International Version®, NIV®. Copyright © 1973, 1978, 1984, 2011 by Biblica, Inc.™ Used by permission of Zondervan. All rights reserved worldwide. www.zondervan.com.
Other Scripture quotations are slightly paraphrased by the author.

Library of Congress Control Number 2021924162

This is my story written from memory. My first-degree relatives have given me permission to use their names and/or likenesses in this story. Second and third-degree relatives have been modified to protect their privacy. All other characters have been fictionalized. Some names, dates, and locations have been changed or fictionalized for privacy.

www.BrokenGirlFly.com

For Lana . . .

Taste and see that the Lord is good; blessed is the one who takes refuge in Him.

—Psalm 34:8 (NIV)

CONTENTS

BROKEN GIRL FLY

DEAR FRIEND

I need you to know something. This is a hard story. It contains child sexual abuse, drug abuse, alcoholism, depression, anxiety, suicidal ideation, and a whole host of ugly.

When God first called me to write my story, I told Him, *No, thank you very much!* And then He pushed and pushed until I shook my fist at Him, sat down, and began typing smack in the middle of the dirty. I popped on my headphones, turned on AC/DC, and got mad as a hornet. But, as I obeyed and did the work, something weird happened. I felt lighter. And the deeper I went, the lighter I became.

Sitting where I am today, with my manuscript complete and the story told, I realize the writing is not just for me. It's also for you. It's for the person sitting in the back of the room, at the back of the bus, on the back pew in church. It's for the person wearing the bold "fake it 'til you make it" attitude. It's for the person donning a brave mask to cover the secrets scarring their soul.

It's for the person who needs to know it's okay to be broken. It's okay to seek help. It's okay to heal. And it's for the friend, relative, partner or spouse walking alongside a loved one wounded by sexual abuse. This book is for all of you, whether you know God or not. Please read it and be encouraged. You are not alone. And you are loved.

Regardless of your religious beliefs, I hope God becomes a safe place and a refuge where you can wrestle. He can handle your pain, your emotions, your questions, and your anger. He's a good Dad, and He's waiting for you to duke it out with Him. Because that's what good dads do.

Shine Brightly,
Melissa

A WORD OF CAUTION

If you are a survivor of abuse, read this story with caution as you may be triggered, saddened, angered, or confused. If you are just beginning your journey to healing and count yourself brave enough to enter these pages alone, please remember to set the book aside if you feel overwhelmed. Take a break, say a prayer, call a trusted friend, or schedule a therapy appointment.

If you are in an abusive relationship or if your life is in danger, please take the steps needed to find safe shelter. You can contact your local authorities via 9-1-1 or reach out for help via the National Domestic Violence Hotline at: www.thehotline.org, 1-800-799-SAFE(7233), or text the word START to 88788.

This book is my story. I am not a licensed mental healthcare professional. While this writing is meant to encourage you to be brave and courageous, I do not know your story, or the risks associated with navigating through it. Please walk with wisdom and seek professional counsel when needed.

Please remember that child abuse is a crime. Should you choose to share your story with others, please do so with careful consideration as there may be serious repercussions that follow.

INTRODUCTION

Tangled in Lies

I lie weeping, my body curled in a fetal position, on the dry bed of a blue kiddie pool. The loose rocks peppering the concrete driveway poke through the plastic, needling my arms, legs, and the side of my face, but I don't care. My heart aches more, trampled and crushed like the soft shell of a robin's egg when it falls from the nest.

"Can someone please shut her up?" a boy asks, nudging the side of the pool.

My best friend, Jess, leans down beside me.

"Missy," she says, "can you get out of the pool?"

"No! I'm not getting up until I know he loves me!"

"Sweetie, he's over this mess. You need to get out of the pool."

My stomach churns with the suds of pale ale and whiskey shots. Liquid crazy pulses through my veins as I lie on Brent's driveway and cry. The party rages on despite my tears, with bass thumping out the windows, clouds of smoke drifting into the autumn air, and the laughter of drunken teens mocking my brokenness.

"I want him to love me," I say, rolling a beer bottle between my palms.

"Someone's going to call the cops, if you don't shut up," the boy says again, kicking the pool this time.

I jump up and holler, "Screw you, Jake," then take off running down the street, screaming at the top of my lungs.

A neighbor dressed in a bathrobe walks out her front door and says, "Hey, little girl! Quiet!"

"Shut up, witch!" I scream, collapsing onto her grass.

"I'm calling the sheriff," she says, marching back inside.

"Screw you!" I yell, tossing my beer bottle behind her.

"Damn it, Missy!" Jess says, helping me to my feet. "Shut your drunk ass up."

"What if the cops show up?" I ask. "I'll be busted!"

"We'll all be busted," Jess says, staggering with me to the camper parked alongside the curb. Brent's parents aren't home. They would never consent to a bunch of middle schoolers partying in their house. Jess pushes me inside the RV and snaps the door shut behind us. Then my other friend, Traci, pulls me in for a hug, hands me a beer, and says, "You're okay."

"Why doesn't he love me?" I ask again, pulling in a long swig.

She doesn't answer. No one ever does. The stupid thing is, I know why Brent doesn't love me, but I dare not say it out loud. If I say it, my stupidity becomes real. And I'm not ready to face my own stupidity.

I wipe the snot off my nose and glance at the faces staring at me. Jess, Traci, and Mandy. These girls are my crew. And the boys outside are, too, only they're brash. Especially when they drink. The scary thing is all these people think my crazy is about Brent. They all think I'm nuts about a boy. That the booze and pot bring out a loopy, pathetic affection for a guy who doesn't love me.

They are wrong.

I squeeze my fist into a ball and peer down at my swollen knuckles. I like to punch things, like the floor, my locker, and school desks, hoping to get someone's attention, hoping someone will notice. The truth is, if I were brave, I'd be covered in cuts. I'd take the X-Acto knife from our utility drawer at home, and I'd slice the sharp blade down the belly of my forearm like a fisherman gutting salmon. That's a funny analogy. My dad's a fisherman. I've watched him fillet plenty of fish, spill their guts out on the ground, peel the skin off them. He's filleted me, too.

I want to tell my friends the truth, want them to know why I scream and cry and drink and run. Why I want someone to see me. I'm looking for a pure love. An unadulterated, untouched, unmarred love. Someone who loves me for me. Someone who knows all the dirty about me and still loves me. I know he isn't Brent or any other boy. At least, deep inside my spirit I know. But for now, I'm following what all those fairy tales, Hollywood movies, and romance novels tell me. Real love is found in a boy.

Someone outside yells, "Cops!"

I peek out the window to see red and blue lights. Someone opens the trailer door and shoves me out, saying, "Run, Missy! Run and hide." I trip going down the stairs, then crawl on my hands and knees toward a parked car, slide underneath, and hold my breath to listen. A car door slams, muffled voices fill the air, but I can't hear what they are saying. Until they move closer.

"Her name is Missy. I don't know her last name," Traci says.

"Where is she?" asks the cop.

"She ran when you got here. Out through that field," she says.

"Crap!" I whisper. The car I'm under is parked beside the field.

His flashlight dances over the pavement as he walks toward me. I nuzzle between the wheels and lie with my body parallel to the axle. Traci and the cop stand so close, I could touch their ankles.

"Call her name," the cop says.

"Missy!"

I push up into a plank position, shove my back against the car's rear axle, and pray he doesn't find me.

"Do it again," he says.

"Missy!"

I hold my breath.

"She's long gone," Traci says.

The cop spins around so his toes are facing me, bends over, and shines his light under the car. My heart pounds so loud, I wonder if he can hear it. He flicks the spotlight back and forth, then stands up and walks to another vehicle. The shuffle of his feet fades away, but I hold my position, and my breath, until I hear him say, "If you see her, tell her to go home."

His car door slams, lights flick off, and tires creep away over damp pavement before I climb out of my hiding place. When I reappear, Traci says, "Where did you go? I thought you were busted!"

"I hid under a car," I say, pointing behind me.

"The car we were standing behind?" she asks.

"Yeah," I say, as Jess grabs my hand.

"But he looked under that car," Traci says.

"I know! I was squeezed between the tires, pressed up underneath it!"

"Damn, you're lucky!"

"Time to go," Jess says, pulling me down the driveway.

"You two walk safe," Traci says, climbing back inside the camper.

My best friend and I shuffle down the road with white puffs of foggy air trailing behind us. Johnny's house is only a few blocks away. His house is the party house. He's got no mom, his dad's never home, and his door is always unlocked. Jess and I plan to crash there tonight.

I drape my arm around Jess and lean into her strawberry blonde hair.

"I love you, Jess," I say with a slur.

"I love you, too," she says.

"I'm sure glad somebody loves me," I say, pulling a Marlboro from my pocket.

The next morning, Jess and I trek back to our neighborhood as the sun rises, then part ways at the edge of my cul-de-sac. I sigh in relief as I round the corner and notice my father's car missing from the driveway. Dad is probably fishing, which is good, since gone is what I like best about him. I sneak through the front door, hold my breath and listen for Mom. I hear the dryer door clang shut. Mom's down in the basement doing weekend laundry. I take a deep breath and tiptoe upstairs to my room where I collapse onto my bed and hope to get some sleep. A rumbling in my tummy forces me to sit up, breathe deep, and count to ten. No luck. I jump out of bed and run for the toilet.

Brown puke runs out my nose as I heave, tossing the remnants of last night's party. I try to barf quietly, which is impossible, so I formulate my lie as waves of nausea roll in my belly. Food poisoning. I'll tell Mom Jess made nachos with some old hamburger. That ought to do it. I brush my teeth, pull my hair into a scrunchie, and tiptoe back to bed. Sleep rolls over me like a blanket, lulling me into a world of dreams, when a knock at the door makes me jump.

"Hey, honey," Mom says, poking her head in. "Can we chat a minute?"

I push myself to sit, grip my belly, and nod my head.

"You smell like beer," Mom says.

Gulp.

"Were you out drinking last night?"

"Me and Jess had a couple beers with her sister," I say.

My parents are not super strict about what we do, so long as we're safe. My lie should slide right past her.

"Are you lying?" she asks.

My eyes grow wide as I say no.

"We drove past Jessica's house last night," she says. "No one was home."

Uh-oh.

"So tell me the truth. Where were you last night?"

"I slept at Jessie's," I say, lying again.

Momma holds my gaze for several seconds before letting out a long sigh. She shakes her head, then stands to go, saying, "Dad and I are going to the Petersons' for dinner tonight. Want to tag along?"

"No, thank you."

"You sure? Your brother is at Chris's, so you'll be home alone. It gets dark early now."

"I'm not a baby, Mom. And I'm not afraid of the dark," I say

9

with an eye roll.

"Okay, fine. No friends tonight," she says, walking out the door.

Fine by me. I probably don't have friends after last night anyway, I think to myself before collapsing back into a long, dark sleep.

♥

I watch the headlights of our blue Chevy back down the drive and breathe a sigh of relief as my parents head out for the evening. As I stare outside, a muddled reflection peers back at me through the window, distorted by the amber glow of my bedroom lamp and the trickles of rain freckling the glass. I stop to drink her in.

My family sees a petite, brown-eyed, zany girl who doesn't care what people think, say, or do. They know a girl who's a bit of a troublemaker, but also happy and free and full of life. But she's a lie. A 1980s' composite of *Wonder Woman* reruns, Guns and Roses rock songs, and Madonna's *Like a Virgin* attitude. She's the girl I make up every time I cake on three inches of foundation, slip on my stirrup pants, and tease my long brown curls into a tower of mall bangs. She's the skin I put on to be cool with my friends and keep things chill at home.

But she's a shadow, a ghost, an aberration. Behind her cheerful demeanor lies a heart drowning in despair, grief, and fear. And secrets. Oh, the secrets. If people only knew how dirty, shameful, and used up she is.

The girl in the window, she's the girl I know, with her mangled features and mascara-stained cheeks. The girl I know wants to die. Sometimes I wonder if this story will end with me jumping off a bridge. Mom says suicide is the unforgivable sin. What if she's right? I don't want to spend eternity with the devil. I'm already living with him. He pops out when I least expect it, turning my father's irises midnight black when he shoves his accusations in my face. Satan himself thunders over me every time Dad screams at me. Satan himself whispers in my ear when . . .

I pinch my eyes at the thought, turn from the window, like a million times before, and grab a tissue off my dresser.

"Where did this sadness come from?" I wonder aloud. It's like a virus or a curse in my DNA, this propensity to drown in my own sorrow. My father has it, too. So does his mother. But they have good reason.

I blow my nose, wander toward the living room, plop down in front of the coffee table, and pull out an old photo album. Mom calls it my baby book. Memories of my first three years on earth rest inside its stained leather cover. Each photo sits in its own paper square with Mom's silky handwriting telling the who, what, and when of each scene. They say things like "Missy's first bath" or "Missy wearing Daddy's army hat," along with a date and place. Momma's good at loving me like this. She's good at remembering and celebrating the people in her life.

I flip past the pages of Mom's pregnancy, her youthful face shining and happy, standing in front of a Pike National Forest sign next to my father. I remember the tale of Daddy meeting Momma when he returned from Vietnam, of him going AWOL to ask Granddad for Momma's hand in marriage. His valiant proposal landed him in the brig.

I flip to the pictures of my momma's family. Granddad cradling me in his big hands, Grandma in her skinny arms. My aunt Kathy feeding me a bottle. She died a few years later when I was five and she was eighteen. I exhale, feel the weight of her loss on my heart. In four short years, I will be eighteen. I pull out Kathy's photo for closer inspection, lay a kiss on her paper cheek, tuck her back in her sleeve, and turn the pages.

I bypass birthday cakes and Christmas trees until I find the picture I'm looking for. The one with my father standing shirtless, a stark black wizard tattoo covering his heart, his wavy black hair pulled into a mass of beaded braids. These were the dreadlocks of the seventies. He holds a pipe in his hands and a deep well of grief in his eyes. He's not doing anything special in the photo. There's no funeral or loss of any kind. There's just my dad, his funky hair, and an air of sadness all around him.

I stare at the photo for a long time and try to understand. Or maybe try to remember an event locked away in the recesses of my mind. I think Dad's despair jumped on me when I was maybe four or five. I would sit and stare at this photo, let all the dark emotion in Daddy's eyes climb off the page and slither past the windows of my soul. It's a strange spiritual kind of thing I can't explain. It's as if I'm addicted to this darkness, this abyss of unhappiness. It's abstract, yet as real as any flame I can touch, and it burns my soul even now.

I snap the book shut on his face, pull a shoe box off the shelf, flick open the lid, and grab a handful of grainy photos. I love to remember; to hear Mom's words ring in my head as I stare at each picture. The funny stories she and Dad tell around the kitchen table on hot summer nights. I love it when Dad talks about how Mom dropped out of college to drink beer and hang her ass out the car window. "That's why I fell in love with her," he says.

I also love the story of me asking Granddad if he was smoking hash in his tobacco pipe. Hey, I was four years old. How was I to know my parents were a couple of liars? Since then, my family of four has grown accustomed to lying to my grandparents. We never mention the marijuana, the cocaine, or the LSD someone slipped into my daddy's drink one time in the desert.

"Who tells their kids stories about dropping acid in the desert?" I wonder aloud. "Only my jacked-up family."

I say this with a conflicted heart, because at the same time I judge Mom and Dad, I also thank them for teaching me to never use angel dust or heroin.

"PCP will make you think you can fly," Momma says. "People jump off buildings and bridges when they do that stuff."

"Don't ever stick needles in your veins, Missy," Dad says.

"You can't come back from shooting black tar."

"Thanks for teaching me to stay away from the dangerous drugs," I say to the photos in my hand.

Sighing deeply, I decide to indulge this harmony of joy and sorrow a bit longer. Maybe in my pondering, I can figure out where my sadness came from. I pull a Fleetwood Mac album from its sleeve and drop it on the turntable. Then I thumb through the photos while Stevie Nicks's gritty voice pulls me back to the sticky scent of honeysuckle.

PART 1

The Breaking

1

Jesus In A House Of Hippies

We stand on the splintered boards of a three-walled shack in the Blue Ridge Mountains of North Carolina. My baby brother, Stacy, snuggles into Momma's chest, sucking his thumb. The three of us watch a man with brown hair, braided to his waist, sit cross-legged on the floor. He lights a long pipe, draws in a puff of smoke, and hands it to my father. There are no doors on his house, no glass in the windows, and the roof is ramshackle old, pocked by holes and tree branches. The summer sun creeps in, broken into splotches by pines, maples, and the spider webs draping across the open windowpanes.

I cup my four-year-old fist around Momma's ear and ask, "Is that Jesus?"

"No," Momma says in a whisper, "that's Erik."

"He looks like Jesus on the wall at church," I say in a hush.

"He's not," she says, shifting the weight of my baby brother on her hip.

The smoke wafts out of Daddy's mouth, drifting through the air and up my nostrils. It smells like skunk, making me want to scrunch my face. Stacy wriggles and turns away when Momma takes a long drag from the pipe and hands it to Erik.

"Why don't they sting him?" I ask Momma, watching fat bumblebees root on Erik's arm.

"I don't know, but he's not Jesus," she says.

My heart sinks. I wish we were sitting with Jesus. I learned all about Him in Sunday school. How He loves all the little children of the world, how He loves me, how He is God's only Son. He died on a cross and came to life again. Momma says

He lives in heaven and on earth at the same time. He's in two places at once. Only we can't see Him. He's like a ghost.

I stare at Erik for a long time before Momma grabs my hand and leads me down the raggedy steps of the front porch. We climb into the van with Daddy, Erik, and our other hippie friends and drive to the river, where we spend the day tubing and getting sunburned.

After dark, we head home to our own rundown shack. It has doors and windows, but no electricity or running water. Momma makes me a quick bowl of oatmeal on the gas stove and mixes up some powdered milk for me to guzzle down before walking me out to the woods for a potty.

"Help me squat," I say, grabbing her hand.

"Don't pee on your shoes," she says, taking a drag off her cigarette.

At bedtime, I snuggle into great grandma's patchwork quilt and work to get comfortable on the green army cot I use for a bed. Momma lights a match, holds it to the wick of our glass kerosene lantern, and adjusts the knob to make it brighter.

"I miss Granddad," I say.

"Me, too," she says, tucking Stacy into his crib.

I pull the blankets toward my chin and run my fingers over the black thread puckering the denim skin of my Baby Beans doll. Granddad gave me Baby Beans for Christmas, and that makes her extra special. If I close my eyes and use my imagination, I can still smell the sweet tobacco from his pipe on her plastic face. I love my bean-filled dolly so much I carry her everywhere. Over time, threadbare holes spring open on her body. One day it's an arm. Another day it's a leg. I don't notice her innards trickling out until they are half gone, making her a skinny, ragged baby. Momma gathers her lost beads off our musty carpet, stuffs them back through the rips, and sews on a patch, so I can keep loving her.

Music springs to life in the front room as my father strums loud on his acoustic and sings "Moon Shadow" with the hippies.

"Daddy sings just like Cat Stevens," I say.

"He does," Momma says.

"Daddy's not so mean anymore," I say, fingering Baby Beans' dryer-fried hair.

"He's lived a tough life, Missy. One day you'll understand," Momma says.

I watch her turn the knob on the kerosene lamp, dimming it low.

"Good night," she says.

"Sleep tight," I say, pulling Baby Beans under my cheek.

"Don't let the bed bugs bite," we say together as she tiptoes out the door.

♥

Daddy finds us a giant old house on Jonas Ridge, for just him, Momma, me, and Stacy to live in. Momma says the house was built during the Civil War, and it's haunted by a ghost. She calls him General Franklin, saying, "I swear he moves my stuff when I'm not looking!"

I think the ghost spooked the old biddy who owns the place, 'cause she took off and left all her stuff behind. Momma roots through the old lady's boxes, freeing flapper dresses, high-heeled slippers, and cosmetics. I play dress up with her black feather caps, smear pink lipstick across my face, and cover my skin in old lady perfume. On Sunday mornings, when Momma sleeps in with Daddy, I paint Stacy's fingernails. He pokes his tiny fingers through his crib slats, and I cover them with red stickiness, careful to blow them dry before he snatches them back. Momma wakes up and laughs at us.

"Messy Missy," she says, "what am I going to do with you?"

When the weather turns cold, we stay in bed until Daddy feeds logs into the pot-bellied stove and lights the fire to warm us up. Sometimes he lets Stacy help chop wood. Daddy uses the real chainsaw and Stacy uses his little blue one, pulling the string and making motor sounds with his mouth when the batteries run out. We never get new batteries for our toys because they cost money, and we need our money for food. And Momma says we don't need batteries when we have imagination.

We don't have a mailbox on the house, so we pile into the hippie van and rumble down Old Toe River Road to the mail stop every few days. On a sunny autumn afternoon, I stand in the back of the van, lean against the shaggy brown carpet covering the walls, and look out the open window at the spindly trees, all bare and naked for winter. I peek down toward the white-capped river below. My tummy gets butterflies when I look at the water.

I hear Momma say, "I hate this road; it's so narrow," like she does every time we drive it.

"Ah, we'll be all right," Daddy says from the driver's seat. Momma's friend, Leanne, holds Stacy on her lap in the passenger seat. Momma sandwiches in the middle, and I ride in the back alone.

Momma says, "What happens if we meet another vehicle?"

"We're just fine, woman. Relax," Daddy says.

I stumble across to the other side of the van, watch the dust poof up in clouds as we bump along the dirt road. I peer up a tall cliff, then cross back to look down at the river again.

"I can see the Old Toe River," I say to Momma.

"Yep," she says, craning her neck to look back at me.

"It looks cold and scary," I say, sitting down to fiddle with the square wooden box holding Daddy's eight-track tapes. Pulling one free, I fight the urge to stick my fingers inside the wide opening and pull out the brown tape that makes the music.

I hear Momma say, "That truck is taking up a lot of the road."

Stuffing John Denver back in his slot, I feel surprised by the sudden urge to lie down. "I'm taking a nap," I say to Momma, hoping she realizes what a good girl I am. Just as I close my eyes, I hit the roof, and the tape box lands on top of me. The carpet smashes into my face before I hit the roof again. I roll and roll, finally stopping with my face in the carpet, the tape

18

box resting on my back, and eight tracks scattered around me.

I don't hear Daddy call my name, just the crunch of broken glass as he opens the back door, pulls me out and sets me down in a sea of colored leaves. He bends down to brush glass off my dress, my arms, my hair. I follow him around the side of the van.

"Watch your step, Missy," Daddy says. "Stay there, baby girl."

I freeze and my eyes get wide when I see the van leaning against a thin tree. "How did that tiny tree stop our big car?" I ask, peering down the bank at the mist floating off the river. "We almost went into the water." I taste blood on my lip. I shiver and run my fingers over a scratch on my arm as Momma and Daddy work to get Stacy and Leanne out of the van.

"Wow," Momma says, cradling brother tightly. "God was watching over us. Missy could have been tossed out the window and crushed."

Daddy picks me up again, looks me over, and says, "Yeah, when I looked back, she was in the air."

He carries me up the hill, hands me to the man driving the truck that pushed us off the road, then turns to help Momma and Leanne. My lip gets fatter as we pile into the bed of the man's pickup and head toward the hospital. Leanne has a big bump on her head, and we need to make sure the baby in her tummy is okay. She did a real good job of holding Stacy. He's safe. Momma and Daddy walk away with only cuts and bruises. I think maybe Momma's right. Maybe God was watching over us when we rolled down the hill.

♥

When the snow arrives, Momma gets a phone call at the neighbors across the drive. We can't afford our own phone, so Momma uses their number for emergencies. Ten minutes later, she stumbles through our front door, her eyes blurry with tears.

"I can't believe she's gone," she says, collapsing into Daddy's arms. "She was only eighteen."

"Who?" I ask, jumping from my warm spot in front of the pot-bellied stove.

Tears rain down her face as she picks me up, holds me tight to her chest, and says, "Your aunt Kathy died in a car wreck last night, honey."

"She died? What does that mean?" I ask.

"She was on a road trip with a friend, they hit a snowbank," Momma says, setting me down to blow her nose.

"It means God took her to heaven, honey," Daddy says, caressing Momma's hair.

As I watch Momma cry, tears spill onto my own cheeks. Momma's tears are contagious, just like her laughter. When she laughs, I laugh, even when I don't know what's funny. And when she cries, I cry, even when I don't understand her pain. I tuck in between my parents and weep with them until Momma says she needs to walk back to the neighbors to call the airline. Grandma and Granddad need her home for the funeral.

Daddy grabs her hand and says, "I'll walk over with you. Melissa, keep an eye on your brother."

I tiptoe toward Stacy's crib to watch the gentle rhythm of his breathing, the way his eyelids twitch when he dreams. I was three and a half when he was born, old enough to feed and rock him, and smart enough to run away when Momma changed his diaper. His pee-pee shot me in the face like a water hose once, and once was all it took!

Stacy is too young to remember this, but Momma took me and Stacy to live with Grandma, Granddad, and Kathy not too long ago. She got mad at Daddy, packed us up, and we flew on a plane all the way to Las Vegas. It was the best time ever. Granddad is my momma's daddy. When we lived in Vegas, Granddad played dollies with me and read me lots of books. I'd nestle into his arms at night, breathe in the sweet scent of tobacco smoke drifting off his pipe, and flip the pages of *Cinderella* or *Snow White* while he told me stories of broken beauties and the handsome princes riding to their rescue.

Granddad helped me feed lettuce to Urtle, a wild turtle who built a hut in their backyard. He and Grandma took me for bumpety-bump rides on Lake Mead. Granddad even let me drive the boat. Grandma packed a cooler of sandwiches and cowboy cookies for us to eat on the beach.

Aunt Kathy took me for rides in her car and wrestled with me on her messy bed. She talked about boys all day or talked to boys on the phone. She was boy crazy! She and I played forty-fives on her record player and danced like disco queens. She let me slip on her dresses, dab her perfume on my wrists, and slather on her lip gloss.

I let out a long sigh and think about how much I'll miss my aunt Kathy. And how much I miss Grandma and Granddad. When Momma kissed and made up with Daddy, I cried. I didn't want to move home to my father, didn't want to come to North Carolina to drink powdered milk, bathe in a stone-cold creek, and live with a bunch of hippies. But, Momma said, "We are a family when we are together"—so here we are.

North Carolina isn't all bad, though. Momma calls it an adventure. Out in these hills, she teaches me to pee in a squat (careful to miss my shoes), catch daddy long leg spiders, and read library books by kerosene lantern. North Carolina is where I reckon oatmeal for breakfast, lunch, and dinner, is okay, since I don't go to sleep hungry. But I am super happy when Momma cashes in her food stamps for some mac-n-cheese, canned ravioli, real cow's milk, and hot dogs. She used to give us raw hot dogs for snack, until Stacy choked on one. His face turned blue, and Momma flipped him upside down quick as a whip. The entire hot dog slid out of his throat and landed on the floor beside me. It was gross! Now she cooks them and serves them sliced up so we can eat them on a plate.

"Staaaa-cccyyyy," I sing, slipping my hand between the slats of his crib to tickle his palm. He stirs a bit, squeezes my fingers, and opens his big brown eyes to stare at me just as Momma and Daddy walk through the door.

"Brother's awake," Momma says, lifting Stacy out of his crib.

"Momma, is Kathy in heaven?" I ask.

"I'm sure she is," Momma says, sitting on the floor with Stacy in her lap.

"Jesus lives in heaven, right?"

"Yes," Momma says.

"Then why do you cry? Don't you know it's better for Kathy to be with Jesus?"

Momma releases Stacy to toddle around the room, then holds her arms out to me. I climb onto her lap and rest my head against her chest.

"How are you so wise, at five years old?" Momma asks, nuzzling her face into my hair.

"Because that's what we learned in Sunday school," I say, brushing curls out of my eyes. "And God's not a liar, Momma."

She pulls me in tight and says, "I think I'll take you with me."

"Where?"

"To Las Vegas."

My mouth drops open as I ask, "You mean, to Grandma and Granddad's?"

She nods and says, "Yes, I think you will bring joy to their sad hearts, Melissa."

I turn around to hug her long, kiss her face, then slip away to pack my dollies for the trip.

2

The Devil's Dirty Secret

Static pops and clicks through the speakers, pulling me back to our front room, as the needle jumps in time with the rotating album. Fleetwood Mac is done serenading my sad, fourteen-year-old heart. I switch the record to Led Zeppelin, "The Song Remains the Same," and drop the needle before yanking another stack of pictures free from the box. The photos in my hand are more current, covering the past six months. I sigh as a picture of Brent drops to the floor.

"Mom, you are so unorganized," I say.

I pick up the photo and inhale deep. I can't help it when my eyes glue to his face. Even from the glossy square, his ocean blue eyes mesmerize me, and I fight the tears rolling down my cheeks.

"I'm so sorry," I whisper to him.

I want so much to say it to his face, but I haven't the courage. What do I tell him? How do I apologize without spilling my ugly beans all over him? My parents are relieved he's gone, a permanent absence from my life. They are probably glad I won't be barefoot and pregnant at fifteen. As my heart aches over losing my first love, I remember my talk with Momma just a few months ago . . .

She asked, "Are you sleeping with Brent?"

I swallowed hard and glanced away as her face went blank. Feeling a sudden urge to cover my tracks, I pulled a pillow tight to my chest and waited for her to speak.

"What is going on with you, Missy? The lies, sneaking around? What happened to my little girl? And why are you so angry with me?"

"I'm not mad at you, Mom," I said.

"Then what?" Momma asked again.

"I hate Dad. He says one thing and does another. He's always angry, and I just get tired of him."

Momma sighed.

"I don't know why you guys can't just let me make my own choices," I said.

Mom sat silent.

"Sometimes, I don't even want to live here anymore," I said. Regret washed over me like rain, making me want to eat those words the moment they landed on her.

My mother stared at me, blinked a few times, and then said, "I need to ask you a question."

Like a storm brewing, I knew what was coming before she said a thing. The air thickened, time slowed, and then she asked, "Has your father ever . . .?"

A car door slams outside, jarring me from the memory. I jump up, dumping the photos, and peek out the large front window. My heart relaxes as I watch the neighbors walk to their front door. I tiptoe back to my warm spot on the carpet, hunker down, and pull Brent's picture to my cheek.

"I'm so sorry my broken got all over you," I say, closing my eyes for a heartbeat. Then I tuck his picture in my lap, grab the stack, and root out the photo of a little gray house.

♥

I am six years old when we pack our things, say goodbye to North Carolina, and move back to the Mississippi delta. We had lived in Arkansas, just across the green bridge, when I was four. Arkansas is where we lived when Momma got mad at Daddy and left him. Probably because Daddy grows dark in this place, morphing into an angry beast at the slightest noise. Me and Stacy can't giggle or squeal or fuss without a whipping. And heaven forbid we should drop a glass or a pan. Loud noises startle Daddy, then he startles us by yelling in our tiny faces.

We start out living in a single-wide trailer, then move into what I call the june-bug house. The day we pull up to the little gray shack Momma calls "our new home," piles of giant beetles lay all bellied up, like someone sprayed them with Raid. My skin crawls as I inspect the hairy legs and brown shelled bodies of these crispy critters.

"Blech," I say, skipping around them to grab Momma's hand.

"We can sweep them up," Momma says, ushering me inside.

"It's hot in here," I say with a whine.

"Yeah, there's no air conditioning," she says, letting go of my hand to collect my baby brother in her arms. I watch Daddy and Buddy, my father's best friend, carry in our furniture. A brand new black and white checkered couch and matching chair, along with a lacquered coffee table and two end tables.

"When are Grandma and Granddad coming to visit?" I ask.

"In a few weeks," she says.

"Good. We can swim at their motel pool," I say.

"Won't that be nice," Momma says.

"Do you work tomorrow?" I ask.

"Yes, honey."

"Did you and Daddy buy our furniture with the money you make at your new job?"

"We did."

I imagine Momma sitting in front of a typewriter at the *Delta Times*, her nyloned legs crossed beneath the desk, a long white cigarette smoldering in the ashtray as she clacks on the keys. When she works, she drops me at summer kindergarten with a Wonder Woman lunch pail, a kiss good-bye, and the burn of her Wind Song perfume lingering in my nose. She drops Stacy at daycare.

"Does Daddy work tonight?" I ask, watching him carry two cots and a pile of blankets in his strong arms. We had ditched Stacy's crib at the dump and got him a green army cot like mine when we left North Carolina.

"Tomorrow, baby," she says. "He works Monday nights,

remember?"

I nod, recalling how we drive down to the river docks late at night to deliver his dinner sometimes. Daddy works repairing the big rusty ships hauling cargo up the Mississippi. Maybe that's why he's so tough. And mean. Like Brutus on *Popeye*, but Daddy is a smaller guy with a grouch face. I watch him and Buddy carry in a mattress for Momma, then long plywood boards and cinder blocks for a bookshelf, and finally our small kitchen table with its yellow-green chairs.

When the guys are done, and Buddy bumps his way out the dusty drive in his truck, Momma sets Stacy down and grabs a broom. She kicks those nasty june bugs onto the long grass, sets a smile on her face and pats my brother's toddling head before looking at me. "See? The bugs are gone. Now we can enjoy our new home," she says. And with that, we lumber back into the stifling house with a slam of the screen door.

A day or two after we move into the june-bug house, Momma brings home an inflatable swimming pool just big enough for the three of us. Using the green garden hose, she fills it to the top, then dips down in the water, despite her cutoff shorts. Stacy and I laugh, spray her with the hose, and jump in beside her. We spend many weekends soaking in our little pool, with beer in the cooler and hot dogs on the barbecue.

One hot July evening, Daddy and his band practice their Cat Stevens songs in the front room, and Momma makes me mac-n-cheese for dinner. She helps me practice my penmanship, using a cornflower blue crayon to write M-E-L-I-S-S-A between the lines of my kindergarten notepad. I use a pencil to trace her letters, often adding M-I-S-S-Y in front of Melissa.

Momma glances at my work and says, "Missy is not your proper name."

"I like to write it this way," I say, scribbling a sloppy M-I-S-S-Y in front of her tidy letters.

"Why don't you like Melissa?" Momma asks.

I shrug. "I just like Missy better."

"Melissa is a pretty name," she says. "It means honeybee."

I stop tracing and ask, "My name has a meaning?"

"Honeybee," Momma says again.

"Bees sting, Momma."

"Yes, but they also make honey," she says.

"So they are sweet, too," I say.

"So should I call you Melissa?" Momma asks.

"Maybe when I turn seven," I say, working my fingers over an M.

Momma giggles. "Time for bed. Missy Melissa."

With Baby Beans tight in my arms, I race down the narrow hallway, stopping to peer out the large window in the room I share with Stacy. I pick at the flaky white paint covering the windowpane and scour the inky sky for stars while Momma roots through my chest of drawers for jammies.

"A full moon! I can see him, Momma, he's staring at me!"

"Who?"

"The Man in the Moon!"

Momma chuckles, tugging a white satin nightgown over my head.

"Handsome fella, the Man in the Moon," she says, batting at a mosquito buzzing around our heads.

When these hungry sucker's sneak past the screen door after dark to hum in my ear and poke my skin for a bloody snack, I might wake up with a bite or two. But when we play outside, they nearly eat me alive! Even in the daytime! We splashed in the pool with the mosquitos lots today, leaving my skin lumpy as cottage cheese. Momma's soft gray eyes survey the bites covering my tiny frame. She uses gentle hands and a cotton swab to smother the itchy bumps in calamine lotion.

"My goodness, Missy, you have at least a hundred bites on you!"

I poke my fingernails into the swollen bumps, one by one, the harder I push the better they feel.

"Don't scratch, it will make the itching worse," she says, dabbing on the last drop of calamine from the bottle. Then she dips down, kneeling with her elbows on the metal frame of my cot, and we close our eyes to pray together.

"Now I lay me down to sleep. I pray the Lord my soul to keep. If I die before I wake, I pray the Lord my soul to take. Amen."

"I love you, little Mis."

"I love you, too, Momma," I say as she clicks off my light and disappears into the hallway.

Itchy bites spring to life on my body as the calamine lotion crusts over, and I fight the urge to dig my nails into them. As the moonlight plays peekaboo on my wall, I watch the shadows grow and wonder if the Monster will creep in tonight. He tiptoes into my room while Momma sleeps and slides his hands under my blankets. Sometimes I doze hard until he touches my privates, then I wake up, hold my breath, and lay still until he leaves.

I poke at the bites covering my body and fight the urge to sleep as the music in our living room stops, and I hear the latches click on Daddy's guitar case. Muted laughter dances in my ears as my eyelids slip down. Sleep lulls me into a dream where I find myself alone in a warehouse, tiptoeing barefoot over cold concrete. I make my way toward the golden light streaming from the door ahead, never pulling my gaze from the wooden boxes surrounding me, fearing something will reach out and grab me. Cool air whisks up the hem of my nightgown and I clutch Baby Beans tight.

I reach the door, step inside, and gaze into a tall picture window as a butter-yellow moon creeps into view. The glowing ball mesmerizes me as a face takes shape and comes to life with squinty eyes and a jagged nose. It's the devil! I gasp and turn to run away, but my feet refuse to budge. He blocks me with his large hand, chuckles low and opens his fingers to show me what he's holding. It's a leaf, all rolled up like one of Daddy's marijuana cigarettes. I feel weak, like I might throw up. As the leaf falls open, a tiny figure appears. A little girl. She is stiff and lifeless, frozen in time. And she is wearing my nightgown.

My eyes pop open. The sky outside my window is pitch black. When did I fall asleep? Where did the moon go? My heart drums in my ears and sweat runs down my forehead. I can't move. I am petrified by fear.

"Momma," I holler out.

"Momma!"

The sound of her feet padding toward me slows my breathing.

"The devil came to get me in my sleep," I say, sitting up.

"You're okay, honey. It was just a dream," she says, hugging me.

"It was so scary," I say, clinging to her.

"Shh," she says, stroking my hair, "It was just a bad dream."

I repeat her words aloud, hoping I can believe them. "It's just a dream. It's just a dream." But deep inside, I know it's not just a dream. Because the devil is real. And he's already got me in the palm of his hand.

♥

On a hot, muggy day, Momma leaves brother asleep on his cot and me alone with Daddy while she goes grocery shopping. I beg her to take me along and promise to be good, but she piles in the car and waves good-bye before clunking down our long dirt driveway.

After Momma disappears, Daddy sits to color with me. I stare at him in wonder. *Daddy is never this nice.*

"Would you like a cupcake?" he asks, pulling a chocolate-covered, cream-filled delight from the Hostess box on top of the fridge.

"Momma already gave me one," I say, licking my lips.

"I think it's okay to have two," he says with a wink.

My eyes grow wide as he pulls the plastic away from the cake and hands me the goodie. I whisper thank you and bite into the soft muffin with a giggle.

Daddy eats one too, matching me bite for bite. We hunker

low, shoulders down, and snicker while we eat in secret. When we finish, he pours us each a small glass of milk. I chug mine down while he watches with a grin.

"Want to play another secret game?" He asks, sucking the milk from his moustache.

I lick frosting off my thumb and raise my brows at him. "What kind of game?" I ask.

"A tickle game," Daddy says.

"Tickle, tickle, tickle," I say, thrusting my fingers toward him.

He laughs, puts a finger over my lips to shush me. "This is a new tickle game," he says.

"Okay."

Minutes later, I lie on the scratchy carpet, and Daddy touches my privates. I don't like it but I'm too scared to say no. What if he gets mad at me? I feel dirty and know we are doing something bad because Daddy checks the window for Momma every few seconds.

He says, "Missy, this is a game for just you and Daddy, okay?"

I nod, but no words come out of my mouth. When Momma's car pulls up, Daddy helps me put my panties back on. Still on his knees, he stands me up, and locks eyes with me.

"This is our secret. Momma can never know. It will kill her if she ever finds out," he says.

I suck air in real fast, cover my mouth, and picture Momma dying like Aunt Kathy. I can't live without my momma. While Daddy's yelling and screaming, Momma's calm and sweet. She never hollers at me like Daddy. I nod at my father and make a vow in my heart to protect her always.

Leaning into him, I cup my fist over his ear, and say, "It's okay, Daddy. I will never tell."

I draw an X across my chest to secure the promise and say, "Cross my heart and hope to die."

The front door rattles open, and Daddy disappears down the dark hallway. I run to greet Momma, draping my small body around her legs.

"Hi, sweetie, did you have fun with Daddy?"

As I search my mind for an answer, my father's voice booms, making me jump.

"Melissa!" Daddy says, hollering at me.

My smile falls, heart pounds in my ears as he makes his way toward me.

"Did you use the toilet and not flush?"

I search for kindness in his eyes. Where did it go? Shakes sweep over me as I stare at my feet, my lips forming a frown.

"No," I say.

His eyes turn black, and he reaches to unbuckle his belt. Quick as lightning, the jangle of the buckle fills the air and I back away with my palms over my behind.

"No, Daddy, please don't spank me," I say.

I glance at Momma unpacking groceries, hoping for mercy. She frowns, shakes her head at me and turns away to tuck the milk in the fridge.

"Momma," I say, as he loops the belt over his fist.

She says nothing.

"I didn't mean to Daddy. The potty scares me," I say.

My tears run out of control, fueling his anger. Before I say another word, his hand is tight around my arm, and I am spinning, my tiny frame cast over his knee as the sting of the belt pierces my skin.

When the whipping ends, he stands me up and says, "Get to your room, young lady."

I escape his grip and run to my cot with my backside burning. His anger always strikes fast, leaving me in shock. With my face buried in the pillow, I sob until the bed of my heart runs dry. After several minutes, I sit up, rub the goobers from my eyes, and crane my neck to listen for his return. I know better than to move a muscle before he excuses me from my room. Finally, he tiptoes in and looks down at me.

"Missy, when I have to spank you, it hurts *me* more than it hurts you."

I nod but I don't believe him.

He kneels beside my bed.

"I'm sorry for getting mad at you." Tears fill his eyes as he lays his head on my lap.

I put my hands in his soft, dark hair and say, "It's okay. Don't be sad."

His eyes meet mine. "Can you forgive me?"

"Yes," I say, leaning in to kiss his forehead. This is how I get the sadness off Daddy. When he does bad things, I smile, forgive him, and do my best to make him happy. And I keep his secrets to myself.

3

Don't Call Me Special

We pull into the drive of a white house with gray shutters and a fancy screen door guarding the entrance. A black aluminum mailbox with scalloped edges hangs beside the door. Flowering hedges nestle under each white paned window. This house is rectangular, not square like the tiny gray shack we live in now. The only thing missing is a white picket fence.

"You mean we get to live here?" I ask Momma.

"We do," she says, thrusting open the car door to free Dooley from her grip. Our orange kitty scampers into the bushes, anxious to stake a claim in his new neighborhood. Momma drops the passenger seat forward, grabs Buttons off my lap, and sets her down so she can pee in the grass. "I'm starting a new job and the extra money will help pay the rent on a bigger house."

"No more june-bug house," I whisper, scooping Buttons back into my arms. I cradle my tiny chocolate poodle like a baby and stare at our new home as hope builds in my heart. We are still in Mississippi, but today is a new day, and maybe I can leave the dirty things Daddy does to me in the old house with the dead bugs.

"Come on!" Stacy says, grabbing my hand. We run to the backyard and our mouths drop as we stare up at a wooden structure nestled into the canopy of an elm tree.

"A tree house!" Stacy says with a squeal, his four-year-old legs scrambling up the ladder. I set Buttons down, follow my brother up the rickety slats, and run my fingers along the splintered railings, all painted a flaky red, white, and blue. The floor is in good shape, and while the roof overhead blocks out the Mississippi sun, nothing stops the sticky air from wetting my flesh. Locust songs fill my ears, reminding me of the baggy skin these bugs leave hanging in the trees. If I were a normal kid, I'd love this little fortress. But I'm not normal. I'm a sissy. So I fold in my arms, scan the tree branches for locusts and ask, "Can we go in the house?"

"Yes, you may," Dad says from the yard below.

Stacy and I scramble down the ladder, race across the yard, and burst through the screen door. In the living room, we are greeted by an icy blast of cold air. "Yay, an air conditioner," I say, standing with my face in the vents. Stacy sneaks up beside me, shoves his hand under his arm, and squeezes out arm-farts.

"You're gross," I say, slapping his bare shoulder before racing off to call dibs on the biggest room. When Stacy slips up beside me again, I lower my voice and narrow my eyes at him. "I wonder if this house is haunted."

He shoots me a dirty look and says, "No!"

"Well, I'm sure Grandma Bea's house is full of ghosts, and we are sleeping there tonight," I say, waggling my finger in his face. "In fact, we are staying there until Mom and Dad move our furniture."

"Okay, kiddos, time to go to Grandma Bea's," Momma says, making me laugh at Stacy's petrified stare.

Grandma Bea lives two blocks away from our new house. She adopted Daddy and his younger siblings, my Aunt Shellie, and Uncle JJ, when Daddy was nine. I don't know what happened to Daddy's real family, the one he was born with. I just know, according to Daddy, Grandma Bea likes Aunt Shellie more than the boys. Shellie is my favorite, too, so I understand.

Bea's mansion is two stories tall, with a maze of rooms to peruse. Her property stretches long, with her bookkeeping office at the driveway gate, a two-room cottage for visitors, and a pond. Her menagerie of animals includes ducks, geese, chickens, two cats, and three dogs. Her ugly pug is Chester. Chester's eyeball falls out sometimes. The thought of an eye dangling from Chester's face freaks me out, so I avoid him like the plague.

Her chickens and geese freak me out, too. I am always on guard, ready to run if a scrawny bird tries to chase me across her yard. One morning, Bea walks into the kitchen with a giant aluminum pan in her hand and her eyes on me and Stacy. "Would y'all like to come help feed the chickens?" She clucks her tongue and raises her brows at us.

"Yeah!" Stacy bolts for the door. Seems he got all the courage, and I got all the fear. I glance at Mom, who nods in encouragement from her comfortable spot on the sofa. I humph and set aside my paper dolls to follow them out. Sticky heat saturates my face as we step into the chicken pen. Bea leans over, holding the pan out with one hand, pushing her large, black-rim glasses back into position with the other. Her midnight blue hair sits high atop her head, with random grays poking out in all directions.

Stacy grabs a fist full of pellets and tosses them on the ground while chickens cluck at his feet, pecking fast to grab every morsel.

"Missy, don't you want to help?"

"No, thank you." I give a small squeal, dancing around chicken poop. "I don't want their poo on my Mary Janes," I say, wanting to preserve the shine on my fancy red shoes. Every time I look at them, I remember Mrs. Olson's lunchtime prayers. She is my second-grade teacher. Before the meal, she makes us line up and bow our heads. I don't close my eyes, instead, I stare at the pearly shine on my shoes while she prays to Jesus. She seems to love Him a lot. Maybe that's why God let her live after He hit her with lightning. I'm not kidding.

Lightning totally struck her, and she survived! The black scars zigzagging her old-lady legs are proof.

Stacy finishes the job, and we head back inside to wander the upper rooms in Bea's mansion. I love the shiny, gold wallpaper on her walls, the tall brick fireplaces, and the furniture decked with clawed feet. Dust on the mantels and creaky stairs are perfect for making up ghost stories. The scent of old runs up my nostrils as I stop to admire the picture of Jesus hanging on her wall. It's the same picture that hangs in the Methodist Church.

I stare at His face and wonder how the artist knows what Jesus looks like. If He's invisible, how do they know what to paint? Is His hair really the color of almonds? Does He have brown eyes, or are they blue? Maybe they are a color we can't see. Is His skin milky white, or is he tan like me? Is He as soft and lovely as He looks in the picture? I want to reach up and touch His cheek.

As I lift my hand toward Jesus, Stacy launches by me, saying, "Race ya!" His exit spooks me. I don't want to be up here alone, so I take off behind him with fear nipping at my heels until we reach the kitchen. Fear is like that. Always lurking, sneaking, chasing. And never leaving.

On the day we move into the tree-house house, Buddy and his family come over to help us pack in our furniture just like at the june-bug house. Only now we have new bedroom sets. Grandma Bea took us shopping at the furniture outlet while we were staying with her. Gone are the squeaky cots and Mom and Dad's funky, old mattresses. Grandma Bea bought my parents a dark walnut bedroom set, complete with bed, dresser, chest of drawers, and matching nightstands. She gave Stacy an old bed and dresser from one of her spare rooms. She got me white princess furniture trimmed in scalloped edges and gold foil. The set includes a nightstand, a dresser with a vanity mirror, and a canopy bed!

When the boxes are inside, the furniture is set, and the sun dips behind the trees, Dad rolls weed into a Zig-Zag paper and pulls out his guitar. Momma tells me and Stacy to get showered while she makes our beds. We head for the bathroom, strip down, and slide into the tub. When I get the water nice and warm, Stacy squeals, saying, "It's too hot." He pushes past me and twists the knob until icy water blasts atop my head.

"Burr!" I holler, shoving him aside to turn up the warm water.

We go back and forth until a burning rage prompts me to shut the cold water off. Completely. My little brother lets out a howl as steamy spray drenches his skin. Our father's footsteps rumble down the hall and my heart stops. Before the door flies open, I know what's coming. I yank the cold water on as Dad rips the shower curtain aside, pulls me over the porcelain edge, and folds me over the toilet. His bare hand stings my wet butt with one, two, three hard licks. Stacy squeals when Dad lifts him out by the arm, smacking him twice before planting his wet feet on the shaggy bath mat next to mine.

"Get your asses in bed, now!"

We scurry for our towels, wrap up tight and head out the door, sniffling as we go. Momma helps us into our jammies and forces me to apologize. At first, I'm not sorry. I just say it to stay out of trouble. But once we snuggle down in Stacy's bed, I roll toward him and say it for real.

"I'm sorry."

"Me, too," he says, pulling me in for a hug.

Even though we have our own rooms, Stacy and I still slumber together every night. We snicker and giggle until Dad hollers at us, "Y'all go to sleep 'for I come whoop your little asses!" Then we snicker and giggle some more. Some nights, we play before we snooze. The hardwood floor is hot lava, the bed is base. We take turns running over molten rocks to rescue stuffed animals and baby dolls, jumping into bed with a squeal and our little dog, Buttons, close behind.

When playtime is done, and the house grows quiet, I hunker in close to Stacy, wrap an arm around his shoulder, and drift off to sleep. And every night, I hope my brother's presence will discourage my father from entering the room.

But it never does.

♥

Momma leaves the *Delta Times* to take a job at the rice factory in town. She must do a good job because they give her a uniform, her own office, and a special badge to wear. Daddy still works at the shipyard, but they move him to days instead of nights. On weekends, he plays music gigs at local bars. Together, my parents make enough money to buy Daddy new guitars and sound equipment for the band. We also buy a small aluminum boat and a second car.

The only downside to my parents' success is that Stacy and I go to Temple Daycare for the summer. Instead of staying home with Momma, we get up early for sugary corn puffs, toss on shorts and sandals, and prepare for a day of torture. The kids at daycare run wild, shooting ketchup from spoons, and spit wads from sticky lips. The teachers are stinky old grouches who carry rolled-up newspapers to slap us over the head with when we misbehave. One afternoon, I grab a red crayon, draw 7734 across a sheet of white paper and flip it upside down. With a sly grin, I turn to show off the word HELL and find a teacher standing behind me.

"You don't curse in church!" she says, smacking me like a dog. I'm confused, because even though *hell* is a curse word, it's also in the Bible. Our Methodist preacher talks about hell, and people going to hell, almost every Sunday.

I hate being at daycare, where everyone is rude and spiteful. There is no reading, no playground equipment, no bookmobile, and only a few people to call friends. All my best buddies are from school or the neighborhood, not this crusty old church. I daydream of playing dress up with Jennifer or Barbies with Julie. And I yearn to be home with Momma.

At home, Momma lets us help cook and clean. I'm not

a fan of chores, but I love kitchen time. She lets us help make cheesewiches. I grate cheddar cheese while Stacy smears tomato paste over toast. We pop the sandwiches in the oven for ten minutes, then scarf them down with a glass of sweet tea. My favorite snack is sugar donuts. Momma melts Crisco in a small pan, piles white sugar on a Corelle dinner plate, and sprinkles on a little cinnamon. She lets me push the spoon into the seam on the Pillsbury biscuit can, pop it open, and punch holes out of the dough. Stacy and I eat the raw scraps, while Momma dunks the donuts in crackling hot oil, then pulls them free with a big fork. After they cool a minute, me and Stacy take turns rolling them in cinnamon sugar. Momma lets us help make Toll House cookies, too. And chocolate cowboy cookies and birthday cakes. We get to lick a spoon or a bowl or a mixing wand. Life is sweetest when it's the three of us, without daycare and without Daddy.

Daddy tries to be normal, but his dirty habit follows us from the june-bug house. He can't keep his hands to himself; there is no safe place for me to be. Anytime Momma leaves the house, I beg to tag along, knowing he will slip me into his bedroom to fondle me. If I sleep next to Stacy or even have a friend over, he waits until everyone is dozing before he touches me under the covers. If I have a bad dream and climb in bed between him and Momma, he puts his hands under my nightgown after she falls asleep.

One night, after Daddy sneaks into my room, I see Momma's shadow in my doorway and my heart stops.

"Clint. What are you doing?"

Dad jumps from beside my bed, pretends to grope around the floor, saying, "I was looking for Buttons. Didn't you hear her whining?"

Momma says, "Buttons is right here."

"Oh," Daddy says, "I must have been dreaming."

Momma doesn't turn on my light or ask questions, but the tone in her voice tells me she's not happy. Daddy follows her out of my room, and I hope her catching him scares him away.

It doesn't.

On my eighth birthday, Momma throws a huge party in the backyard, complete with streamers, balloons, and a cat cake she decorated herself. While my friends play tag outside, Daddy pulls me into the living room to slip a silver ring on my finger. The light catches on the center of a small heart perched atop the band as he says, "That's a real diamond."

"Wow," I say, staring at it.

"Be careful with it," he says. "That's my special gift to you."

Special.

I put on a grin, fix my eyes on the light glimpsing off the tiny gem, and work to swallow. The word *special* makes my stomach queasy. Dad says I'm special when he touches me, says we are special, have a special secret. I hate the word *special*. And because his molesting me does not die with the june bugs, the ring on my finger only reminds me how gross I am.

♥

One of Dad's favorite things to do is drag us fishing. He ties our aluminum boat on top of our Volkswagen Bug, tosses a cooler of beer in the trunk, and hauls us off to Lake Washington. Me and Stacy hunker on the floor of the boat with fluorescent orange life jackets cinched to our eyeballs, as Dad rows us along the edge of the lake, looking for bass. When Dad stands to cast his line, he rocks the vessel, making my heart pound. I grip the sides and pray he doesn't tip us into the murky water. Lord knows what lives in the silt—gators, snapping turtles, snakes, or the decomposing body of some lost fisherman.

Bald cypress trees grow inside the water's edge. I stare up at their tall branches and long to rest under their canopy, to take a reprieve from the thick sunshine baking my skin. But the snakes prevent us from anchoring any one place for too long. *Cotton mouths*, Daddy calls them. These water moccasins are hulky and long, black and gray in color. They curl on logs and dangle from tree branches. More than once, a slithery viper has dropped from a tree on high to land where our boat was just parked. So we bake in the sun most of the day while Daddy waits patiently to catch a slimy fish for dinner. When my parents finally free us from our aluminum prison to eat sandwiches, guzzle sweet tea, and climb into our car, my pulse slows to its normal rhythm.

Dad likes to meander the dikes of the Mississippi on the drive home. Me and Stacy curl up on the black vinyl seat as my parents spark a joint and chatter about life. They pay us no mind, passing the roach back and forth, talking about things kids don't understand.

"I'm not sure I ever want to meet her," Daddy says one day.

"She's your birth mother," Momma says, blowing smoke out the window.

Daddy grips the wheel and works his jaw, glancing side to side as he drives.

"Your brother and sister met her, and their kids. Don't you think our children should know their biological grandmother? Do it for them, if not for yourself," she says.

"Shellie and JJ don't remember her, the foster homes, or the orphanages. I don't know if I can face that woman after she left us," he says. "Maybe if I'd had a family, I would have skipped Vietnam."

When Daddy mentions the war or the army, I envision the shiny Purple Heart he keeps in a small leather case atop his dresser. When she catches me and Stacy snooping, Mom says, "Dad sacrificed for that medal. It's not yours to touch without permission, okay?" We both nod with wide eyes and a proud spirit.

"You can't blame your mother for Vietnam," Momma says. "That's not fair, Clint."

Dad furrows his brows, glares at my mom, and barks at her, saying, "You weren't there! Don't tell me how to feel. Or what to do!"

Momma is not venomous like Daddy. She holds her tongue, hunkers down in her seat, lights a cigarette, and stares out her

41

window. The wind blows her smoke and ashes into my face, making me scoot toward Stacy. I put my hand on his leg and give it a squeeze. We look at each other, grin, and shrug our shoulders. We don't understand what they are talking about, except I think Daddy knows where his birth mom lives.

♥

Momma packs our heavy white suitcase, lugs it out to the car, and says, "Make sure you go potty. We won't be stopping for a while." We do as we're told, then pile inside and make the drive south with my aunts, uncles, and cousins, to meet the woman who gave birth to Dad's family. The drive takes forever!

At nighttime, we arrive at my new grandma's house. Jeannie Lue Prichard opens the door of her tiny, one-bedroom bungalow, and ushers us inside. I am immediately taken with her dog. "He's a mix of Chow Chow and some other mutt," she says. He smiles at me with his blue tongue draped over his sharp teeth. I take to massaging his golden fur, try to avoid the emotions filling the room as my dad and his biological momma drape each other in hugs and tears.

"I'm so sorry," she says, cradling him. "I've missed you."

This is a big deal for my daddy. He hasn't seen this woman since he was five. While his siblings have no memory of her, he does. He remembered his Momma all these years, and now here she is, holding him as he weeps.

When the emotion settles, I tiptoe toward the door framing the kitchen and stare at Jeannie Lue. She looks like a porcelain doll, dressed in a bright orange muumuu, her rosebud lips caked in thick red lipstick. Her bottle-black hair rests in perfect curls around her ears. She catches me watching her and tiptoes over, saying, "It's a wig." She breaks into a low giggle. "Girl, I ain't got no hair!"

I imagine her shiny bald head and laugh aloud.

"Do you like my dawg?" she asks.

I nod as she takes a slender white cigarette from a leather

pouch and lights it, pulling in a long drag.

"Yeah, he's cute," I say, cuddling his golden fur.

"His name is Bear," she says with smoke rolling from her nostrils.

"Bear," I say with a grin.

"You're a pretty thing," she says, looking me over. "Look a lot like your daddy."

"Yeah, people tell me that all the time," I say.

"Bear's taken a liking to you," she says.

Laughter from the other room grabs her attention. She holds her cigarette to red lips, takes a long drag and winks at me. "You can call me Grandma J."

I can't take my eyes off her as she walks away with her muumuu swishing over the linoleum floor. Everything she does mesmerizes me. From how she props her cigarette between her fingers and thumb, to the low cadence of her voice when she talks. She's dark, deep, and sultry like the lady off *Gone with the Wind*. Romantic. I glance in the mirror hanging beside her front door. I have the same rosebud lips. The same tawny skin. The same squinty brown eyes. We are built from the same bones, Grandma J and I.

I watch the way she talks with my mom, how her face lights up at the sound of my dad's voice. My smile perks as I realize the impact of my daddy finding his momma. Maybe she can love him the way my momma loves me. Maybe she can make him into a better man.

On our drive home, Dad talks to Mom hush hush about his birth father. "He was a mean ole drunk," Daddy says, flicking a lighter open to spark the joint in Mom's hand.

"I got no desire to ever meet that bastard."

Momma takes a puff and hands the joint to Dad.

"I remember him beating Jeannie Lue, leaving her for dead. That same night, Daddy packed us up, took us to stay with his sister, then we started hopping from orphanages to foster homes."

I lift my right lid and sneak a peek as he takes a deep toke and passes the joint to Momma.

Daddy was taken from his momma? She didn't give him away?

"I feel sorry for Jeannie Lue," Momma says, holding the paper cigarette to her lips.

"She was unfit to care for us," Dad says. "Her life was hard, too."

"Shellie says Jeannie Lue's afraid to leave her house," Momma says, "And Jeannie Lue doesn't drive or hold a job. It must be terrible to be a prisoner of your own mind."

Daddy doesn't say a word.

Momma reaches for his hand, pulls it to her cheek, and gives it a kiss.

We drive in silence a long time before Daddy clicks on the radio. "Bette Davis Eyes," pot smoke, and the gentle motion of the car rock me to sleep. I curl up opposite my dozing brother, with my head pressed into the door jam. Just as I drift into deep slumber, Stacy rolls over and shoves his knee in my back. I wake with a start and slap his bare thigh, yelling, "Stop!" My response is automatic, not allowing me time to process Daddy's presence in the front seat or the fact that Stacy was sleeping. My brother cries out as a red welt the shape of my hand rises on his leg. Daddy swings his arm back over the bench seat to smack me, prompting tears from my own eyes.

"Don't make me pull over, young lady!"

I glare at Stacy's teary face and fight the urge to kick him in the shin.

"Hey! You hear me?" Daddy yells.

"Yes," I say, sitting up.

"Yes, what?" he asks, tilting the rearview mirror to glare at me while he drives.

"Yes, sir," I say in a whisper.

I stop reacting immediately, remembering the time Dad did stop the vehicle. He snatched his belt from the loops, bent my brother and me over his knee and whooped our butts us as cars flew by. I know when to stop pushing his buttons.

I fix my gaze out the window as rows of cotton flick by, starting wide at the road and converging to a narrow point on the horizon. As I stare at the white tufts, I wonder why Dad gets mad at me and Stacy over nothing. I mean, we can't have a giggle fit without risking a lashing from his belt. Whining, bickering, or voicing our opinion all result in the same thing —punishment. Dad is not a negotiator or a listener or a concerned parent.

He is a punisher.

I want to hate him for being mean, but I remember Momma's words—"your daddy has had a tough life"—and I think of Jeannie Lue. I imagine my dad as a brown-haired boy, watching in terror as his daddy beat his momma, and all I can feel is sorrow. I pity my dad and wonder about the orphanages and foster homes. I wonder who punished him the way he punishes me. A single tear rolls over my cheek as I choose to love him despite his meanness. And I choose to forgive him because it makes my life easier.

♥

"We are moving!" Daddy says with a boom.

I drop Barbie and her blonde horse on the coffee table in front of me and grip the tiny pink hairbrush still in my hand from styling his mane. My heart sinks.

"Why?" I ask in a soft voice, not wanting to anger him with stupid questions.

He turns on me, his tone commanding, and says, "This town is not fit for raising kids."

How is our town unfit?

Five years of memories tumble through my mind. The day we arrived in Mississippi when I was six. How I started first grade at Madison Elementary, moved to Clayton in the fourth grade. Maybe that's it? Madison teaches only through third grade, and Momma isn't happy about Clayton. It's an old, rundown school with peeling floor tiles and flaky paint. There are lots of poor kids at Clayton, but that's okay with me. Poor kids are nicer than rich kids. And I want to finish fifth grade with my friends. And what about the rest of my life? Whitney and my neighborhood pals, weekends at Roller World, summer visits with aunts, uncles, and cousins. And what about Buttons? My eyes dart around the room searching for my little poodle.

"Where are we headed?" Stacy asks.

Mom comes in from the kitchen, wringing a towel in her hands, her light brown curls pulled into a ponytail. She wears contacts instead of glasses, making her eyes appear blue. "We are going to Washington," she says, staring at Dad.

I crumple my brows and ask, "Washington, D.C.?"

"No. Washington State, two thousand miles away," Dad says, his tone triumphant. "Pat and Lucy moved there a year ago."

"You remember Pat?" he asks. "He plays the drums. Wears braids in his hair."

I nod, remembering our hippie life from North Carolina. *Why can't we just put down roots? Make a home where we can stay? We don't have family in Washington, and we haven't seen Pat in years.*

Dad cuts into my thoughts. "Pat and Lucy say Washington is beautiful! Our family needs a new adventure."

"I don't want to move," I say, fighting tears.

Momma nestles beside me on the couch, plays with the frayed ends of my tangled hair and says, "We are stopping in Las Vegas to see Grandma and Granddad on the way."

I sigh, pick up Barbie and work the pink brush into her matted hair. My heart resigns in sadness. "Okay."

A week later, a giant orange moving truck pulls up to our house. Stacy and I hide in the tree house while sweaty men carry furniture and boxes to the big trailer. My brother is excited for our road trip. I am not. I get the sense we are running away, like a bunch of thugs scattering in the night, and I wonder if someone found out that Dad is a monster.

4

Guess I'll Go Eat Washington Worms

The moving truck pulls up behind our car five days after we arrive in Vancouver, Washington. We stayed with Pat and Lucy until my parents found this rental on 67th Street. The one-story house is brand new, with black shutters and white paint. Red cedar bark dust scallops the Crayola green lawn. Stubby fir trees and shrubs offer natural fencing along the curb.

Inside, everything smells crisp and new. My feet leave imprints in the thick, brown, unstained carpet. I stop to dig my toes into the plush texture, inhale the scent of fresh paint, and admire the brick fireplace decorating the far wall.

"This is a pretty house," I say to Momma as she whizzes by carrying a box.

"Go find your room, Dolly," she says, nodding down the hall.

"Yes, Ma'am," I say, meandering by the galley kitchen with its pass-through window and bar seating. I wander past the bathroom with its double vanity and slide open the doors on the hall closet.

"This is such a nice house," I say, flicking on the light at the end of the hall.

"Your father and I get the master bedroom," Momma hollers.

I wander the two extra bedrooms, decide one is not better than the other. Both feature a popcorn ceiling, a window looking out over the front yard, and mirrored doors covering the closet. I pick a room, lie down on the carpet, and think maybe Washington isn't so bad after all.

Hours later, the moving van pulls away, and Momma helps

me put the lace top on my canopy bed, then the sheets, then the pillows. She pulls my jammies out of a box, tosses them my way, and tells me to dress for bed. I yawn big as she tucks the blankets tight around me, clicks off my doll lamp, and wanders out the door. The next morning, Stacy and I wake up early, rummage through boxes to find our school clothes, then brush our teeth, and comb our hair so Momma can drop us off at Sunnyside Elementary.

My tummy quivers as I think about walking into a new fifth grade classroom.

"I miss my old school," I say as we make the two-mile drive north.

"You'll be fine," Momma says, "You'll see."

I sigh and shrink down in the passenger seat.

"It's a brand-new school," Momma says, lighting a cigarette. "They built it last year, so it's really a new school for everyone honey, not just you."

"But everyone else isn't starting in November," I say.

Mom cracks her window to suck out the cigarette smoke, then drives in silence as I fight the nausea rolling around in my belly. As usual, I'm alone in my fear. I long to trust my mother, to believe her when she tells me everything is going to be okay. But I can't. No matter how hard I try, I can't believe her. Because she doesn't see what I see or feel what I feel. She doesn't even try to understand. She just buries her head in the sand and goes on with her life.

I swallow hard as she pulls into the parking lot, finds a space near the door, drops her cigarette butt out the window, and turns off the car.

"What if the kids hate me?" I ask, studying the fancy brick building.

"No one is going to hate you, honey," she says, thrusting her door open. Stacy scrambles out of the backseat and races toward the sidewalk. I wish I had his enthusiasm. And his courage.

"You're going to be fine, Missy," Momma says. "Don't forget

to grab your brother and take bus 79 home."

The office lady walks me to class, where my teacher parades me in front of a sea of kids, saying, "Students, this is Missy. She's from Mississippi. Make her feel welcome, please."

Kids snicker into their palms. "Missy from Mississippi."

"Get it? Missy-ssippi?" a boy with an oversized head says to the girl beside me.

I slip into my seat, wishing I could dissolve into the plastic chair.

"Shut up, Brandon," she says.

I glance at the freckle-faced girl defending me. She greets me with a wide grin that spreads out the spots on her face like a peanut butter smudge and offers me her hand.

"I'm Jessica," she says with a wink. "Call me Jessie or Jess."

I shake her hand and admire the strawberry blonde curls cascading over her shoulders, the emerald sparkle of her eyes.

"I'm Missy," I say with a drawl, making her giggle.

"I love your accent," she says.

"Thanks."

"Swings at recess?"

"Yes," I say with a sigh of relief.

When the bell rings, I chase her out the door, and hop onto a U-shaped rubber swing.

"Swinging is my favorite thing to do at recess," I say.

"Me, too," she says.

We pump our legs until we almost touch the sky, giggling and laughing as we compete to get higher and higher. When our bodies tire, we slow to a gentle sway, and take turns leaning back so far, our hair drags the ground.

"Do you like it here?" Jessie asks, stopping to pick bark chips from her curls.

"Not really," I say. "I'm homesick. We don't have friends or family here in Washington."

"I miss my home, too." Jessie says. "We used to live in California. But last year, we moved up here to live with my Nana."

"How come?" I ask.

"My mom died."

I sit up straight and stare at her.

"Your mom died?"

"Yeah, she had cancer."

"Wow. I am sorry. You must be so sad."

"I miss her," she says with a nod.

"Where's your dad?"

"He's in the military. Stationed overseas."

I twist in my swing to face her.

"We should have a sleepover sometime," I say.

"Sure! You can come slumber at my grandma's house."

When lunchtime comes, I grab my brown bag, eager to eat with Jess and steal our spot on the swing set. We gobble PB-n-Js, chug chocolate milk, and chatter like bees. When we finish, we toss our bags in the trash and run outside to play.

As soon as we step out the door, Stephanie stomps over to us.

"She was my friend first, Jessica," Steph says.

Jessie looks at the ground. I stare between them, confused. Steph is lying. I only talked to her for a minute during math. We aren't friends.

"Come on, Missy," Steph says, reaching for my hand. "You don't want to be friends with Jessie-Scum. She's got cooties."

I snatch my hand back and glare at Steph.

"Jessie is not scum," I say, resisting the urge to sock Stephanie in the nose. "And Jessie made friends with me, first."

Steph throws her hands on her hips, tosses her head to the side, and says, "You can't be friends with both of us, Missy."

I glance between Jessica and Stephanie and wonder why not. I was friends with all the kids I knew in Mississippi.

"Pick!" Steph says, hovering over me. "Her or me?"

A pack of kids gather to watch Steph, who, with her gigantic body and toothy, sarcastic grin, appears to be the popular girl.

How did Jess make enemies with the entire fifth grade? Don't they know her mom died?

"I choose Jessica," I say, narrowing my eyes at Steph.

"Oh, man! Steph!" a girl shouts.

"She told you!" hollers another.

My heart pounds in my ears.

"Missy-ssippi," Steph says, mocking my accent, "ya know, ya sound stupid when ya talk?"

Another girl steps forward with a sneer. "Where'd ya get them ugly green pants? Ain't ya got style, hick?"

A tall blonde follows the chant. "Ya know, you's ugly, and ya momma dresses ya funny!"

Laughter spills out of them like wolves howling for blood. Fingers poke into my chest, a shove in the shoulder knocks me off balance. I stand my ground, hold my tongue, and fight the tears threatening to fall from my watery eyes. A recess aid blows her whistle to break up the gang, freeing me and Jessie to run for the swings.

After school, I ride the bus home with Stacy and hurry to tell Mom about my day.

"Tomorrow will be better, Missy. You did a good thing, sticking up for your friend. Remember, dynamite and diamond rings come in small packages," she says.

I grin, feeling tough and sassy. But when I climb into bed, tears and anxiety replace my tough and sassy emotions. Because, again, Mom doesn't understand, and she's not helping me. *Maybe God can help me,* I think. *Maybe I should pray.*

"God," I say, "I want to go home, back to Mississippi. I hate Washington, hate being hated by other kids."

Waves of guilt wash over me for using *hate* in my prayers. Momma says it's not okay to hate. I sigh and wonder if God is listening. Or if He even exists. It's not like I talk to God. Me and Mom stopped praying together years ago, and we only go to church sometimes. *God, are You even real?*

Silence.

If You are real, could You move my mobile? I stare at the silver unicorns hanging from my ceiling and wait for the slightest movement. I dare not blink for fear of missing Him. Tick. Tick.

Tick. My eyes dry out while I wait. Light dances off the silver beasts, but they don't move. Nothing. Not even a shift.

Then I remember hearing somewhere that I'm not supposed to test God. Fear creeps up my body like ice. I don't want to anger Him. He could strike me with lightning or kill me or send me to hell. So I say, "That's okay God. You don't have to move my mobile. I still believe in You," and I drift off to sleep singing the song I learned in music today. "Nobody likes me, everybody hates me, guess I'll go eat worms."

♥

The only worms I gobble down are gummy, but fifth grade is still the longest year of my life! On a good note, Momma gives me a house key, saying, "Watch your brother until I get home from work." No more daycare. Yay!

At the start of sixth grade, I board the school bus behind Stacy who promptly leaves me to sit with his friends. I glance around for my new buddy. Even though making friends at school is tough, I make lots of neighborhood pals. Mom says I bring home stray kids the same way other people bring home stray animals. Kim is one of them, and I'm thankful that she is in my grade.

Kim waves and scoots toward the window.

"Missy," she says, "come sit with me."

I walk down the aisle, losing my balance as the bus jerks to life. The movement tosses me toward Brent, who smiles up and winks, making my toes tingle. I hurry to collapse by Kim.

"You have a crush on Brent, huh?" She asks, whispering in my ear.

"What?!"

"I can tell." She weaves her arm through mine. "Best friends know these things."

Well, Jess is my best friend, I think. *But Kim makes a great neighborhood pal.* I smile at her and nod. "Don't tell anyone!"

"I promise," she says with a wink.

Kim's parents are gone a lot, so we do our own thing at her house, like eating candy for dinner and making prank phone calls. Kim has four siblings. There are no blankets on their beds, no real food in their fridge. I'm usually cold and hungry when I sleep over, but I don't mind because no one messes with me in the middle of the night. Her house is safe, like Jessica's. Well, except the one time, Kim's older brother Ted held me down and stuck his tongue in my mouth. Kim jumped on his back, punching him over and over until he let me go. He called it my first kiss. I called it gross!

Kim and I survive the sixth grade with slumber parties, secret sharing, and note passing. I still see Jess sometimes, but I think she's jealous of Kim. She talks mean about my neighborhood buddy and never invites her over. To make Jess feel better, I pinky swear to be Jess's best friend forever, no matter what.

Summer arrives, leaving me to watch Stacy and *Wonder Woman* reruns while Mom works all day. On a hot Friday afternoon, Mom comes home at five o'clock with a U-bake pizza and two liters of soda. Dropping her purse on the counter, she says, "Hey, Mis. How was your day?"

"Good." I say from my comfy spot on the couch, eyes glued to MTV.

"Thanks for washing the dishes," Mom says, scampering in and out of the garage, arms loaded with paper bags. "Dad's playing a gig at City Zoo tonight."

I love Dad's band. When the guys are over, they pass around plenty of beer and weed, putting a smile on Dad's face. Plus, the band is good! They play "Stray Cat Strut" perfectly. Kim and I dance our legs off when the band practices!

I sit up on the couch and watch Mom put groceries away.

"So, are you going to watch them play tonight?" I ask.

"Of course, I am," she says.

"Can Kim spend the night?"

Mom frees the pepperoni pizza from its cellophane wrapper.

"Sure," she says.

I race to hug her. "Yay! Thank you, Momma!"

I snatch the phone off the wall and dial Kim. Ten minutes later, we sit crisscross-applesauce on my bedroom floor.

"What do you want to hear first?" I ask.

"Let's do Steve Miller Band," she says.

I put the record on, set the needle and jump up to twirl around the room. "Abracadabra" booming out of the speakers muffles the sound of Dad's car pulling up. When the garage door slams, I stop mid-twirl and keep my back to the doorway, ears pricked so I can hear his mood.

"Sounds like your dad's home," Kim says, dropping to sit.

"Yep," I say, frozen in place.

I hate it when he comes home. The sound of his car, the garage door clicking shut, the cadence of his voice, all gives me shivers, making me want to run and hide.

Mom hollers down the hall. "Girls, can you put the pizza in the oven while I run Stacy to Chris's house?"

"Okay, Mom," I say.

I free the record, slip it back in its sleeve and hunker down across from Kim, feeling safer with her here. Dad plays nice in front of my friends. I hear Mom start the car and back down the drive, leaving me and Kim alone with Dad. Heavy footsteps shuffle over the thick carpet, bristling the hairs on my arm.

"Hello, sugars," Dad says in a syrupy tone.

Gag.

"How are you, Kim?"

"Fine," she says with a grin.

Double gag.

"Good, good," he says softly.

"Well, I have to shower, get ready for the gig."

I watch him disappear into his bedroom across the hall. From my vantage point, I can see through his room into the entrance of the master bath. The large vanity mirror above the sink reflects the shower and the closet.

I hope he closes his door.

I sit down across from my friend and try to ignore my suspicions.

"What do you want to hear next?" Kim asks.

I stare at the stack of albums as she thumbs through my music collection.

"Abba, Pat Benatar, or Queen?"

I look up to find my dad's reflection in the mirror as he stands buck naked, his eyes eerily fixed our direction.

"Pat Benatar!" I yell, hopping over Kim to slam my door.

Kim jumps, dropping the stack of vinyl.

"Sorry," I say. "We can turn the music up loud when my door is closed."

As Kim puts on the record and turns up the volume, I let out a long sigh.

Why does my dad have to be such a weirdo?

♥

"Dad has a date planned for you tonight," Mom says from the doorway of my room.

"He does? Who's going" I ask, blinking twice.

Dad never, ever makes plans with me.

"Just the two of you. I know it's odd, but go along with it, okay?"

I stare at her, a mixture of fear and excitement brewing inside me. "Where is he taking me?"

"The Aqua Chutes!" Dad booms behind her.

I toss *Are You There, God?: It's Me, Margaret* on the bed.

"Seriously?!"

"Just the two of us. Get your swimsuit on, we leave in twenty minutes."

"Yay," I say, racing to hug him.

Is this how it feels to have a normal dad?

Amazement washes over me. Where did this cool guy come from? My elation rides with me on the drive to the waterslides, into the locker room, and up a dozen flights of stairs. As we stand in line with a hundred booger-nosed kids, I marvel at Dad's patience, his tolerance for the shrill sounds, the pungent smell of chlorine. This place is normally way out of his comfort zone.

At the top of the landing, I grin at him before hopping into the mouth of the slide. Squeals escape me as water tosses me through darkness and light, around sharp curves, and over bumps, stealing my tummy, before dumping me into the shallow pool below. Dad shoots out of the tube next to mine with his legs splayed out like a chicken, making me howl with laughter. We hop out, head for the stairs and do it again. And again. And again.

We ride the hydro tubes until Dad says he can't climb another step.

"Go get changed. We'll grab a bite to eat on the way home," he says.

I race for the locker room, wriggle out of my soggy swimsuit, and meet him at the front door. The sky is dark when we hop into our Bronco. He turns the heat up to dry out our water-logged bodies.

"Did you have fun?" he asks, pulling a cigarette from his shirt pocket and cracking the window.

"I did." I smile and relax into the seat.

"Great." He winks at me and slides his smoke between his lips before shifting into first gear. "I noticed you enjoy reading. Tell me about your book."

"It's written by Judy Blume. She's the best author ever. It's about Margaret, a girl who talks to God while coming of age."

"You mean, maturing?" he asks.

"Yeah, she turns into a woman, stuff like that," I say with a shrug.

"Does she start her period? Are you learning about that?" Dad asks.

"Yeah," I say with a gulp.

"Have you started yours?"

"No," I say, squirming in my seat. My stomach churns in a

sickening blend of hunger, from all our time in the water, and nausea, from my father's intrusive questions.

I thought girl talk was for girls, I think to myself, remembering Margaret from the book.

"Margaret also talks to God," I say to my dad, hoping to change the subject as we approach Burger Barn. I press my palms together, lick my lips in anticipation, and crane my neck as Dad whizzes by the restaurant without stopping. "No fudge bar?" I wonder aloud, pointing back at the neon burger twisting in the sky.

"Where are we going?" I ask with a squeak.

"I figured we could take a drive," he says, flicking ashes out the window.

Where could we possibly go in the dark? I sit up straight, tuck my hands under my legs, and push down the panic rising inside me. Dad takes a long drag off his smoke, flicks the butt out the window, and cranks the handle shut, locking out the sound of tires on wet pavement. I feel trapped, have trouble breathing. Maybe it's the stale air pulling the oxygen from my lungs. The sound of my racing heart swooshes blood over my eardrums.

I should have known, I think, balling my fists. *I should have known he would pull some trick on me.*

Leaning back in my seat, I pull in a deep breath, count to ten, and exhale slowly. I dig my thumbnails into the soft skin on my fingers, allow the pain to distract me. This is what I do when I'm in a scary place. I breathe, I count, I dig my nails in deep, and repeat. If I can just escape before the pattern breaks, I am safe.

We pull onto a country road and follow it for several miles. I feel the Bronco climb higher. Dark shadows and silvery evergreens tell me we are in the mountains.

"Did you tell Mom where we're going?" I ask, reminding him I have another parent who cares about me.

"She knows we'll be gone awhile," he says, glancing at me. "Are you nervous?"

"No, I'm fine." I lie.

My hands are pinched together now, thumbnails drawing blood from the tender skin covering my fingers. Outside the truck, it's pitch-black, without a star in the sky. There are no cars, no people around, when Dad parks on the edge of the road, clicks on the dome light, and reaches over my legs to open the glove box. The latch clicks, dropping the door free. Dad runs his hand up my thigh, making me shrink back. He's never done this before.

"Hand me that pipe, will you?"

I wriggle free of his grasp and grab the sticky glass pipe. I hold it as Dad pops the gray top off a film canister. The skunky smell of weed fills the car, making me want to gag. Dad shoves his fingers into the canister, grabs the pipe from my hands and packs the bowl tight with greens. He flicks open his lighter, lays the flame to the pipe. I listen to the marijuana crackle and pop as he draws smoke into his lungs. He holds his breath, cranks the window down a smidge, and blows a long cloud of white smoke outside.

I want to go home, I think, squeezing my eyes shut.

Dad thrusts the pipe my way.

"Why don't you smoke a little with me?"

My brows furrow, lips pull into a tight knot as I curl up in my seat and shrink as far away from him, and the pipe, as I can.

Has my dad forgotten I'm twelve?!

He looks at me with a hazy grin.

"Come on, it'll be fun." He leans over the console, gazing at me. "Maybe you'd let me touch you a little bit? There's no one out here to see us," he says, clicking off the dome light.

Earp.

I barf a little in my mouth. This is not the Monster I know. The Monster I know sneaks into my room to molest me at night or when Mom leaves. He does not drive me into the woods! Tears brim as I pull back against the door, wet hair pressed to the glass, and shake my head.

"No," I say with my body quivering. "No!"

Shocked by my boldness, he withdraws as I sob.

"Take me home. I want to go home!"

Dad tosses the loaded pipe and canister into the glove compartment, slams it shut, and grinds the engine to start. He looks me over with black eyes before thrusting the Bronco into first gear, launching us back onto the road. Tears rain down my cheeks as he drives home in a silent rage.

When we pull into the driveway, he shoves a finger in my face and says, "Quit your sniveling, young lady. I don't want your mother seeing you this way."

5

Latchkey Kid

Seventh grade at Chinook Junior High brings class periods, locker combinations, and a student store packed with candy. Junior high is cool, but Chinook is a dark place compared to Sunnyside. There are no swing sets, dodge-ball squares, or recess aides. It's a free for all with the freshmen leading the pack.

Stoner girls with black parachute pants and Iron Maiden jerseys claim the girls' bathroom. They cloud the stalls with smoke and tatter the walls in bubble-letter graffiti. Their artwork features things like *Tammy loves Tyler forever* and *Mrs. Graves is a skank*. These tough chicks hate preppies. Lucky for me, I'm just a unicorn-loving, nerd girl. Steph and her gang are the preppies (ha!), with the collars on their Izod polos flipped snobbishly high. Yeah, those raunchy girls hate girls like Steph. Watching Steph eat a bowl of her own medicine cracks me up, especially when her phone number appears on the boys' bathroom wall, along with an invitation to "call for a good time."

Steph stops picking on me, but the memories of her cruel words jump around inside my head like fleas on a dog's back. They can't be seen or heard, but they leave a mark. And her suffering at the hands of junior high bullies does nothing to erase the wounds on my heart. Thanks to her, and my weird father, I wander into this season of life believing two things: I'm a loser and caving to peer pressure buys me more friends.

Kim and I remain thick as thieves through seventh grade. Jessica is changing, turning mean and cold. Rumor has it she's dabbling in drugs and steals her nana's whiskey. Sometimes I catch her smoking in the bathroom with the ninth graders. Although I am guilty of puffing a menthol or two, I do not have the gonads to smoke at school. And since I'm still collecting Hello Kitty and decorating my room in rainbows, Jess's gothic choices push me further away from her.

My parents still smoke pot, and I suspect Dad is using cocaine. Stacy snoops in Dad's weed stash after school, swiping a bud now and then. I haven't crossed that bridge yet. One day Stacy found a mirror covered in white residue under our father's dresser. It was packaged with an empty baggie, a razor blade, and a rolled-up dollar bill. I've seen enough R-rated movies to know Dad's snorting coke.

With Mom working all the time and Dad using drugs, life offers me little choice, except to follow in my parent's shit-laced footsteps. I don't do a lick of homework since there's no one to help me understand prealgebra, memorize all those boring dates in history, or complete science projects, so I'm failing most of my classes. Me and Kim are thirteen now, so riding bikes and dancing to vinyl records is boring. To act like the cool kids, we steal smokes from Mom and beer from the fridge. We also invite two new girls into our sisterhood, Lisa and Mandy.

Lisa is benign and honest. When we slumber at Lisa's house, we watch VHS movies (since her parents can afford the VHS player!) and scarf nachos smothered in queso. Lisa is the baby in her family, the only kid still at home. Her parents are always around, but they are older and lenient. Her mom buys us popcorn, candy, and soda. And she lets us stay up as late as we want. Best of all, she lets both girls *and* boys sleep over sometimes. We don't do anything raunchy since we are all still virgins, but we entertain the idea.

Mandy's parents, on the other hand, are rarely home. Her dad travels for business and when her mom is there, she pays us little mind. Mandy's house is where the PG-13 version of those raunchy ideas come to life. When the sun shines, we lay on towels in her dandelion infested yard, smoking cigarettes and talking about sex. We sneak a beer when we can, or a bottle of wine, and sneak boys through her bedroom window at night for impromptu make-out sessions. One day Mandy and I cut classes to spend the day puffing menthols and watching soaps at her house.

"My parents will bust my ass if they find out I skipped school," I say when it's time to go home.

"Just make sure you answer the phone if the school calls," Mandy says with a shrug.

I make the ten-minute walk home with fear chasing me like a ghost. What if the school doesn't believe me when I answer the phone and pretend to be Mom? What if they call after my parents get home? What if I can't pull off this lie? When I round the corner and spot Dad's car in the drive, my heart stops.

"Oh, no! Now what am I going to do?"

The moment I walk inside and drop my backpack, he appears.

"Where have you been?" he asks, following me to my bedroom.

"School. I got off the bus at Mandy's."

"Chinook called five minutes ago. You were absent today," he says in a silky voice.

Earp.

I confess, saying, "I was with Mandy," and perch on the edge of my bed to cover my butt, expecting the sting of his belt. To my surprise, he stays calm, and even grins a little.

"How about this?" he says. "I won't tell Mom . . ."

Horror swells inside me as he unbuckles his belt, saying, "And I won't punish you. We can trade favors instead. I'll keep your secret and you keep mine."

My tongue sticks to the roof of my mouth. I don't tell him *no* because I don't know what's coming. If I knew, maybe *no* would run off my tongue in a rush of self-protection. Instead, as my father dismantles me piece-by-piece, I fix my mind on a place that isn't here. And when it's done, like the secrets of old, I lock the event away in the darkest part of my heart. Because on this day, the day I bargain with the devil to save my own ass, shame slithers up me in long black tendrils and forms a pit so deep in my soul, I won't be able to find its end. And on this day, the day the devil shifts the guilt of abuse from my father to me, I no longer keep the secret to protect my mother.

I keep the secret to protect myself.

♥

It's Christmas break, and Stacy, Dad, and I are all at home with the flu. Fever chills me to the bone. Strep coats my tonsils in sticky, white pus patches. I snuggle my head against the pillow, work to swallow past the pain knifing my throat, and close my eyes for a little snooze, when the phone rings. I scurry off the couch to grab it before it awakes Dad, but I'm too slow.

As I reach for the receiver, Dad's groggy voice pricks my ears. "Hello," he says.

Dang it. He's awake!

I tiptoe down the hall and hear him say, "This is Mr. Self."

Uh-oh.

He says, "Yes, ma'am" and "You bet I will."

The phone slamming into its cradle sends me scampering back to the couch. I hear the squeak of his mattress springs, his heels pounding down the hall, and the jangle of his belt buckle.

One of us is busted.

I glance at Stacy's wide eyes. My heart thuds a rapid beat in my chest, swooshing blood past my eardrums. It doesn't matter who's in trouble. When Dad wields that torture device and we scream, my heart rips in two, regardless of who's getting beaten. I pull the blankets up to my chin and crouch low as the Monster stands over me, his red robe tied loose around his waist, revealing more of his body than I care to see.

"That was Mrs. Knutson!"

Oh, crap!

"She says you're failing social studies?"

I stare back at him, eyes wide with terror. Would he spank me when I'm shaking with fever? Would he whip me after sneaking me into his bedroom this morning?

"Answer me!" he thunders, making me jump.

I shake my head, eyeing the belt looped in his hands. "No," I say.

"No?! Are you lying to me, Melissa?" he yells, his pupils darkened by rage.

"No, I mean, yes, my grade is bad," I say with a stutter, pushing my body deep into the couch.

I glance at Stacy, hunkered into the love seat across from us, and watch his lip quiver.

"Get up!"

"No, Dad, don't."

He peels my blankets free, grabs my arm, and yanks me up as I bellow.

"No, don't spank me. I'm sick."

My satin nightgown muffles the sound of leather welting flesh, but Stacy still jumps every time the belt hits me.

Dad turns me around, shoves his fist in my face, and says, "You will meet with Mrs. Knutson when you get back to school, and you will bring up your grades. Do you understand me?"

"Yes, sir."

I return in January hating my teacher with a passion. If I could dig out her eyes and spit down her neck, I would. Why do people not care enough to ask a kid what's going on at home? Why does she not care enough to offer help? Judgment and punishment are served up like hot slop in a mess hall, but compassion is as rare as ribbon candy.

Shaken by my father's rage, I obey like a good girl. I focus on bringing up my grades, lugging all my books from class to class, never stopping at my locker. Every step I take is motivated by fear so intense, I can't take a pee break.

Living in this state of confusion over right and wrong is grueling. So it's okay for Dad to offer me drugs? And it's okay to lie to Mom? But it's not okay to lie when I find it convenient? It's not okay for me to fail when I have no help, no compassion, no mercy in my life? There must be boundary lines somewhere, but they are invisible to me.

♥

Momma lets me wear makeup, starting on my thirteenth birthday, but she buys me only gloss and mascara. If I want to be a glamour girl, like the teens on the cover of *Seventeen* magazine, I've got to be resourceful. So one Saturday afternoon, I take matters into my own hands.

"Can you take me and Mandy to the mall?" I ask Mom.

"Sure," she says with a smile, "As long as you ride the bus home."

Mom drops us outside JC Penney with a "behave" and two quarters for the bus. Mandy and I watch her leave before sneaking behind the arborvitaes to share a cigarette.

"I'll watch first," Mandy says, taking a drag. "If anyone comes to your aisle, I'll distract them. You do the same for me."

I nod, take the last puff off our smoke, and crush it in the bark dust.

"Let's go," she says, grabbing my hand.

I take a deep breath and exhale loudly.

"Act normal," she says as we waltz into Newberry's drug store.

Mandy stands at the end of the makeup aisle. Looks right, looks left, gives me a nod. I grab a seafoam green clamshell stuffed with pods of purple, pink, brown and gray shadows, a two-pack of black eyeliner, a tube of black mascara, and a gloss, and stuff them in my purse. We switch positions, and I play lookout as Mandy steals neon purple mascara, another clamshell of shadows, and black liquid liner. Loot in hand, we scurry to the bathroom to hussy up for the bus ride home.

When I walk in the door, Mom stops folding clothes to stare at me.

"What happened to your face?" she asks.

"Mandy gave me some of her old makeup," I say with a shrug.

"Less is more, Melissa," she says.

"You look like a hooker," Dad says.

"I guess you haven't seen Madonna," I say and sashay to the bathroom to pile on more gloss.

♥

Momma carries a black duffel bag out to the car and stuffs it on top of Dad's guitar case and amplifier.

"Dad and I will be gone through Sunday," she says.

"You're leaving us alone all weekend?" I ask.

"Are you okay with watching Stacy, or should I call a sitter?"

A sitter? Um, no thank you. "We'll be fine," I say. "Can we have friends over?"

"You can have a friend or two over. But nothing crazy, you hear?"

"Okay."

When Mom and Dad back down the driveway, I run to the phone and dial Mandy.

"Holy cow! Your parents are leaving you alone all weekend?"

"Yeah. Mom says you can spend the night. And Lisa and Kim," I say.

"Let's call some boys," she says with a squeal.

"Um, I don't know," I say.

"You can call Brent," she says, reminding me of my fifth-grade crush.

"Okay, you call them," I whisper. "But they can't come over until I know my parents are in Seattle."

"After dinner, then?" she asks.

"Yeah, Mom's supposed to call me from the hotel when they arrive."

"I'll see you in an hour," Mandy says with a click of the receiver.

It's dusk when the guys drop their bikes in the drive and clamber up to the door. My heart pounds a nervous rhythm as Lisa ushers them in, her eyes glued to Chad. We lounge on Momma's wicker furniture, drinking sodas, and trying to decide what trouble to dig into.

"We could make prank calls," I say, slurping down a Dr. Pepper.

"How about strip poker?" Jake asks, eyeing us girls.

Mandy's arm shoots up. "Yeah!"

Lisa stares at Chad, raises a brow, and says, "Sure," with a wink and a purr of her tongue.

I freeze, doe eyed. Stacy went to Chris's house. What if he walks in the front door to find his sister half-naked with a bunch of boys? He'd freak out. He might be the younger sibling, but he's still my brother and my fiercest protector. What if my parents come home early? My heart drops at the thought. I want to say no and send these boys packing. I glance around the room, lock eyes with Brent as he drops his chin and smiles at me with his blue eyes. I watch him bounce a Hacky Sack toe-to-toe and remember how I've loved him since fifth grade.

"Come on, Missy," Jake says, grinning wide.

I stare at Jake's broken front tooth and consider my options. It's my house, after all. I could say no. But I don't want to be a downer, don't want to be teased or ridiculed for being a wussy. I sigh as two years of laughing and jeering snare my heart. The desire to be liked and accepted outweighs the risks, propelling me to relent and say, "Okay, let's do it."

I grab Mom's playing cards from the kitchen drawer and toss them on the table. Chad snatches them up, shuffles, and deals.

"Ante up," he says.

I fan out my cards and look at them with furrowed brows. Brent slides up beside me.

"Need some help?" he asks, peeking over my shoulder.

"Um, yes," I say.

"Bets!" Chad barks, making me jump.

"Chill, Dude," Brent says, glaring at Chad.

Brent turns to look my way, drenching me with those ocean blue peepers. "Do you have a pen and paper?" I hop up, thankful to escape his penetrating gaze, and grab Mom's yellow note pad. As he explains the royal flush, full-house, and four of a kind, I stare at his lips. Heat creeps up my face as I realize I want to kiss him. He hands me the instructions with a wink and takes a seat across from me.

I mouth, "Thank you," peek at my cards, and remove my cross necklace to toss in the pot. As the game circles around, I lose both earrings, my barrette, my socks, and shoes. The game picks up speed, with each of us stripping off hats, wristbands, pants, and shirts. I sneak a peek at my half-naked friends, feeling cocky with my almost full house. Until I draw a two. And lose. I look down at my bra and think . . . *I have boobs.* "Dang it!" I whisper.

The guys study my face as red splotches bloom on my chest, neck, and cheeks. It doesn't take them long to realize I've lost.

"Whoa, ho, ho," they say before chanting, "Take it off! Take it off! Take it off!"

"Give it up, girl!" Jake hollers.

I glance left and right, hesitate a heartbeat before knocking my wicker chair back to make a run for it. Ten steps in, a boy is behind me, grabbing my bra strap to pull it off. I fight him, screaming, and dash into the bathroom, pinching his arm in the door. Mandy knocks him off balance, buying me time to click the lock, and lean my weight against it for good measure.

"Wussy," Jake says, pounding on the door.

I slide down, head in my hands, and begin a silent cry.

"Go away!" I say, grabbing a towel to wrap around my shoulders.

Moments later, I hear mumbling and the front door close. Mandy comes to get me.

"They are gone, Mis."

I creep out of the bathroom, put my clothes on and say, "I'm going to bed."

The girls hunker down in sleeping bags beside me, and we

giggle over stupid stories until two o'clock in the morning. When Lisa and Kim doze off, Mandy and I share secrets.

"I'm sorry for being such a baby," I say for the hundredth time.

"Don't be. It was getting out of hand."

"I suppose," I say, scooching into my sleeping bag.

"I'm really surprised Jake chased you down like that," she says.

"He terrified me," I say, breathing deeply.

"Why were you so afraid?" she asks.

"'Cause I didn't want him seeing my boobies!"

Mandy laughs, snorting like a bull with each breath.

"Can I tell you a secret?" I ask in a whisper.

"Sure."

I watch her pick lint off her t-shirt, as I work to find the words.

"My dad touches me."

She stops fidgeting to stare at me.

"My uncle touches me," she says.

"He does?" I ask.

"He has since I was little. He doesn't live with us, though, so I guess I'm lucky."

I roll back onto my pillow and think about Mandy's confession. Somehow her abuse doesn't seem as bad as mine. Mandy seems so normal. She's not afraid of the whole world, like I am, and her uncle is rarely around to hurt her. I've never even met him, so in that regard, she is luckier than me.

"Thank you for telling me," I say. "I don't feel like such a weirdo now."

"You are not a weirdo, Missy. You are one of the sweetest, coolest girls I know," she says, smacking my arm.

I giggle before letting out a deep sigh and relaxing into the moment. It sounds selfish, but I'm happy to know I'm not alone. Someone else is in prison with me.

♥

Eighth grade begins the same as seventh, except I'm afraid to go to my locker. Traci Shaw started picking on me the first day of school, saying things like, "Hey, bitch! I'm going to kick your ass. You better watch your back!"

And her locker is right next to mine.

Traci is no taller than I, but she's thicker and meaner. And I can't figure out why she hates me. I try having a friend intervene, but Traci just keeps calling me names, threatening to beat me up, and she never gives me a reason why. I endure her nasty words, deal with the embarrassment of her harassment in the hallways, and creep around the school haunted by fear until the day I can't take it anymore. I've had enough. My emotions are raw from dealing with Dad, my sense of self crumbles with my failing grades, and my raging hormones make me want to snap. I need my lunch money, and it's in my locker. The only way to get it is by confronting Traci Shaw.

"Hey, you little whore!" Traci shouts as I spin the combination on my lock.

I hold my breath and try to ignore her.

"I'm talking to you, Skank!" she hollers behind me.

I whip around to face her, drop my backpack, and take a step forward.

"What is your problem?" I ask, balling my fists.

Slap! Her palm lands crisp against my cheek.

I gasp, put a hand to my face, and step forward to grab her. Swift as lightning, she shoves me against the lockers. The echo of metal rattles in my ears as I work to right myself. Movement in the hallway stops. There are no cheers, no jeering. Just a sea of faces watching us with wide eyes and slack jaws. I rub my cheek and glare at her, my brown eyes locking on her steely blues as I await her next move. Her expression softens as she says, "Keep your mouth shut, Priss," and walks away. I drag oxygen into my lungs. Heat creeps up my neck as I lean over to collect my bag, and wipe tears off my stinging face.

After fifth period, I wander into the bathroom behind Mandy to sneak a menthol. Traci pokes her head out of the second stall, looks me over and says, "Hey, Prissy Missy, sorry I smacked you."

"Why do you hate me?" I ask.

"I heard you have a crush on Shane."

Mandy bursts out laughing. "Yeah right!"

"Shane?" I ask, looking at Traci with disgust.

"Yeah, he's mine," Traci says, blowing a fat, pink bubble between her glossed lips before sucking her gum between her teeth with a pop-pop-pop.

"Yuck," I say, "I don't like Shane!"

"Missy totally loves Brent," Mandy says, letting my secret go like a butterfly from a net.

I whip around to glare at Mandy. "Dude! You're not supposed to tell anyone!"

"Wait?!" Traci smirks, winding gum around her index finger. "You like Brent?"

I want to grab Mandy's words and shove them down her throat until Traci says, "You know, Brent is my neighbor, and my best friend. I could totally hook you up with him."

As I stare at her, I wonder how we went from hating each other to this—this weird conversation that gets even stranger when she says, "We should totally hang out sometime."

♥

In the months that follow, Mandy, Traci, and I meet up with the guys at Willow Creek Park almost every day after school. The place is huge, with a pond for skipping rocks and fishing, a creek for scavenging salamanders and frogs. The endless dirt, gravel, and asphalt trails offer a paradise for mountain biking or skate boarding. This is a perfect spot to hang with boys, especially Brent. And Brent and I flirt a lot, playing Frisbee, riding bikes, and chasing each other around the swing sets.

Over time, our group grows to include several boys and girls.

We buddy up, like a band of smoking, cussing, troublemakers, and stick together at school now, too. One day, I stand in the hall yakking with the gang when Brent draws close to me. I glance up to catch him grinning my way, braces sparkling, brown skater bangs falling over his light blue eyes.

"What?" I ask with a furious blush creeping up my cheeks. When he bumps me with his elbow, my breathing stops.

"You like me?" he asks, leaning against me now.

Electricity sizzles to my toes. I can't hold his penetrating gaze, so I glance away.

"What do you mean?" I ask.

"Traci said you think I'm cute. Do you?"

I snap my head to the left, glare at Traci, and say, "You traitor."

I inhale deeply and will myself to look up at Brent. My eyes wander over the soft brown lashes framing his playful eyes, land on his full lips, his scrumptious dimples.

"Yeah," I say, letting out a sigh. "I think you're cute."

"Wow," he says. "I had no idea!"

The shrill hammer of the lunch bell makes me jump. He squeezes my wrist before wandering away backward, his eyes never leaving mine.

Mandy slides up beside me, asking, "What was that all about?"

"I have no idea," I say, grabbing her hand to skip down the hall.

After school, Mandy and I walk to Willow Creek Park, as we always do, to meet up with Brent and the gang. We play Frisbee, scour the creek for critters, and hang out until the frogs start singing. When the streetlights come on and the sun dips low, Mandy gathers her bag, grabs Jake's hand, and asks, "Are you walking home with us?"

"No," Brent says, "she's staying with me."

"Promise you'll walk her home?" Mandy asks, staring at my face to make sure I'm okay.

"Cross my heart," Brent says, grinning down at me.

My heart pounds in my ears as the gang walks away, leaving us alone at the picnic table. He smiles at me and reaches for the Frisbee in my hand. I tuck it behind me and walk backward, daring him to come get it.

"Oh, I see how you are . . . You think I can't take that from you?" he asks, stalking me across the damp grass.

"Let's see you try," I say.

He strides toward me, wraps an arm around my waist, and locks a palm on the disc. I fight him for it, pulling him closer. A smile lights his face when he tucks a foot behind my heel, gives me a push, and falls on top of me in the grass.

We wrestle a minute, giggling and breathing hard until he stops, locks his eyes on mine, and asks, "Can I kiss you?"

"Do you think our braces will lock?" I ask with a snort.

"Let's find out," he says, covering my mouth with his.

My spirit bounces with the brilliance of a million fireflies as I lie back in dewy grass and receive the kiss I've longed for since the fifth grade. It is the sweetest kiss, the only kiss, I have ever wanted on my fourteen-year-old lips.

Falling in love with Brent, spending time alone with him and his family, complicates my life at home. Dad is jealous, of course, and overzealous in his suspicions about Brent and his intentions toward me. The bottom line is, Dad doesn't like Brent. So, he questions me about everything we do. How do we spend our time together, what do we talk about, have we had sex yet?

None of this is my father's business, but my life is a tangled ball of lies and abuse. I think I know right from wrong, but I really don't. I only know what my parents show me. And what they've shown me thus far is pretty messed up. So I escape into the idea of Brent and me, together forever. I need a handsome prince, or a white knight, to save me from the monster eating me alive. I need Brent to save me from my dad.

♥

My family of four climbs out of the car and wanders up the pebbled driveway of a house in Jessica's neighborhood. The real estate sign planted near the mailbox blows in the breeze, its chains clanking out an eerie sound with each blustery gust.

"This is cool!" Stacy says, peering up the giant fir trees swaying in the yard.

"It's a little creepy," I say nudging my brother. "I wonder if it's haunted."

"Shut up, Missy," he says, jogging up the porch steps.

The house is two stories tall, painted white with brown shutters, has a long concrete patio, and four stately white pillars decorating its face. The same agent featured on the real estate sign opens the front door and ushers us inside.

"This is weird," I say as we cross the threshold to encounter one set of stairs going up, and another set going down.

"It's called a split entry," Mom says, closing the door against the wind. Dad and Stacy follow the agent upstairs, taking the steps two at a time. I trail behind my pokey mother. Halfway up the staircase, Mom stumbles over her foot. I put my hands on her butt to steady her as she catches herself on the step above.

"Dang, Momma!" I say, prompting Dad to turn and grab her hand.

"Thanks, honey," she says as he helps her up the last few steps.

"Are you okay?" I ask, cradling her elbow as we meander into the kitchen.

"It's my gimpy leg," she says, reminding me of the funky stuff going on with her body. Momma's been night-blind forever, but now her right eye is fuzzy in the daytime. Even with her glasses on. And her hand geeks out too, turning her silky cursive into sloppy chicken scratch.

She shakes me off, asking, "Do you like the house?" as we walk from room to room.

"I don't know," I say. "None of the flooring matches, and the wallpaper is hideous."

"Well, get used to it," Dad says. "We are buying our first house, and this is it."

"We are buying it?" Stacy asks.

"I think so," Mom says.

We make our way downstairs, where the air is chilly as a grave.

"The basement is spooky" I say, crossing my arms over my chest.

"It's not a basement," Momma says. "It's a split level."

"Well, the floors are concrete, and the windows are eye-level with the dirt outside," I say with a huff.

Mom ignores me, opening cabinets and closets to assess the storage space before leading me back upstairs. I feel like a zombie rising from the crypt, turn to make sure no ghosts are stalking me, and practically shove my mother up the last step leading to the kitchen. After my goosebumps relax, I remember the real reason I don't want to live in this house.

"I'll be moving away from my friends," I say, shoving my lower lip out.

"Don't be dramatic, Melissa," Mom says. "It's only a mile away from the house we live in now."

"I won't be on Brent's bus, though," I say.

"Brent can ride his skateboard to see you," she says.

I sigh, fold my arms, and glare at her.

"And Jess lives just around the corner, so you have a friend in the neighborhood," she says, brushing past me to follow Dad onto the back deck.

"Jess and I don't even speak to each other," I say, following her outside.

"Well, maybe you should call her," Momma says.

"I don't want to be with Jess. I want to be with Brent."

"Suck it up," Dad says. "We move in a month."

♥

78

My first day on the new bus, I hide in the back, hunker against the window, and shove my nose in a book. Jess doesn't see me until we pull into the neighborhood, but when she does, she jumps up from her seat and stumbles down the aisle, prompting the bus driver to grab his mic and holler, "Please remain seated while the bus is moving."

She gives him the finger (which he totally doesn't see) and plops down beside me.

"Hey stranger," she says, ribbing me with her elbow.

"Hey," I say, glancing at her. Jess looks weathered as a stray dog, with her emerald-green eyes caked in black eyeliner and her skank reputation caked in nasty rumors. Someone said she made out with Zane on our sixth-grade field trip, tongue, and all. We were, like, twelve! Now she gets it on with every boy in town, so I hear. I fight the urge to shake my head. This strawberry blonde is a stranger to me.

She elbows me again, smacking her gum. "What are you doing on my bus?"

"We bought a house in this neighborhood."

"Serious? Which one?" she asks, craning her neck to see out the window.

"Back in the cul-de-sac, white with black shutters," I say, studying the perfect feather of her long, thick hair.

"Cool," she says. "You're just a few blocks from our farm."

As the bus rolls to a stop, I stand to go.

"Why don't you come hang out with me Friday?" she asks.

I'm not sure I want to, but I say, "I'll ask my mom."

"Bring your stuff. You can sleep over," she says.

Great.

♥

I set my bag inside Jessica's screened porch and follow her down the wooden steps to say hi to her horse, Cud, and her Shetland pony, Banjo. A cluster of goats, chickens, and feral cats follow us around the pasture. After feeding treats to her barnyard bunch, we take turns on the tire swing hanging from one of the giant fir trees growing on her property. I peer through the branches overhead and remember how Jessie and I spent hours on this swing when we were in fifth grade. My heart relaxes as each memory floods my brain. Playing hide-and-go seek around her ten-acre property, telling ghost stories inside her giant farmhouse, annoying her older siblings until they chased us out of the barn. This place was like my second home. And Jessica was my very best friend.

I watch her toss her long hair over her shoulder before grabbing the tire to give me a push.

"How's life?" she asks.

"Good," I say, shaking the hair from my eyes.

"How's your family?" she asks.

"Mom's having some weird episodes with her hands and eyes."

"What do you mean?"

"Like, her right eye gets cloudy vision. And she trips over her right foot."

"Do you know what's wrong with her?"

"Not yet," I say, hopping off the swing to sit beside Jess in the grass.

"That's tough," she says. "I miss your mom."

"She misses you, too."

"My grandpa died last year," Jessie says. "Drank himself to death. Nana went back to work. My brothers and sisters all moved out, leaving me to care for the animals and the house by myself."

"That sounds overwhelming," I say.

"I raid Nana's liquor cabinet," she says with a sly grin. "It helps me cope."

"I steal weed from Dad," I say, one-upping her.

She stares at me with wide eyes. "What?! Sweet little Missy is smoking dope?"

"Me and Mandy smoke it sometimes."

"Can you get some for us?" she asks, giving me a hand up.

"I can try," I say.

We jump the creek, meander across the pasture, and pull open the heavy door to her barn. "I always wanted to hang out in here, but your sisters wouldn't let us."

"I remember," she says. "They're bitches."

"I thought they were cool," I say.

"Trust me," she says, clicking on the giant tin lights swinging from the rafters, "they were bitches then, and they are bitches now."

Jessie's family stopped storing hay in the loft years ago, leaving space to raise six wild teenagers. I study the place as we shuffle toward the loft. An old pinball machine, soda cooler, and cigarette vending machine sit beside her grandfather's rusty, green tractor. One of her brothers hauled a crusty brown loveseat up to the loft using the old hay trolley. Empty whiskey barrels, silvered by time and weather, rest in random locations throughout the barn, serving as tables for games, drinks, food, and such.

"This place hasn't changed at all," I say, following Jess up the steep ladder leading to the loft. I have a natural fear of falling from high places, so I crawl away from the edge before standing up. Jessie's grandfather never installed a rail around the perimeter of the loft. The thought of tumbling over the side gives me the willies, even from twenty feet away.

"I see you haven't changed either, chicken shit," she says with a smirk.

I flip her the bird and say, "Shut up. You know I'm afraid of heights."

"You're afraid of everything, you pansy."

I stick my tongue out at her.

"You and Brent are super cute together," she says, flopping onto the dusty sofa.

"Thanks," I say, sitting gingerly on the braided rug covering the plywood floor. I watch the area for movement, then relax a smidge while keeping one eye glued to the dark corners, lest a mouse or a hairy spider should make its way up my leg.

"Are you still a virgin?" she asks, tucking a pinch of Skoal into her lower lip. She offers me a scoop of her mint-flavored chewing tobacco.

"No, thank you."

"Virgin?" she asks again.

"Yeah, aren't you?"

"No," she says, tossing her hair over her shoulder. "Why haven't you and Brent done it yet?"

I blush and stare at the rafters above us.

"Are you just a wussy?" she asks with a low giggle.

"No!" I say with a laugh. "He hasn't even tried."

I glance around the barn, hoping to change the subject.

"Don't you worry you'll get caught smoking in here?" I ask, pointing at the overstuffed ashtrays peppering the room.

"Nana never comes up here," she says.

We spend the next few hours chattering about life, puffing on menthols, and sucking down bottled sodas. Jess tells me about her boy drama, how she hops from bed to bed, and never plans to fall in love. I tell her all I want is to love one boy – Brent – for all my days. My sappy heart makes her gag and roll her eyes, but it also softens her up a bit.

"I'm glad you are back in my life, Missy," she says. "You've always been my best friend."

"Can I tell you something," I ask, "since we are sharing all our secrets?"

"You can tell me anything," she says.

I climb onto the sofa, blow out a long sigh, and pull my legs crisscross.

"My dad touches me," I say in a whisper.

"He molests you?"

"Yeah."

"Dude. That's awful. I'm so sorry," she says, furrowing her brows.

I'm not sure why I told her or what I expect her to do. Sometimes I think I need to say it out loud, just to confirm the evil is real. I also need my best friend to understand me and what I'm going through.

"I love you," she says, pulling me in for a long hug. "I know I'm no help, but you can always talk to me."

♥

Jess and I tether together like bees and honey. After school, I race home to do my chores before slipping out the door to meet my bestie. Some days, the two of us ride her horses around the trails on her property or hunker down in the loft to share the day's secrets. But most days, we cruise our ten-speeds to Willow Creek Park to hang out with the gang. Since our group is getting rougher, adding things like weed and pills to our cigarettes and cussing, Jess is a welcome addition.

One warm afternoon, I plan to meet her at her house for a sleepover. I slip between the rails of her wood fence and meander past the tire swing when I spot Jess jogging toward me with a large brown jug in her hand.

"I swiped a goodie," she says.

"You stole it?" I glance around, wondering if anyone gave chase.

"From Nana's cabinet, dummy," she says.

She tosses her head back, takes a swig, and wipes the excess on her palm before thrusting the bottle at me. With wide eyes, I read Jim Beam on the label and pull the rim to my nose for a sniff. I scrunch my face at the sour smell. I've sipped beer before, but I've never been drunk.

"Just drink it, you baby," she says, lighting a Marlboro.

I take a deep breath, lift the jug up, and try not to gag when the liquid burns my throat. Jess snatches it away, guzzles deep, and hands it back to me. We pass it back and forth until my head spins and time disappears in a haze of silly jokes and stupid conversation. As night falls and mosquitoes arrive to feast on our skin, Stacy appears with a band of his little buddies.

"Dude! My sister has booze," he says to his friends.

I glare at him and tuck the bottle close to my chest.

"Let me have some," he says, holding out his hand.

"No way, baby brother! If Dad found out I gave you booze, he'd bust my ass," I say.

"He's not gonna find out!" Stacy whines.

"I don't care. Mom and Dad hold me responsible for you. So the answer is no," I say with a smirk.

Stacy snatches the bottle from me with a giggle and puts the rim to his lips. I stumble into him, yank it from his hands, and scream *no* in his face.

"You're a bitch!"

His sour words ignite the alcohol pulsing through my veins, and before I can blink, my palm crashes against his tender cheek.

Slap!

Stacy gasps, pulls his hand up to cover the welt, and locks his brown eyes on mine. Shame drops on me like a block of iron.

"Sorry," I say, glancing at the red spot on his face.

He says nothing in return. His eyes glisten, but he allows no tears. He just gets on his bike and rides off as I succumb to the monster of anguish living inside me. I protect my mother with my bloody soul. I am spread too thin to cover Stacy with the same fortitude.

Tears roll down my cheeks and my stomach churns with the taste of too many cigarettes and whiskey shots. I follow the split-rail fence to the base of a tree and heave brown booze out my nose and mouth. When I stumble back toward Jess, she just laughs as I collapse into the grass and fall into a deep, dark sleep.

A few days later, Brent rides his skateboard to my house. I hardly ever see him anymore. We sit with Jess under the weeping willow draping the vacant land across from my cul-de-sac. It feels awkward, hanging out, the three of us. My relationship with Brent feels innocent, untouched by peer pressure. Jess, on the other hand, is dark hearted, almost wicked. I do my best to navigate between them and try to remain untouched by my best friend's bad attitude. When the sun sets, Brent gets on his skateboard to head home. I walk with him a block, leaving Jess under the tree. He leans in to hug me and says, "You're different when you hang out with her."

"How?"

"You were always such a sweet girl."

I stare straight ahead and wait for him to tell me more.

"You're changing, turning into her," he says, pointing at Jess.

Unsure of how to respond, I shrug my shoulders and look away.

"Well, later," he says, hopping on his board.

His words sink into my heart as he rides away.

I'm not sweet? Is that bad?

I wish I could tell Brent the truth. I wish I could explain the dirt and grime living inside me, the brokenness in my heart, the nasty things done to me. Would he think I'm cheating on him? Is that what it means to a boy when a girl is molested by her father? I don't know and I don't plan to find out, so I skip back to Jess, drop down next to her, and pull a cigarette from my pocket.

♥

Stacy and I arrive home from school to find two cars in the driveway. Our parents are never home, together, at three o'clock on a weekday.

"Something's up," I say, unlocking the front door.

When we walk inside, Mom and Dad call us to join them at the kitchen table. Stacy and I slide our chairs out, sit across from our parents, and stare at their somber faces.

"Remember how I've had some trouble with my right hand and right eye?" Mom asks.

We nod.

"The doctor ran some tests, and they found white lesions on my brain. I have a disease called multiple sclerosis or MS."

Stacy and I exchange glances.

"The disease eats away the myelin covering my nerves, stripping their ability to send signals from my brain to my body. It's like I'm short circuiting. Does that make sense?"

We stare at her in silence.

"For example," she says, "my right eye can't see because signals from my brain aren't making it to my eye. Same thing with my hand."

"Are you going to die?" The question drops out of my mouth like an anvil.

"No." she says.

"But . . ." Dad says, cutting her off, "MS could debilitate your mother."

"So—you could die?" I ask.

"MS could disable me. Or it may go away all together. Just like my symptoms are here for a time, and then gone for a time. The doctors don't know where the disease comes from or what it will do to me. I could live to be one hundred. Only God knows," she says.

"There are a lot of things we don't know," Dad says. "But your mother needs help and support from all of us. And she needs you both to behave. You can't stress her out, or it will make things worse."

I'm not sure how to respond to my father's orders, since I haven't figured out how to behave yet. But I nod, and so does Stacy, as we give Mom a hug and tell her it's going to be okay. But I know this is a lie. Momma is dying. Maybe not today, but this disease is going to steal her away; I just know it.

6

The Question

In the days I spend with Jess, saturating my brain in hard liquor and marijuana, I become a master liar, and my momma eats my stories like cake. If I come home late from Brent's, I weave a tale of a rabid dog chasing me. "It was a giant German shepherd, Mom. I swear," I say. "I had to take the long way home." I use a ballpoint pen to change the Fs and Ds on my report card to Bs, and I cheat in the classes I am passing. Mom congratulates my achievements, never once suspecting my failure. She's like a fish on a line!

My lies pass the sniff test because Mom's naïve and Dad's got his own ass to cover. I came home from school one day to find Dad standing in the hallway with his weed-box in hand.

"Who's raiding my stash?" he asked.

Me and Stacy both steal from him, but I claimed it was all me. And I paid the price. Now my dad is a child molester, and he gives me drugs to keep me quiet. Just like a street pimp and a hooker.

Since my father is contributing to my delinquency, my sham grows unchecked. I get ballsy and tell Mom I'm sleeping over with Jess when we are really crashing at a party house. With boys. And Brent. And it's not long before I give him more than just my heart. But I can't do it sober. So I suck down some booze, then hand over my virginity like it's worth nothing more than a bag of cookies from the five and dime. I don't do it because it sounds fun, or pleasurable, or even because I want to. I do it to be cool.

I'm so ashamed by all my lies, I can't even look at my mother, much less talk to her. So when she knocks at my door on a Sunday afternoon, my heart stops.

"Come in," I say.

"Can we talk?"

I nod and say, "Sure."

"The breeze is nice," she says, eyeing my open window.

"Yeah," I say, glancing around the room. Posters of Bon Jovi, Jack Wagner, and various unicorns decorate my walls, along with a life-sized Iron Maiden poster, a host of deflated Mylar balloons, and every greeting card I've ever received. My bed is a mattress and box springs stacked on the floor. I dismantled that god-awful canopy months ago and tossed it out in the garage like childhood trash.

Mom perches on the corner of my bed. I soften as I study her, dressed in a raggedy old t-shirt, faded blue jeans, and an oversized flannel. She wears a thin line of black liquid eyeliner along her top lashes and a smidge of black mascara. The dark makeup makes her gray eyes sparkle. Momma is a simple, graceful kind of elegant. Not flashy and dramatic, like me. Sometimes I wonder how I popped out of her.

She peers at me through her glasses. "Everything okay with you?"

"Yeah? Why do you ask?"

Mom draws her fingers along the stitch lines in my pink checked comforter and shrugs. "It's been a while since we had a girl talk."

"We don't chat like we used to," I say.

"How are things with Brent?" she asks.

Maybe now is a good time to ask for the pill, I think.

"Terrific." I grin. "I love him, Mom."

"You are in love, huh?" she asks.

"We are."

"Are you two saying the L word?"

"Yes."

She glances away, saying, "Love is a complicated thing, Missy. You need to be careful. Don't forget—"

Releasing a long sigh, I say, "I know, I know. No sex before marriage."

"That is God's commandment, not mine," Momma says.

"Yeah, well I don't understand His commandments, or why I have to obey. And what about you and Dad?"

"This conversation isn't about me or your father."

"So, it's about God?" I ask.

I stop to consider God for a moment, and the little I know about Him. When I was a tiny thing, He was Jesus on the wall in my Grandma Bea's house. He was the Ten Commandments we learned at that awful daycare. He was the minister preaching hellfire and brimstone at the Methodist Church in Mississippi. To me, God is nothing more than a cold rule-maker.

"Mom, you and Dad break God's commandments all the time," I say. "Like when you have me lie to the bill collectors when they call."

Momma parts her lips to speak and I cut her off.

"You had me stealing ashtrays off restaurant tables when I was seven."

She shakes her head as I ramble on.

"Why don't Grandma and Granddad know you smoke weed?"

"That's enough, Melissa," Mom says. Her tone kills my tirade, forcing me to drop back and cross my arms. "God puts his laws in place to protect you," she says, "because he loves you. And you are right, your father and I set a horrible example. Can't you be better?" She asks with a limp smile.

I drop my head as silence fills the room.

"What if I don't believe in God?"

"God is not your enemy," Momma says.

"How am I supposed to believe in Him when He never

answers my prayers?" I ask, picking at the threads poking from the hem of my sweats.

"It takes faith to know He's there," she says. "You have to believe without seeing."

"That's impossible," I say.

Momma rubs her brow.

"What about love? I love Brent. I'm fourteen. I am not a baby."

Mom waits in silence for me to continue.

"My friends are having sex."

"Are you?"

Her question turns my skin crimson.

"Are you sleeping with Brent?"

I nod, then swallow hard and glance away as her face goes blank.

"I was thinking about taking the pill," I whisper.

Mom shakes her head and stares at the ground. I study her face, the furrow of her brow, the purse of her lips. I know she doesn't approve of me having sex. Or taking the pill.

"Why can't you just let me make my own choices?" I ask with a huff.

"Because you are only fourteen years old," she says.

"I hate being treated like a baby."

Mom holds her ground, saying nothing in return, so I decide to stick her sharp.

"Sometimes, I don't want to live here anymore."

The instant the words leave my mouth, I want to take them back, certain they will crush my mother. But she doesn't flinch, or blink, or tear up. She just peers at me with soft eyes, studying me like I'm a puzzle, or a mystery she can't solve. She tilts her head to the side and narrows her gaze. "I don't understand. Are we really that bad? So bad you don't want to live with us?"

I let out a sigh and drop my arms.

"It's not you, Mom."

"Then what is it?"

"It's Dad. He's a hypocrite. He's always angry." I shake my head and peer into her eyes. "I hate him."

Something inside Mom shifts. A quiet, protective, fierceness slips in, replacing the tenderness on her face. It's the rare kind of mother bear expression she gets when Stacy and I are in danger or suffer an injury. Like the time she dislodged the hot dog from my brother's throat. Or the time I fell off the back of the car and needed stitches in my chin. It's the same look she gets when Dad takes his rage too far.

And it's the same look she got when she found Dad creeping around my room in the darkness when I was little.

I pull in a deep breath as the air between us thickens.

"I need to ask you a question," she says in a low tone.

Time slows. My heart pounds in my ears. I look away as she asks, "Has your father ever touched you?"

My world screeches to a stop. I can't speak. Can't utter a single word. I can't even look at her. My mother has never, ever, asked me this question.

"Melissa. Has your father ever touched you?"

I weigh my options in a blink. What if Mom doesn't believe me? What if she blames me and stops loving me? What if Dad convinces her I'm lying, and she chooses his side? What if they send me to foster care? What if the truth makes Mom's MS worse and she dies?

The word *no* rushes out of my mouth before I can stop it. I want to pull it back in, want so bad to scream *yes! Are you effing blind?* But I can't do it. So there it is. The whole truth. Dropped on the ground like a hot potato.

Even I can't touch it.

"No," I say again and toss in, "gross, Mom," for good measure.

"I'm sorry," Momma stammers. "I had to ask."

"It's okay," I say.

I swallow hard and fight the tears brewing behind my eyes as Mom reins in her emotions.

"Can we take a walk? I'd like to share something with you," she says.

I nod, grateful to wrap up this horrifying conversation, and follow her outside. We stroll in silence under the canopy of fir trees peppering our cul-de-sac until we are a good distance from the house. Then Mom slows her pace, turns to face me, and says, "When I was in high-school, there was a boy next door."

She clears her throat.

"He and I used to meet up in the backyard and . . ."

I stop midstride to lock eyes with her.

"And?" I ask.

"Have sex," she says.

What—?

"Until I got pregnant."

I drop my jaw and stare at my mother.

"You got pregnant?" I ask. "By a neighbor boy? As a teenager?"

"I did," she says.

"Then what?" I ask.

"The boy refused to admit we had sex. He refused to take responsibility for the baby."

"Did you have an abortion?"

"No. This was in 1968. Abortion was illegal."

"So . . . ?" I ask.

"I gave him up for adoption."

"Him? You gave *him* up for adoption?"

Time stops as I consider the obvious.

"I have a brother?"

"Yes. I named him Timothy Mark. I held him for three hours, then they took him away."

"Wait, who's they?"

"Grandma and Granddad sent me to a home for unwed mothers," Momma says.

"Why didn't you keep him?"

"In 1968, women didn't keep babies outside of marriage. I had no way of supporting him."

"Do you know where he is?"

"No."

"Can you find out?" I ask.

"The adoption records are sealed. And I wouldn't do that to him. He may not even know he's adopted. Interrupting his life would be a selfish thing to do," she says with a shrug.

I step back to study my mother, let the weight of her imperfection settle on me.

"Does Dad know?"

"Yes, but Stacy can't know yet. Please keep it to yourself, for now."

"Of course," I say.

"Missy, I'm telling you about Timothy, so you know there are consequences to the choices you make. Birth control is not fool proof. I don't believe in abortion, and I don't want you giving up a baby like I did."

"Was it hard? Giving him up?"

"Yes, but it was the right thing to do," she says.

Momma doesn't cry or express any anger toward her parents. As we meander back to the house, I reach down, grab her hand, and think . . . *My mom gave up a baby.*

I can picture my mother with a tiny bundle in her arms, soaking in his eyes, his hair, his skin, before handing him over to a stranger. Why didn't my grandparents help her keep him? Why did they shun her by shipping her off to such an embarrassing place?

Her confession explains so much about our life. Her running away with my dad when she was twenty, hopping from state to state, escaping her judgmental parents. I love Grandma and Granddad, but we see them only once a year. Momma keeps her distance, and when they come to stay with us, our entire world shifts. We use our manners, watch our language, scrub every inch of the house before they arrive. We are fake when my grandparents come around, and this explains why.

The next morning, I wake to find a white envelope resting against the clock radio on my nightstand. *Missy* is penned across the front of it in Momma's silky handwriting. I sit up, stretch my arms high, and release a yawn before opening the letter.

> *Dear Missy,*
>
> *There's always lots of things I would like to say to you, but my mouth won't always work with my brain, so it sometimes comes out easier for me on paper. This is not a lecture, but it may give you some insight as to how I feel about a few things.*
>
> *One of the things we talked about last night was God. He's very important in my life, and I want Him to be in yours, too. Faith is not a material to be seen, heard, smelled, or touched, but is as real as anything that can be imagined. You can be aware of Faith as easily as you can be aware of earth. Faith is as certain as is the existence of water. Faith is as sure as the taste of an apple, the smell of a rose, the sound of thunder, the sight of the sun, the feel of a loving touch. Hope is a wish, a longing for something you don't yet have—but with the expectation of getting it. Faith adds surety to the expectation of hope.*
>
> *Have we been drifting apart so long there is no getting back? Was there a curve we didn't go around together, one corner one of us didn't see? Worse, has someone else been hiking down your highway? Change is change, unaccountable, but nonetheless surprising. I had hoped all our surprises would be planned together.*
>
> *I love you, Mom*

I read it over and over, unsure how to respond. The words *God, faith,* and *hope* stick in my soul like a burr. But the last paragraph hits me raw, sparking angry embers to life.

Yes, there were a lot of curves we didn't go around together, Mom. The devil is hiking down my highway, and I don't have the courage to tell you the truth or confront the dirty beast.

I tuck her letter, and her God, into a drawer and sigh. I love her words, but I wake up in the same nightmare every day. Her letter and her God cannot erase the past or release me from my father's persistent trespasses. So I hop up to shower and head to Jess's for the day. I've got weed to share with my best broken friend.

♥

Summer creeps in with suffocating heat and long, lazy days. With little to do except find trouble, Jessie and I spend our time lallygagging at the party house. Most days, Brent shows up on his skateboard to sip beers and make out with me on the ratty couch decorating the back porch. One sweltering August afternoon, as Jess and I ride our bicycles over to drink the night away, one of Stacy's dweeby friends skids his bike to a stop in front of me and says, "Hey, Missy. Brent is over at Kaylie's house."

"What?" I ask, hopping off my bike. "He's at Kaylie's house?" My heart pounds as I narrow my eyes at the kid. I hate Kaylie with a passion and Brent knows it.

"Yeah," he says, "they are flirting in her front yard."

I toss my hair back, thrust my nose high, and say, "Tell Brent we are done!"

The kid smirks, flips his bicycle around and pedals hard up the hill toward Kaylie's house. *That ought to get Brent's attention,* I think with a huff. Then I wait for my guy to realize his mistake. I watch for his silhouette to appear on the hill as he rides his longboard my way, eager to kiss and make up. Minutes pass before Jess kicks my back tire and says, "Let's roll. He ain't coming."

And she's right. Brent never comes. Never says a word. He

lets me go without a fight. So I guzzle one beer after another. Then Jessie and I pile in some dude's car. We cruise to a local diner for a midnight breakfast. This is where an older boy puts an arm around me, pulls my limp body close, and plants a slobbery kiss on my drunken lips. I don't say no, don't shake him off.

We drive back to the party house. Jessie hangs out until two in the morning, then goes home with some random guy. Now I am alone with the boy and his sloppy kisses, and before I know it, I am in his bed. Again, I don't say no, but I don't want his hands roaming my body. I don't want him to undress me, but he does. And as usual, my voice is gone. I lay under him, my tears rolling onto his pillow. Minutes pass with me frozen to the mattress, unable to move a muscle, until Phil Collins comes on the radio singing *Against All Odds*. Those lyrics shatter my heart as images of the only boy I've ever loved spring to mind.

"Stop!" I holler, "Please, get off me."

Confused, the boy dismounts. I grab my clothes and run from his room, but the damage is done. I crash on the couch until the sun breaks through the curtains. When I awake, Brent is no longer my boyfriend. Our declarations of *I'll love you forever and always* dissipate like the dew. And when word gets out about what I've done, I'm nothing more than a pathetic cheater.

As summer draws to a close, my heart aches every day. I want so much to undo the past. If I could just go back, rewind the clock, make a different choice. But I can't. Sadness eats me alive as Jess and I keep on wasting our time, and our brain cells, at the party house. The boy and I never talk about what happened in his bedroom that night. We just let it go and I act cool, like all the other girls who sleep around.

A few days before the start of our freshman year, Jess and I pedal fast toward the party house, with a blazing sun at our backs and wind in our hair. We arrive to find the gang whipping up a delicious concoction of jungle juice, mixing vodka, rum, grape juice, fruit slices, Sprite, and ice in a giant garbage can. Someone hands me a red plastic cup filled to the brim. I take a sip. Yum! The juice leaves no burn in my throat, just a sweet fizz cascading past my tongue. I drain the cup, then another, and another, until the hue of liquid courage settles into my bones.

I look at Jess and say, "I need to see Brent."

Brent hasn't been back to the party house, and I want so much to apologize and tell him the truth about what happened the night I broke up with him. I want him to know I'm not a cheap floozy. Then maybe he can forgive me. Maybe he can even love me again.

Jess nods, sets down her cup, and grabs her bicycle. We ride past Brent's house, but he's not home. So we ride to Willow Creek Park. We check the parking lot, the playground, the pond. There's no sign of Brent or his buddies. On our way out, we haul butt over the cracked asphalt, cruising fast with our feet off the pedals; until we hit the gravel exit. Jess whizzes out of the park without a hitch. But the pebbles pull my bike off course. I squeeze the front brake and the ground flies at me. Time slows as I tumble over the handlebars yelling, "Dang it," in slow motion.

I lie with my face in the gravel for a millisecond before standing upright to stare into Jessie's horrified expression. Her gaping mouth and wide eyes tell me it's ugly. My tongue follows the taste of blood up a fat lip and over my teeth. The orthodontics once adhered to my upper jaw ravage into a mass of twisted metal. The wire hangs jagged inside my mouth, with every single bracket broken free.

"Oh, dang," Jess says. "Dude, we have to call your mom."

I retrieve my bike, straddle the seat, and yank a powder compact from my purse to examine the damage. My eye is swelling shut and the once delicate skin on my cheek looks like mashed raspberries.

"Oh, no," I whisper.

We ride back to the party house to use the phone. When

Mom buzzes up in our VW, she climbs out, grabs my chin for inspection, and gestures for me to get into the car without saying a word.

"I'll make sure your bike gets home!" Jess hollers as we zip away from the curb.

At the house, Mom packs a bag with ice and hands it to me with a frown.

"What happened?"

"Jess and I were riding bikes in the park. I hit the front brakes," I say, mumbling through swollen lips. I omit the jungle juice party. Mom watches me for a minute, lets out a sigh, and picks up the phone to call my doctor and my orthodontist. I have appointments tomorrow. Stacy comes out of hibernation to inspect the damage and stifles a grin when he realizes I'm drunk.

The front door slams, and he scurries to his bedroom. Dad marches up the steps, stops when he sees my face. "What happened to you?"

"I wrecked my bike," I say with a shrug, brushing by him.

He follows me to my room, eyeballing me as I pull off my sneakers.

"Have you been drinking, Melissa?"

This is the weird thing about my dad. He's fine with me drinking one minute and not fine the next. He's fine with me smoking one day and not fine the next. He's hot and he's cold, sometimes in the same day. I never know which way is up!

"Answer me," he says with a boom.

"No, I just crashed," I say, my words slopping out over swollen lips and jungle juice. When he stares, I roll my eyes at him.

"Jodie!" he yells, "you need to get in here."

She walks through my door. "What?"

"Your daughter's drunk," he says, glaring at me.

"I am not drunk," I say, parroting him.

"Clint, she hasn't been drinking," Mom says.

I plaster on a smirk.

"Woman, are you blind, or can you not smell? Smell her breath!"

I peer at Mom doe eyed as she leans in for a sniff, saying, "I don't smell anything."

"By God, woman! Pull your head out of the sand!" Dad hollers.

Turning to me, he shoves a finger in my face and yells. "You are lying!"

"No, I'm not!" I holler back.

"Tell your mother the truth, young lady!"

"I have not been drinking," I say, raising my brows at him.

"Don't raise your brows at me, little girl," he says.

I raise them again.

"If you raise your eyebrows at me one more time, I'm going to slap the shit out of you," he says, his face turning purple.

I raise them higher.

Momma sits speechless. Stacy slips in behind her to watch the drama unfold.

Dad steps closer, his fingers unfolding inches from my nose. "One. More. Time." The clock stops as I lean forward, purse my lips, narrow my glare, and pull my furry little brows as high as they will go.

Slap!

His palm crashes against my left cheek. My mouth drops open in disbelief as shock waves fill the room.

My mother yells, "Clint!" at the same time my brother's horrid scream pierces our ears.

Stacy hollers, "No, no, no, no!" and bolts for the front door. Dad scrambles down the stairs, grabs my brother, and pulls him back inside.

"You hit my sister!" Stacy screams. "You hit her face! Why would you do that?"

My brother's sobs echo up the stairs, settle into my room, into my ears, and into my heart. It's a sound I'll never forget.

"You don't get to hit us in the face," Stacy hollers again.

I hear them collapse on the linoleum floor, my dad saying,

"I'm sorry, Stacy, please forgive me. You're right, I don't get to hit my family in the face. I'm so sorry for slapping your sister. Please forgive me."

Stacy keeps sobbing. The sound of him weeping propels me to get up, creep down the stairs and wrap him in my arms. "I'm sorry, Stacy," I whisper. "This is all my fault. Please don't cry."

♥

It's Friday the thirteenth, a day for spookiness and bad luck, according to Mom, who spits when a black cat crosses her path. Mom loves God, but she's also superstitious. And I think she's right. I busted the face of a hand mirror when I was seven. Maybe all the evil in my life came from that broken piece of glass. But I turned fifteen last October, so the curse has expired. Seven years' bad luck, so the story goes. Well, if today is the devil's day, that's good! Because I plan to bust this night into a thousand shards of wild.

I drop onto my bedroom floor, scoot toward the full-length mirror, yank out my makeup bag, and plug in my curling iron while Jess yaks at me on the phone. We gossip about the boys we crush on and the girls we hate while I curl my hair and smother my face in cakey foundation, thick purple eyeliner, brown shadows, and three layers of mascara.

Jess says, "I can't believe you told the home-economics teacher to go screw herself."

"The skank wouldn't let me bake!"

"Did the school call your house?" she asks.

"Yeah, I took the call, and pretended to be Mom."

"So, your parents don't know you're suspended?"

"Nope," I say.

Dad's car pulls into the drive. "Crap. My dad's home."

"Get a move on, slowpoke!"

I jump when his car door slams.

"I'll be over in ten," I say, dropping the phone in its cradle.

Stuffing my purse with makeup, house keys, and cigarettes,

I tiptoe toward the kitchen to find Dad leaning into the fridge, his ball cap perched high atop his head. "How was school?" he asks, cracking open a beer.

I'm certainly not telling my dad about my trip to the principal's office, or the in-house suspension I got today. But, just in case he knows something I don't know, I drop a crumb, saying, "My home-economics teacher is stupid. I was just telling Jess . . ."

"Stupid?" he asks, slurping foam off the rim.

My palms break a sweat.

"Did you just call your teacher stupid?"

Uh-oh. Here comes a lecture.

"You damn kids think you know it all. What do you know at fifteen? You ain't lived a day of life yet." He pulls in a swig, mounts a hand on his hip, and shoves a finger in my face, saying, "You respect your teachers, you hear me, young lady? Respect them, or I'll whip your ass."

He doesn't even know what I was going to say!

I narrow my eyes and purse my lips as he sucks the suds from his thick, black moustache, then says, "Your failing grades are proof you don't know jack shit. You and those loser friends of yours." He takes another long drink, lets out a belch, and points his finger at me again. "All you care about is hanging out with your friends. Those friends of yours are dragging you down, Melissa. You have your priorities in the wrong place. Family is what matters. And getting your education." He shakes his head, pulls a cigarette out of his shirt pocket, and slips it between his teeth. "Little girl," he says with the unlit smoke dangling from his lips, "you best get your shit together, or you'll be a nobody, just like your dumbass friends."

My faint eye roll sharpens his anger.

"Don't you roll your eyes at me," he says, snatching the smoke out of his mouth. When Dad gets pissed his eyebrows take on a life of their own, with one arching and twitching independent of the other. I watch them wriggle and jump with each syllable as he asks, "Am I wrong? Do you put forth any effort in school? Do you put forth any extra effort to help your mother?"

I stare at him as he rants on.

"You don't do a damn thing around this house."

What's he talking about? Mom cooks, mom does the laundry, mom does the shopping, mom pays bills. I do the dishes, I vacuum, I clean the bathroom and Stacy mows the lawn. Stacy even takes out the garbage. Dad is the only one who doesn't do a damn thing around this house.

My pulse pounds, but I know better than to share my thoughts, so I knit my lips together and stare straight ahead.

"Look at me!"

My eyes jump to meet his.

"Am I wrong? Do you do anything extra to help your mother?"

I shake my head and tell him what he wants to hear. "No."

"No, what?"

"No, sir."

"You're a lazy ass! You can't even keep your room clean! It's an effing pigsty!"

That's not true.

"Your mother and I bust our butts all day long to put clothes on your back and food on the table. We've given our whole lives up for you kids. And what do we get for all our effort?"

I stare at him, but I don't say a word.

"A couple of lying, failing, self-centered brats," he says, pulling another long drink off his beer before slamming his can on the counter. I jump and blink twice before looking at him again.

"I would have given anything to have your life."

I look down at the floor and wonder ... *What's so great about my life?*

"Look me in the eye when I talk to you," he says with a boom.

I jolt again, stare into his eyes, and hold my face perfectly still until he barks, "Go on! Get!"

I turn on my heel, slip on my coat and zip it up tight.

"Where are you headed, anyway?"

"The dance at Chinook," I lie.

I grab my purse and jog downstairs, thankful to be free of him. An icy blast of wind threatens my feathered hair as I traipse down the drive. "What do you know at fifteen?" I ask, mocking my dad with a deep voice and animated hands. I stomp toward Jessie's, my imitation leather boots slapping the pavement with each step. I swear their heels are worn to a half-moon edge from months of hiking this same angry path. I fight the tears lurking behind my lids and ball my hands until my fingernails pierce the skin on my palms.

"Damn, I hate him," I say, marching in fiery anger all the way to Jessie's house. I open the door, step inside without knocking, and wander the halls until I find my best friend in the bathroom, engulfed in a cloud of Aqua Net. Her thick locks, a weave of yellow and strawberry, stand like a feathered helmet on her head.

"Did you get us some buds?" she asks with a wicked grin.

"Yep." I nod, fumble a small bag of weed out of my pocket, and toss it her way.

"Your dad's awesome," she says, sniffing the bag.

I cross my arms and lean against the wall. "He's an ass."

"Did he find out you're suspended?"

"He didn't have to. He bitches me out no matter what I do."

Jess socks me in the shoulder, tosses the baggie of weed to me, grabs her jacket, and says, "Lighten up. It's time to party."

Jessie's nana drops us at Jake's, where we plan to get wasted before walking to Smokey's Pizza. The snooty kids go to the dance, the cool kids go to Smokey's where we get high and graffiti the bathroom stalls. As Jess and I meander up Jake's driveway, I pop a square of bubblegum in my mouth and pull out my bag of weed.

"Oh, here's the popular girl!" Jake says, wrapping his arm around my waist. He takes my dope, pulls a fifth of Jack Daniel's out of his denim jacket, and hands it to me. I cradle the bottle, inspect the gold liquid, and take a long swig, careful not to swallow my gum. Sour mash tastes worse than vomit. The group laughs at my puckered face, then chants in rhythm.

"Chug it down! Chug it down! Chug it down!"

I follow their cheers, guzzle deep, and wait my turn for another round. Before long, my head spins like it's detached from my body. Someone passes me a joint. I inhale deeply, peer at my blurry circle of friends, and think, *Dad is full of crap. My friends love me.* I smile over at Jess, blow a long cloud of smoke into the frigid air, and my world goes black.

Moonlight streams onto my face as I rouse from sleep.

What is stuck in my throat?

I open wide to retrieve the swollen bubblegum seeping into my tonsils. *Gag! Where am I?* I pull my head off the pillow, note the vomit caked in my hair and down the side of my face. The smell of stale whiskey pulls up a gag as I roll over in yesterday's clothes and peel open my mascara-crusted eyes. My bedroom takes shape in the shadows, the red digits on my clock read 4:52 a.m.

"Crap!" *Do my parents know I got wasted? How did I get home?* "Ugh." I moan, push myself to sit, as waves of nausea ride up my belly. *Lord, I need a toilet.* As I move toward the door, I feel sticky wetness in my jeans. *Did I pee my pants?* I close my eyes and swallow furiously to keep from puking on the carpet. Hand to mouth, I open my door, stumble to the bathroom, and circle my arms around the icy commode as brown liquid gushes out of my mouth and nose.

"Oh, God, oh, God, oh, God," I say between heaves, sinuses burning. Despite the prayers, I heave and heave, until nothing comes up except moans from my throat. I cling to the toilet for several minutes before standing to wash my face and blow my nose. A shower sounds divine, but waking my father is not worth the risk. So I grab a wet washcloth and tiptoe toward my room.

"Back to bed, young lady," my father says from across the hall.

I am so busted. Waves of nausea threaten to drag up more whiskey. I breathe deeply, peel off my wet pants, pull on a clean night shirt and settle into my comforter. Tears rain through the crispy vomit in my hair as I whisper to the God I don't believe in: "God, I hate this life. How do I make it stop?" My pain is soul deep, spirit deep, oceans deep. I press the wet washcloth against my face, stifle the whimper rolling over my lips, and pray again: "Lord. Please save me."

Three hours later, light hits my face and pulls me from nauseating sleep. I run my tongue over parched lips, roll out of bed, and amble toward the bathroom. The toilet beckons once more, pulling dry heaves from my alcohol-ravaged body. I brush the slime out of my mouth with a heavy glob of Crest, toss my shirt on the floor and crank open the faucet on the tub. A hot, steamy shower clears my nose, my throat, and my brain. The balmy water melts the gunk off my hair. I wish it could melt the grime off my heart.

I sit in the tub until the water runs cold, then slip into sweats, and shuffle to the kitchen to find my parents waiting at the dining room table, coffee in hand. The scent of French roast halts my steps. I pause, hold my breath, and try not to gag.

"You know they abandoned you last night." Dad says, blowing steam from his mug.

"What are you talking about?" I ask, collapsing into a chair.

A frown edges Dad's lips as he repeats his statement. "Your amazing friends abandoned you last night."

"They did?"

"You blacked out. Your buddies wanted to go to the dance. They pulled your limp body several blocks, dropped you on the gravel at Willow Creek Park. And left."

"How did you find me?"

"Ryan ran to a neighbor's house and called me. Jessica sat with you in the park until we got there."

He stares at me, slurping his coffee from the rim before setting his cup aside.

"Jessie said your head bounced off the street like a

basketball. Bump, bump, bump, all the way to the park."

I run my hand over the back of my skull. No bumps, no cuts. I pull my feet onto the chair, ball a fist into my belly, place the other over my face, and fight to remember. Nothing springs to mind. I try to fathom the fact that my friends bailed on me, dropped me on the cold, hard ground in a dark park. And left me to die.

Would I leave any of my friends to freeze in a park at night? No!

"They dropped you in the woods like a sack of trash," Dad says.

I look at my mother for confirmation. She stares at me for a long time with her brows furrowed and her mouth pulled into a frown. As usual, her tender eyes melt my heart into a puddle of guilt. I look at the ground, unable to hold her gaze as she says, "Your father is telling you the truth. You completely blacked out. Lost all consciousness. Puked all over yourself. Only Ryan and Jessie cared enough to stay and help you."

I picture Ryan mustering the courage to call my dad, Jessie sitting in those dark woods by herself.

Mom clears her throat. "Your dad gathered you off the frozen ground and put you in the car. We brought you home and put you to bed."

"I'm sorry, Mom."

"Aren't you embarrassed?" Dad asks. "You peed your pants." He lets humiliation do its work before pronouncing his sentence. "You are grounded for a month."

I nod in relief. Maybe Dad's right. Maybe if I take a break from my crazy friends, I can get my crap together and stop breaking my mother's heart.

♥

My dance with Jack Daniel's changes something in my body chemistry. Now, just the smell of sour mash makes me puke. No joke. I can't take a whiff off the bottle without retching. So when Traci throws a party, I trade in the hard liquor for orange coolers and beer. And I don't guzzle down one drink after the other. I sip it nice and slow, add in a hit of weed, and I'm as happy as a clam.

Around my fourth drink, a group of boys stops by, and Tommy pulls my tipsy ass into a bedroom. I don't want to go with him, but as usual, my voice is gone. He kisses me once, then twice. The third time he drops his sloppy lips on mine, I shove him aside and run for the toilet. Hanging deep into the bowl, I heave and gag as my stomach expels stale beer. The orange wine cooler burns as it runs out of my nose. I sit up, gulp for breath, and work to unstick my hair from the sides of the urine-spotted, rust-stained bowl. *God. I'm sorry. Please make this stop.* I lean in to heave again, praying, *Please God, please. I hate barfing. I can't breathe.*

I don't bargain with God. I just beg Him for help until my tummy relaxes. I snatch a handful of tissue off the roll and blow my nose. Fearful the waves of nausea will pull me under again, I don't stand to rinse my mouth. Instead, I curl up in a ball, rest my head on the padded pink rug circling the pot, and sleep until Traci escorts me to her bedroom.

Around three a.m., I wake up on her floor, still dressed in my clothes. A chill runs up my legs. I have no blankets or pillow. A desperate thirst parches my throat, but I'm too scared to walk to the kitchen. I'm sure Traci's parents are home by now. What if I run into her mom? I wreak of booze and have puke crusted around my lips. I remember the giant bowl of cherries on Traci's dresser and grope for them in the dark. Finding the plastic dish, I shovel wet, soggy, day-old fruit into my mouth and suck the juice from them like a skeleton in the desert.

Why am I here? I wonder, spitting the pits into my hand. *These people are not my friends. They mock me and laugh when I hurt, feed me poison, leave me to freeze in a cold park or on this floor. This is not fun. There is nothing awesome about barfing every time I drink, nothing beautiful in a boy feeling up my limp body. I hate this life. Hate it. But I don't know how to make it stop.*

When I've eaten all the cherries I can stomach, I lie down

and open the faucet of my heart. Tears run down my cheeks, pool around my ears and into my hair as my mind wanders back over all the times I've drank too much. Too much Jim Beam, too much jungle juice, too much Jack Daniels, too many orange wine coolers. I remember sleeping with Brent and the other boy I cannot name. And I remember the question my mother asked me—the question no one will ever ask me again.

♥

The needle clicks at the end of Led Zeppelin, and I stare down at the pictures in my hand. The one of Brent rests in my lap. I remember the blue kiddie pool from last night, drinking too much beer, running down the street screaming, hiding from the cops. I remember puking this morning, then lying to my mother.

Lord, when will this nightmare end?

The blue letters on our VCR tell me it's midnight. I slide the record into its cardboard sleeve and turn off the stereo. A car door slams outside. Mom and Dad's muffled voices carry as they unlock the door, then shuffle upstairs to find me sitting in a mess of pictures.

"Doing a little reminiscing?" Mom asks.

"Just a little," I say, stacking the photos back in the box.

"Are you okay?" she asks, studying my tear-stained face.

I nod and put the box back on the shelf. Then I stand up, give her a long hug, kiss her cheek, and wander to bed, saying, "I'm fine."

But I'm not fine. I'm nowhere near fine. And, oh how I wish she'd ask me that other question again. That ominous, life-changing question. This time, maybe I could find the courage to tell her the truth.

PART 2

The Rescue

7

We're Going To Church

Our family pulls into the gravel parking lot of a tiny, rectangular building. Going to church was my dad's stupid idea. Or maybe it was Mom's. I'm not sure. But here we are, the four of us, all gussied up like some cologne and new clothes will cover our ugly. Dad met up with friends from the old neighborhood a few weeks ago. That meeting led to breakfast with a pastor. A pastor! My dad eating with a man of God blows my mind.

"It's a small church," Mom said when I whined about going. "And our friends go there. You'll be fine."

I sigh. Church reminds me of the hateful teachers at Temple Daycare. The ones who whacked us kids with paper bags and never had a kind word on their tongue. To me, church is nothing more than a brick building decked in chandeliers, velvety pews, and leather altars. Church is washing down a white wafer with a thimbleful of grape juice. It's coming hungry and leaving thirsty. To me, the house of God is just another unachievable benchmark.

Clearly nobody cares what I think because here we are, piling out of the car in the parking lot of Friends Community Church.

Yippee!

I take my time gathering my purse and jacket, then slam the car door when Dad barks, "Hurry up!"

I huff and stumble through the gravel in my stiletto heels, careful to keep my mini skirt from riding up too high. As I walk, I stare at the backside of my motley family. Stacy's mullet sways in a rare August breeze, his Metallica t-shirt hangs loose over his jeans. I watch him kick dust off his checkered Vans. That's how Mom got him here. She bribed him with a new pair of shoes. Dad walks tall in cowboy boots, with a crisp red t-shirt tucked into his dark Levi's, and a shiny leather belt snug around his thin waist. Mom wears the same business casual she dons Monday through Friday. A tan pencil skirt, white cotton blouse, and nylons a shade darker than her arms.

As we approach the building, I begin to think my rag tag family might fit in here just fine. Friends Community Church, sitting nestled into a grove of fir trees, is ramshackle old, with peeling white paint and a double-door entry. A cross sits high atop the pitched roof, reminding me God lives here. Somewhere inside my memory, a little girl sings Jesus Loves Me. As I stare at the steeple, I realize that little girl is me, and an odd reverence for God blooms in my heart. I decide to drop my snarky attitude and step into this moment with an open mind.

We take our time climbing the steep cement stairs to the door, where a man in a gray suit guards the entrance.

"Good morning," he says, shaking my mom's hand.

Next, he grips my palm, saying, "Welcome!"

"Thank you."

He studies me with bright blue eyes and says, "I'm Pastor Drew."

I nod.

"And you are?"

"Missy."

"Glad you are here, young lady."

I step onto musty green carpet, glance at the two shallow rows of pews lining each side of the sanctuary, and think . . . *This is doable.*

Drew's wife, Pennie, grabs my hand. "Missy. It's wonderful to meet you," she says through a toothy, well-glossed mouth.

In flat shoes she stands as tall as her husband. The whispers of silver in her black hair pair well with the fine lines stretching up her high cheekbones. If I had to guess, I'd say she's a tad older than my parents. She steps back to study me and says, "My, you are a beauty," making me blush.

When Dad walks up, she grabs his hand and says, "You must be Clint! Drew told me all about you. Welcome!"

"Thank you, Miss Pennie," he says with a goofy grin.

I roll my eyes and follow Momma to sit. The congregation is small. Stacy and I are the only teens. Several blue-haired ladies sit among the crowd, smiling at us through wrinkled skin and gray teeth. They nod and wave at me as I relax on the hard bench and let my eyes wander over the place. Light cascades through the tall windows. Flecks of lint and dust dance in the sun stream. There are no photos of Anglo-Saxon Jesus hanging on the wall, no Ten Commandment scrolls or bench altars for communion, and no judgmental faces. An odd sensation settles over me, inviting me to be still and rest. I can't explain it, but this place feels like home.

Service begins with announcements. Everyone is invited to next Sunday's potluck in the basement. Someone named Denise is getting married in two weeks. Shirley's husband finally passed. His funeral is next Tuesday. I don't know these people but everyone around me responds like they are family. Next, we open our hymnals and stand to sing "How Great Thou Art" and "Great Is Thy Faithfulness."

Pastor Drew steps up to the mic. "Are there any prayer requests in the house?"

Hands shoot up. People take turns sharing worries like they're at the dinner table. This is nothing like the Methodist Church, where ministers in white robes walked the aisles looking too cold to touch.

I look at Mom, and say, "This is weird."

She shrugs.

"Let's pray," Pastor says.

We bow our heads. Pastor Drew recites the Lord's Prayer.

I know it by heart because Momma says it with Stacy every night before bed. Next, Pastor prays over the people who shared their cares and concerns, then he says, "It's your turn, folks. Pray as you feel led," and sits down.

A shaky voice says, "Lord, help my sister Delilah in these last stages of dementia. Help my son Peter find a home for his dog. And help me be more like You. Thank You, Jesus."

As I fight the urge to turn and stare at her, another voice springs to life, saying, "Lord, I started drinking again. Please help me attend all my AA meetings."

For fifteen minutes, people pray like they're popcorn in a microwave, shooting up requests in random succession. When the woman beside me says, "Lord, please help my husband find a job," I wonder if I'm supposed to go next.

Holy moly. I can't pray aloud!

Panic rushes over me, stealing my breath. Sometimes Dad makes me say dinner grace, but the only time I acknowledge God is when I'm puking after a bender. I squirm, moving the hard bench from one butt cheek to another. I nudge Mom, exchange glances with her and shake my head. She squeezes my hand and closes her eyes. I breathe deeply to still my pounding heart and press my lips together until silence blankets the room.

Finally, Pastor Drew says, "In Jesus's name," and we all say amen.

Hallelujah amen!

The sermon moves at a turtle's pace, leaving my head bobbing as I fight sleep. Mom pinches me several times before handing me a stick of gum and a pencil, so I can doodle on the church bulletin. When the service finally ends (and I never thought it would!), we join Chuck and Darla (from the old neighborhood) at their new house across the street. My family spends the afternoon feasting on barbecued chicken, potato salad, corn on the cob, and buttery rolls. We sip sweet tea or lemon water. There is no beer at this party. No weed or guitar playing. Just a group of people high on life. And loving Jesus.

♥

After our second Sunday of church service and barbecue, Stacy and I pile into the backseat of our blue Chevy Cavalier. My parents crank the windows down, letting the warm August air blow like a whirlwind through my hair. I close my eyes to avoid the mascara flecks falling from my heavily dressed lashes.

"Your mother and I are turning over a new leaf," Dad says.

I squint and glance between him and Mom. He grabs her hand, pulls it up for a kiss, and says, "No more drinking and no more drugs."

What's happening?

Stacy and I lock eyes. My brother's face drops. He shakes his head, crosses his arms, and stares out the window. Dad folds the rearview mirror down to make eye contact with us kids. "You are included in this equation, do you understand?" His attention drops to the road, then back to me, waiting for a response. I nod slowly and glance away.

"That means no more drinking for either of you," he says.

This is weird.

"No more drugs," he says, "And no more lying. Do you hear me? We are going to be a new family."

What does he mean, "a new family"? How exactly are we supposed to be a new family? How do we overcome all the dark things haunting the way we live? I don't roll my eyes or huff or get angry. I'm not sure how this works, but a new emotion blows over my heart like a dewy breeze on hot sand. It's a good feeling. Something I can't define.

When we get home, Momma pulls a six-pack of Bud from the fridge, cracks them open one by one, and tips them upside down in the sink. The drain consumes them heartily, leaving Mom to retrieve the containers, rinse them out and toss them in the trash. Dad struts down the hall to their bedroom and returns carrying two baggies of green dope, a pipe, a bong, and some Zig-Zag papers. He tosses them atop the beer cans, gathers up the Glad kitchen bag and frees it from the trash can.

"No more," he says, knotting the top. He clambers down the steps, swings open the garage door, and tosses our sins outside with a thud.

Wow—just, wow.

On the third Sunday, after a full week of sober parents, I sit in the pew as Dad talks with Chuck outside and Mom circles the sanctuary to greet Darla. Stacy wormed his way out of services with a slumber party at Chris's. Go figure. As I sit and listen to the chatter of soft voices around me, I notice no exchange of unkind words, no judgment, and no criticism. Just the ease of love, acceptance, care, and concern.

Mom plops down beside me, rummages through her purse, and asks, "Do you have any gum?"

"Yeah," I say without moving.

She keeps digging through her bag.

"I don't want to go to hell," I say.

She snaps her head up, a stick of Big Red in hand, and stares at me with furrowed brows.

"What?"

"How do I know I'm going to heaven when I die?" I ask.

"Oh, Dolly," she says, putting an arm around me, "You ask Jesus to come into your heart and to be your Savior."

"How?"

"You pray," she says, rubbing my shoulders.

"Can I pray right now?" I ask.

"Sure," Mom says, popping the cinnamon gum in her mouth. "Want a piece?"

I grab the stick from her hand, drop my head, close my eyes, and pray silently.

Jesus. Saying His name ties my tongue. I try again, fighting the tears brimming my lashes. My mind can't bear the words, so my heart prays for me. *I am . . . so dirty.*

A tear rolls down my face. *Can You come into my heart and be my Savior?*

There are no words to describe what happens deep inside

me. It resembles an emotion, but it's more a knowing, a surety. It's like I'm lighter. My heart is weightless. I feel giddy, peaceful, and safe. It's like Someone holy is standing beside me and inside me. I take a deep breath, lift my head, and catch the tears before anyone can see them.

♥

Two weeks into my sophomore year of high school, I feel a niggling in my lower right abdomen during PE, like a small bean rolling around my guts. Something isn't right, but I finish the day, eat dinner, and hit the sack without giving it much thought. Around two o'clock, I wake up nauseated. I hobble to use the restroom, praying I won't barf, then climb back into bed. I wake up two hours later to intense nausea and a sharp pain writhing in my gut. I need to vomit but I can't stand. So I roll to the side, moaning in agony, and barf on the carpet. Around my third heave, someone flicks on my bedroom light.

Dad appears beside me, asking, "Honey, where does it hurt?"

"Tummy," I say, heaving.

"Does it hurt in your side?"

"All four corners," I say, pointing to my hips.

He bends over to pull my hair back and looks at my mother standing behind him.

"It's probably her appendix," he says.

What's an appendix?

Mom dashes out of the room to get dressed. Dad starts the car and reappears with a hot washcloth. He wipes the barf off my face, hands me the rag, and draws me up in his arms. Every step makes me whimper.

"I'm sorry, honey," Dad says, jogging down the steps.

My tears fall onto his shoulder.

"I know, Baby, hang on," he says, placing me in the backseat. Mom lifts my head onto her lap as Dad throws it in reverse and backs out of the driveway. On Interstate 5, Mom snuggles me as highway rivets jar my angry stomach.

"How far?" I ask. "I need to puke."

"Not far, Baby, can you hold on? We just have to cross the green bridge, and we'll be there," Dad says, tipping the rearview mirror toward Mom.

"Okay," I say, taking deep breaths and counting streetlights as Dad speeds down the freeway. Ten minutes later, Dad wanders around northwest Portland, looking for the hospital. He stops to ask a motorcycle cop for directions. The man flicks on his red and blue lights, escorts us to the emergency room entrance and carries me to the front door where a nurse wearing pink scrubs greets me with a wheelchair and a barf pan. Dad shakes the officer's hand and tells him thank you.

The doctor takes an x-ray, gives me my first pelvic exam, and insists upon a pregnancy test, despite my promising, "I am not pregnant". A hospital gown and an hour later, Doc announces I need surgery and asks the nurse to start an IV.

"I am terrified of needles," I say, wide eyed.

She smiles at me, saying, "I'll be gentle, I promise."

I lie back on the gurney, bury my head into the soft, white pillow and pray. *God, please don't hurt me.*

I can't look at the needle, so I stare at the wall. The crinkle of paper packages and tools echoing off the metal tray gives me the willies.

"Okay, honey. Can I see your arm?"

She pops her gum between her teeth as she ties a rubber tube around my bicep, lays a small ball in my palm, and says, "Squeeze this every few seconds."

I look up at the ceiling, swallow rapidly to keep from barfing, and listen to her tear open another package. The smell of rubbing alcohol burns my nose, reminding me of the time Dad shoved an earring into the infected hole of my pierced ear. This is not a good memory.

She takes the ball from my hand, saying, "Just relax and breathe."

I feel the moist alcohol pad against my skin, then slight pressure along the side of my arm.

Jesus, please . . .

"All done," she says, sticking wads of tape on my skin before snapping off her rubber gloves.

"What?" I ask, gawking at the tube hanging from my arm.

"Did it hurt?" she asks with a wink.

"No," I say, dumbfounded. *Holy cow! God answered my prayer. He can hear me!*

I relax back into bed, watch the nurse hang a bag of clear liquid from a tall metal pole, and let out a long sigh as my pain disappears in a sea of intravenous drugs. *So this is why my parents told me to never shoot drugs into my veins,* I think as a warm glow covers my mind, body, and soul. *I feel fantastic!*

"Time to go," says the nurse, yanking up the rail on my bed. Momma kisses me in the hallway. The nurse wheels me into a room where a giant yellow light hangs above my face and the doctor puts a rubber mask over my nose.

"Count backward from ten," he says.

"Nine, eight . . ."

I wake up in recovery, full of morphine, and minus an appendix.

♥

I run my fingers over the scar on my lower right side. I'm all healed up and heading back to school today.

"Ugh," I say with a sigh.

After a long stretch, I traipse down the hallway toward the sound of muffled voices.

What the heck? I round the corner and step into the kitchen to find Mom and Dad on their knees. *My parents are praying!*

Dad says, "Amen."

"Morning, Dolly," Mom says.

"Morning," I stammer, turning toward the bathroom. *That's weird.*

At the bus stop, Jess hugs me tight, kisses my cheek, and says, "I missed you so much!"

"Me too," I say, still taken aback by God's goodness in my life.

"Want a drag?" she asks, passing me her cigarette.

"Sure." I grab it, but I don't look at my best friend. My eyes fix in a daze as my mind wanders over the memory of my parents praying.

"What's going on in your head?"

"I caught my parents praying this morning," I say, pulling in a drag.

Jess throws her head back. "Ugh!"

"What?" I ask, blowing smoke rings into the crisp, morning air.

"Not more God talk. Come on, Missy."

"You should come to church with me," I say, passing her the smoke.

"Yeah right," she says, flicking the butt on the ground as the school bus rolls to a stop and folds the door open.

We climb the steps and I follow Jess as she struts toward the back, drops into the seat, and stares out the window. She doesn't talk much on the ride to school, leaving me to think about Jesus and everything He's doing in my life. My parents are stone cold sober. No beer, no weed, and best of all, Dad hasn't touched me in weeks. God is the only explanation I can muster for all the changes in my family.

As we approach the parking lot, Jess cuts into my thoughts, saying, "We should party this weekend."

"Sure." I nod with a smile, agreeing in my body, but not in my heart.

♥

Mom gives me a New International Version Bible to read (King James is too confusing). I lie in bed on the weekend, skim through the gospels of Matthew, Mark, Luke, and John in the New Testament, and fall in love with Jesus one syllable at a time. I read about Him healing lepers, blind men, and a woman who bled for twelve years! Holy cow! He even raises

Lazarus from the dead. There are lots of things I don't get, but the miracles are undeniable. And so is Jesus's love for people, especially women. I devour the stories of Jesus interacting with broken females like me.

Like the woman at the well in John 4. She was married five times, then shacking up with some dude she wasn't married to. Jesus told her He would give her living water. He revealed Himself as the Messiah to a woman who was divorced and sleeping around. And He told her everything she'd ever done, and *still* offered her living water. He knew all about her... and accepted her just the way she was. She was so ecstatic she told the whole town she'd met the Messiah!

Or the woman caught in adultery in John 8. The Pharisees caught her in the act, then paraded her in front of Jesus hoping they could stone her to death. Jesus gave them permission, with one exception: only the man who never sinned could throw the first stone. They all dropped their rocks and left. Jesus would not allow the religious leaders to condemn her. And then Jesus Himself refused to condemn her. He spoke kindly to her, protected her, He loved her in all her brokenness, and then He let her go.

One of my favorite stories is about the immoral woman in Luke 7:36-50. When she heard Jesus was eating at Simon the Pharisee's house, she brought an alabaster jar of expensive perfume, knelt behind Jesus at His feet, and wept. She wiped her tears off His feet with her hair, kissed His feet over and over, and covered them with that expensive perfume. In his mind, Simon the Pharisee thought for sure if Jesus knew about this woman's sins, He would never let her touch Him. The Lord tackled Simon's question head on, telling Simon that those who are forgiven much also love much. But those who are forgiven little, love only a little.

This must be why Jesus is capturing my heart. Because I am impure. Just like them. But Jesus still loves me. Just the way I am. Jesus is so amazing I just want to know Him more.

But there are also scriptures that are harder for me to

understand. In Matthew 7:13–14 (NIV), Jesus says, "Enter through the narrow gate. For wide is the gate and broad is the road that leads to destruction, and many enter through it. But small is the gate and narrow the road that leads to life, and only a few find it."

What's the narrow gate? I wonder. *Is Jesus the narrow gate?*

I surely don't want to follow the crowd through the wide gate to destruction, so I set out to discover Jesus's narrow gate. Maybe I can find it by following God's ten commandments, especially number nine. *Thou shalt not lie.* Jesus says the one who loves Him obeys His commands, so I need to stop lying to my parents.

The first test of my new-found honesty occurs when my report card arrives in the mail. I pull it from the box, open the envelope, and read it aloud. "F in biology, C in PE, D in Washington State history, F in English, F in math, A in drama, B in art." I sigh. "I'm so busted."

I consider taking a ballpoint pen to the page, changing those Fs to Bs. I've done it before, but this time Jesus sticks in my craw, and I can't bring myself to lie. *Grr.* So I leave the letter on the table for my parents to find and head to my room. Mom reads it when she gets home, hands it over to Dad. The snap of his belt leaving the loops grabs my attention.

My heart pounds in my ears. *Is he going to spank me?*

He stomps into my room, shoves the paper in my face and snatches at my arm.

"Don't you dare!" I shriek, struggling against his grip.

"I was honest with you," I say.

"You are failing!" he shouts.

"Don't touch me!" I yell, kicking at him, but I'm no match. He pins me face down on the mattress and slaps my thighs with the leather strap.

"*I hate you! I effing hate you!*" I yell it over and over, tears running fierce while he continues to smack me.

"Clint!" I hear my mother's voice ring out behind us. "That's enough!"

As he lets me go, I flip around and shove my finger in his face.

"Don't you ever touch me again! You son of a bitch!"

He loops the belt around his hand and stares at me. I glare at him through a mess of tears and snot, my face hot with anger. Pursing my lips, eyes slit dagger thin, I shake my head at him. He looks at the floor with a sigh and follows my mother out of the room without another word. I spit on the carpet behind him, jump up to slam the door and shove my thumb in the lock. Guilt dances around my heart, but I push it away. This time I was honest, and sometimes honesty comes with fire.

♥

On New Year's Eve, Dad falls from sobriety, toasting our family with a glass of champagne.

"It's just one glass," he says.

And with that sip, Dad slips into his old skin, toting home a six-pack of beer and a dime bag of weed every day after work. Mom follows his path, with limits. She "allows herself" a beer after five o'clock and a hit off Dad's pipe after dinner. She says marijuana helps with her MS. I'm not sure how, as she seems okay to me. Sometimes she complains of a gimpy leg, a wobbly hand, or a fuzzy eye. But she manages to go to work, maintain the house, pay the bills, and be our mom, so I assume she is fine.

After Dad's fall from glory, we still go to church. And the people at church welcome my parents despite their flaws and shortcomings, just as Jesus does. Mom and Dad still pray together every morning, still do their best to read God's word and walk a good walk. But they are still broken. Knowing Jesus accepts my family in this condition, that He came for the sick and the sinners like us, makes me love Him even more.

Two important things I learn in my Bible reading is that Jesus makes me a new creation, and I am not of this world. Jesus says the world hates Christians because of Him and that the world hated Him first. People of the world don't know or understand Him, or me. I find some comfort in this truth. Maybe God made me weird and gave me these horrible circumstances for a reason? Maybe He plans to do something amazing with all my dirt?

Maybe Jesus is why Jessica disdains my love for Him and the church? She is in the world and I'm in Christ, so we are in conflict. Jess and I don't spend much time together because she still loves to party. Drinking and drugging muddle my mind, leaving me groggy and confused. It's harder to focus on following Jesus and doing the right thing when I cloud my brain with substances, so I party a lot less. When we hang out, I don't drink until I puke or smoke weed until I can't function. I still dabble a little. Letting go of what I know is scary. But I don't fall down the pit face first anymore.

And this pitfall is what confuses me about my mom and dad. I'm a teenager, and peer pressure makes change hard. But my parents are adults. They can buy beer or not buy beer. They can smoke pot or not smoke pot. There isn't anyone teasing them for making good choices. So why is it so hard for them to change? They say they love God, but they can't seem to overcome the bad habits haunting them. If Jesus makes us new, why do they act like they always have? Why aren't they different?

Mom doesn't need to change much, and she's working on it. She gives up reading Stephen King in favor of her Bible, and I see her jotting down notes with every sermon. But Dad? Man, he could use a serious overhaul. How does it happen? Does Jesus work a miracle like He did when He healed the blind, or is change up to my father? If that's the case, we are all screwed.

And how does it happen for me? I'm trudging along at a snail's pace. Cutting back on the mind-altering stuff is easy, but honoring my parents, watching my mouth (I love to swear!), not gossiping, those things are hard. I want to do better in school, but I have zero study skills, am behind in every way, and show little hope for improvement. Can God make me smart with a snap of His majestic fingers? Because I haven't paid attention in class since fifth grade and doing five years of work in one semester seems impossible to me!

Wish as I might, I'm still failing most of my classes at the end of sophomore year. So when my report card comes in the mail, I have a choice to make. Do I lie? Or practice honesty and risk another spanking? Once again, Jesus is all up in my craw, propelling me to tell the truth.

"So you have an F in biology and history, Ds in math and English, a C in PE, and an A in drama," Dad says, holding the paper near his glasses.

"Correct." I say, sitting up straight.

"What's your plan for passing next year?"

"Do the work," I say.

"You succeed at the classes you enjoy," Mom says.

I shrug and stare between them.

"It's your future, Melissa. Not mine. Not your mother's," Dad says, tossing the paper on the table.

"How long am I grounded?" I ask.

"Oh, no. We are not punishing you." Dad chuckles. "You are sixteen, my love. Your failure and your destiny, those rest on you now."

I glance at Mom, who nods in return.

"We know you can do it. But are you willing?" Mom asks.

"Seriously?" I flick my head between the two of them.

"One hundred percent," she says. "It's your future."

"I get to choose," I say, "Pass or fail. You are not punishing me?"

"Correct," Dad says.

Something inside me shifts. They are not angry. No yelling, no swearing, no spanking.

Just faith.

In me.

Wow! I'm not sure what to do with that!

♥

The summer between sophomore and junior year finds me spending lots more time with my new best friend: my mother. On rainy weekends, we lallygag around the mall, watch chick-flicks at the movie theater, or take walks around the neighborhood. But when the sunshine finally arrives, we spend Saturdays at Klineline Park.

Baking like sugar cookies on hot sand, Mom and I rest on a spot halfway between the pond and the bathroom, close enough to see my brother, far enough to keep kids from flicking us with sand. Rows of fellow sunbather's line the beach of our favorite swimming hole. Lifeguards watch the water from tall towers, allowing weary moms a few minutes to tan.

"Mom, look!" Stacy bellows from the shallow end of the lake.

"We can't even see him," I say, holding a hand over my face.

"Good job!" she hollers back before resting on her towel.

"Come throw me!" he yells.

"In a minute," she says without moving.

"Isn't he too big for you to be tossing him in the water, Mom? He's thirteen years old, for crying out loud."

"He's getting heavy, that's for sure," she says.

"He's as big as you are," I say, furrowing my brows.

"I don't mind doing it," she says.

I shake my head side to side. On occasions like this, I remember Stacy is Mom's baby. At no time do I ever feel less favored than my brother. But I know any attempts to boss her where he's concerned will be met with, "Mind your own business, Melissa", so I relax into the sand and soak up the warmth.

Minutes tick by, each second growing longer as comforting warmth turns to penetrating heat. I love a tan, but I don't love roasting like a chicken. Twenty minutes in, my heart pounds in my ears as the blistering sun sears my skin golden brown.

"Ready for a dip?" I ask Mom, shading my eyes as I roll in her direction.

"In a few," she says.

I don't know how she lays here so long. The heat is eating me alive. Tick, tick, tick.

"Ready now?"

"It's been two minutes, Missy." She sighs, not lifting her head. "You can go alone, there are no sharks."

"I can wait," I say, studying her.

Mom's glasses are off; her eyelids closed against the blaring sun. The freckles on her arms darken as she tans. Her bright yellow swimsuit is one piece in front, to cover the stretch marks from three children, and two-piece in back, to show off her sexy butt. The rosebud tattoo on her hip peeks out of her waistband.

She opens her eyes and looks at me. "What?"

"Nothing," I say, rolling onto my back.

"Why are you staring at me?" she asks.

"Because you're awesome," I say.

"Ha!" she says, sitting up. "Come on, let's take a dip."

We tiptoe over hot sand, dodging kids with buckets and shovels. I walk in up to my waist, dunk my tender skin under the chilly water to cool the burn. Mom wades in further to toss Stacy from her shoulders. She sinks below the surface, letting him monkey up on her, then shoots up out of the water, launching him in the air.

Mom and Stacy are water dogs. Not me. I hate the water. Especially dark water. Lord knows what's floating around under there. On the Mississippi River, Momma never let us go barefoot because of all the broken bottles and rusted cans, so I don't even like the sand. There were snakes and gators, too. And I hate the deep end of the pool. Panic when I can't touch the bottom. When I was seven, a girl pushed me off the side of a hotel swimming pool. I freaked out, struggled to find the concrete edge. When I did, chlorine burned up my nose and down into my lungs.

I rest my butt on thick sand, and giggle as Mom launches my

squealing brother in the air.

Stacy almost drowned once, too. At a public swimming pool in Arkansas. We went with my aunts and cousins. Momma and I rested on lounge chairs at the shallow end while my little brother frolicked in the deep water with orange swimmies wrapped around his biceps. He jumped off the diving board over and over, hollering, "Momma! Look at me." It's a good thing she kept watching, because the last time he pulled his little body onto the diving board, yelled, "Look at me," got a running start, and leaped off the edge, his orange floaties surfaced without him. Momma bolted up, dove into the shallow end, swam under the dividing rope, and resurfaced with my brother in her arms, all coughing and sputtering. A nose blow and root beer later, he asked, "Want to watch me jump off the diving board?"

He's a brave one. Maybe a little dumb, but brave for sure.

"Hey! Mis!" Stacy yells, flying catawampus into the air. I give him a thumb's up and head back to my towel. Plopping face down, the sand warm on my belly, I grab my Sweet Valley High novel. I attempt to lose myself in the story, but the sun glaring off white paper tires my eyes after a page or two. I toss the book aside and save the reading for tonight. I love snuggling up with a good romance on Saturday night. I haven't had another boyfriend since Brent. I'm over him, for sure. Jesus helped me recover from that heartbreak. But I haven't found another boy who sparks my interest. Not yet anyway.

Three hours and a deep tan later, we cross the cedar bridge out of the park, snow cones in hand. I hold the seat forward for Stacy. He climbs in the back of our orange Volkswagen bug with root beer syrup running over his wrist, freckling his legs and swim trunks with sticky, brown dots. Rolling my eyes in disgust, I climb in the front and balance my icy treat to keep from spilling blue syrup in my lap.

"Jeannie Lue is coming for a visit," Momma says, shifting into reverse.

"Grandma J? When?" I ask, unsticking my wet legs from the

black vinyl seat.

"In August," she says, cranking the window down.

"Wow, we haven't seen her since I was ten," I say. "Isn't she afraid to leave her house?"

"Yeah, this trip is a big deal for her," Mom says.

"Where is she staying?"

"Downstairs," Momma says.

"How long will she be here?" I ask.

"Ten days."

"Well, that's a mighty long time," I say.

"Yes," Mom says. "Yes, it is."

8

Finding Hope On The Slippery Slope

I roll over and glance at the red digits on my clock. Eleven a.m. Time to rise and shine. The banging and clanging in the kitchen tell me Mom's busy peeling potatoes for potato salad, boiling eggs to devil, and prepping a turkey breast for Grandma J's visit. The lemony scent of Pledge tells me Mom's also been dusting. Momma cooks and cleans the same way when Grandma and Granddad come to visit. Only before her parents arrive, I scrub our moldy shower tiles with a toothbrush. The smell of Comet tells me she's already scrubbed the bathroom. Thankfully, Mom's not so picky with Daddy's momma.

I slide a bra on under my shirt and meander toward the fridge to find Mom's slender frame leaning over the oven. She shoves the naked turkey breast, slathered in buttery goodness, deep into the heat. In a couple of hours, she'll cool the meat and slice it for sandwiches.

"Morning, Momma," I say, tossing Cheerios into a stained plastic bowl.

Mom saves food containers from the grocery store and calls them dishes. Recycled pimento cheese jars, jelly jars, and Mason jars serve as our beverage cups. Butter and margarine bowls hold our cereal and soup. Our plates and flatware come from thrift stores and garage sales. A random collection of mugs and coffee cups completes our hodgepodge kitchen set. Momma's mismatched dishes irritate me because she could buy new crockery. Just like she could buy new clothes from Macy's instead of used duds from the Salvation Army. But she doesn't. She's a bit of a pauper.

"Morning, Dolly." Mom says, snapping the oven shut. "You get to help me today."

"Okay," I say, balancing a heavy milk jug against the counter. "What should I do?"

"Prep the downstairs for Grandma J."

Mom walks to the record player, slips Dan Fogelberg from his cardboard sleeve, and drops the needle onto the vinyl album. The sounds of static pops and grainy guitar fill the room as she says, "Vacuum, dust, and scrub the shower."

"With a toothbrush?" I ask with a smirk.

Mom shakes her head and lights a stick of sandalwood incense.

"You know, it still smells like dog dander and musty carpet in here," I say, shoveling cereal in my mouth.

She blows out the match and purses her lips.

"Just kidding. Geez," I say, wiping milk off my chin. "I'll hop to it, Momma."

It's dusk when Dad pulls into the drive. I lean against the picture window, watch him strut to the passenger door, prop it open, and extend a hand. A tiny lady steps out beside him, adjusting her wig and smoothing her black pantsuit.

"She's here," I say, hollering to Mom.

I scamper downstairs to greet her. As she walks onto the porch, we stand eye to eye, brown to brown, same round cheeks, droopy eyes, and rosebud lips.

"Darlin', this is your grandmother. I believe you look just like her," Dad says, grinning between us.

"Missy," she says, her Louisiana drawl pulling my name into a romantic swirl of Es and Ss.

"I am so happy to see you," she says.

I put my arms out to hug her.

"Give Grandma a kiss," she says, puckering up.

I let her cover my cheek in sticky red lip prints, hug her long, then step back to study her. Me and Momma are not so much alike. Mom is earthy and simple, quiet, and easy going. I am a glam girl drama queen with a loud mouth, and an obstinate personality. I wonder if I'm more like Grandma J?

♥

We take Grandma J on the same excursions that thrill Grandma and Granddad. The Grotto on Sandy Boulevard, Bonneville Dam to count salmon climbing the fish ladders. We skip Beacon Rock. My mother's parents are sturdy, often climbing to the tip-top of the eight-hundred-foot boulder. Grandma J ain't gonna make it, so we drive her up the Oregon side of the Columbia River Gorge to stop at Multnomah Falls instead.

"I'll wait here, baby," Grandma J says, reclining on a bench outside the lodge.

"Don't you want to see the falls up close?" I ask

"I'll wait here, too," Momma says.

Dad stands with his hands on his hips and a frown pulling his face down. My father loves to wander the backwoods of the Pacific Northwest. But he's not one for the commercial sights or busy parks, where people gather to click a thousand pictures of one magnificent creation. Dad knows there are plenty of falls to see besides this one, most of them tucked behind the briar bushes and rocky crags no sane person cares to navigate.

Many a summer day Dad drags the family beyond the thicket to drop a jig and bobber into the clear water gathering below the steep rapids of his favorite fishing hole. The Lewis River serves up some of the best steelhead an angler can catch in the state of Washington. And although I hate fishing, sunbathing on the damp rocks of Lewis River Falls on a sweltering August afternoon is a family favorite. Momma packs a picnic lunch, spreads out one lone towel and offers up a smorgasbord of turkey sandwiches, potato chips, cookies, and fruit. Much like today, except Dad wears a smile when we visit the Lewis River.

"Y'all run on up to the lower falls. We'll head out of here when you get back," he barks at me and Stacy.

My brother and I wander the asphalt trail to the lower pool of Multnomah Falls. The sound of alpine water pounding down the six-hundred-foot cliff deafens our ears as we traipse over mossy rocks to venture behind the falls.

"It's nice back here." I holler at Stacy, the mist in the air mixing with the sweat on my face.

"I'd rather be at Lewis River Falls," my brother says, scrunching into the alcove next to me.

I stick my hand under the spray to cool my hot skin.

"Why? 'Cause Dad's being a jerk?" I ask.

"He hates being around us," Stacy says.

"No. He hates being around extended family," I say.

"Do you think Grandma J puts him on edge?"

"I'm sure Dad has a lot of scars related to her," I say.

"I'll be glad when she leaves," he says.

Dad appears at the edge of the falls, cups his hands around his mouth and hollers at us. "Let's go!"

I let out a sigh and follow my brother down the trail to Dad's crusty old Audi. Stacy, Grandma J, and I pack into the backseat like salty sardines in a tin can and I pray for a smooth ride home. Traveling in this rust bucket is fine when it's cool outside. Once the heat rises, the car vapor locks and the engine shuts down. We make it one mile, two miles, three miles . . . "Damn," Dad says as we roll to a stop on the shoulder of Interstate 84.

Well, we made it five miles.

"We may as well eat here," Mom says.

We drape a blanket over roadside trash and ant piles to picnic under the blaring sun, batting away bees and flies while we wait for the car to cool down. Vehicles whiz by at seventy while we choke down turkey sandwiches, Doritos, and bottled soda. After twenty minutes or so, Dad turns the key and the engine roars to life. We tuck our sweaty bodies back inside and pray to make it a few more miles. On Interstate 5, we break down again, two miles from the house. This time under the cool shade of an overpass, thank the Lord!

These day trips are rough. Not because the car stalls out or because we picnic on the side of the highway or because the heat melts my makeup like a Crayola crayon. It's Dad. His impatient barking, his intolerance of his family, his unpredictable temper makes time drag on like a slug over concrete. I agree with Stacy. When our father is outside his comfort zone, family time sucks.

Dad's cranky mood disappears once we get home. Welcome to the harmony of our chaotic life. He smiles as he fries up the steelhead we saved for Grandma J's visit. Mom slices potatoes for the fryer while I shuck corn. Stacy sets the table. We savor our dinner in familiar silence, allowing our forks to rest just long enough to say *yum* before relishing another bite. When our tummies are full, I clear the table and get busy washing dishes as Dad pulls out his guitar. He serenades Momma and Grandma J with his rendition of Dan Fogelberg's "As the Raven Flies." And when I stop to join them, Grandma smiles and winks at me, pointing at her son with a grin.

"He's good," she mouths in my direction.

I smile and give her a thumbs up.

When Dad tucks his guitar away an hour later, Grandma retires downstairs. I shuffle down behind her, carrying a package of E.L. Fudge cookies and two cups of French roast thickened with cream and sugar. I hand her a cup, sit on the floor at her feet and study her pale features. At night, Grandma trades her pantsuit for a pink muumuu. Her bouffant wig sits atop a foam stand. I study her squinty eyes and wrinkled cheeks. The absence of her black brows, sultry lashes, and velvety lips makes her look like a mannequin with button eyes. Her fine, black hair lies plastered in thin strands across her head. Under all her spoofing, Grandma J is as plain as me and

Momma.

"Tell me a secret," she says, pulling a drag off her smoke.

"Hmm," I say, staring at her.

"Come on," she says.

"I used to party," I say, taking a sip of joe.

"I used to lie to Mom and sleep at a party house, in fact," I say. Grandma raises her brows. "You did?"

"One night, me and my best friend lied to our parents about a sleep over. It was summer, so we planned to sleep at Willow Creek Park so we could party. Only as it got late, the air turned cold and damp. We tried to sleep in the restroom, but the concrete floors were cold and wet. So we wandered the neighborhood until some guys in a car stopped to offer us a ride."

Grandma pulls in a breath.

"Did you get in their car?"

"No. Because we didn't know them. But when we declined, they started yelling at us, so we ran. And they chased us. All around the neighborhood. For a long time, we couldn't shake them. When we finally did, we remembered an older boy who lived down the road from the park. His parents were never home, so he let us crash on his floor. It was fun, so we went back the next weekend. And the next. Jessie and I did that every weekend for two summers."

Grandma giggles into her palm and asks, "Do your parents know?"

"No! And don't you tell them!"

"I won't, darlin'."

"I don't drink like that anymore," I say.

"Well, that's good. We've got too many drunks in our family already," she says.

"Your turn to tell me a secret," I say.

"When I was your age, I'd gussy up, go out on the town with Annette. She was my best friend, and we did our share of drinking, too," she says.

"Annette is Mack's sister. Mack is your daddy's daddy. He was so handsome," she says, taking a swig off her cup.

"Dad says he was a drunk," I say, wanting to stuff the words back in my mouth the moment they hit my grandmother's ears.

Grandma looks at me and her eyes go cold.

"Your daddy's right," she says, "Mack drank whiskey. And he was a violent drunk. He beat on me, beat on anyone around him. He loved to fight, and the hard alcohol made him fight harder."

"Dang," I say.

"I was beautiful, men flirted with me, and Mack would get so jealous," she says.

I stare at her, entranced by her words.

"Mack went to the bar one night after work, left me alone with screaming kids all day. He never was any help. I was so angry, I decided to get even with him. I curled my hair, put on my corset, slipped into a yellow A-line dress. Low cut, tight at the waist, to show off my bosom. When he staggered in, I poked my finger in his face and said, 'It's my turn to go out.'"

I grab a cookie.

"He said, 'You ain't goin' nowhere!' and grabbed my wrist. I shook him off, told him I's going dancing with Annette and he ain't stopping me."

She stops, eyes fixed in a daze.

"Did you go?" I ask. "Dancing with Annette?"

"Nope," she says, dropping her eyes to mine. "He beat me. Almost to death."

I gasp.

"He tossed me through a plate-glass window, packed up my babies, and left town."

"Grandma, that's awful."

She nods, working her red polished fingernails under the cellophane for a cookie.

"We divorced, and I met my second husband, Nicholas."

She bites into the wafer, fixes her eyes in the distance again.

"We were so in love. He took real good care of me."

I nod and dip my cookie into tepid coffee.

"He committed suicide," she says. "I found his body."

"Dang, Grandma!" I say, dropping the cookie into my cup.

"But I still love him," she says. "I always will."

How on earth do you love someone who bails on you?

I stare into her haunted eyes and ponder our similarities. How our broken hearts beat to the same drum of betrayal and loss. How our petite frames, sassy mouths, and rebellious spirits match so perfectly. How her confused mind reminds me of my own. And how the drama of her fractured life spills into mine through Dad. *She is me and I am her. We share the same splintered DNA,* I think.

But Dad is only half of me.

"Missy, life's been hard for me," she says.

I nod. "That ain't no lie."

"I never learned to drive."

"Me neither! I failed driver's ed three times," I say. "I hate driving."

She chuckles. "Me too! I walk wherever I need to go. Or someone drives me."

"I ride the bus." I giggle. "Do you have a job?"

"I draw disability. My roommate, Joe, works part time. And Social Security helps, too."

I fish the wafer out of my cup.

"I attempted suicide. Ate a bunch of pills," she says, lighting a cigarette. "They lock me up when it happens. My doctor calls me manic-depressed."

"When it happens?" I ask. "As in, more than once?"

"I've tried several times," she says, smoke rolling in soft white tendrils out of her nose.

I sit. Speechless. I remember the moments I wanted to die. *Holy cow, we really are alike.* Then I remember Jesus.

"Do you believe in God?" I ask her.

"Yeah," she says.

"Do you believe Jesus is His Son?"

"I do."

"He changed everything for me after I accepted Him as my Savior. He could change your heart, too, Grandma."

"If you say so, baby," she says, patting my hand. "If you say so."

When it's time for her to return to Louisiana, I watch Grandma J pile into Dad's car wearing the same pantsuit and black wig she arrived in. My heart aches. I want to know her more. Want to understand her broken. Was she born with it? Did the devil give it to her? Am I going to end up just like her? Unable to drive or work? Riding the endless turmoil of an emotional roller coaster? So high one minute I could conquer the earth, so low the next I want to be buried in it?

I don't know what our future holds, but Grandma J is my authentic, flesh-and-bone grandma, and tears fill my eyes when part of me drives away.

♥

"Come hang out with me," Jess says as the bus rumbles to a stop.

"Maybe," I say, standing to go.

"I miss you," she says, grinning.

"Fine," I say. "I'll see you in a bit."

We hike around her farm, feed some apples to Banjo, and catch up, talking about boys and school. When we settle onto the dusty sofa in the barn loft, she pulls a small sandwich bag from her pocket, and gives me a tantalizing grin.

"Want some?" she asks.

"Is it coke?" I ask, studying the off-white dust packed in the lower corner of the baggie.

"Crank. It's better. Gives you tons of energy," she says.

"Hm, I don't know," I say.

"Come on, don't be a wuss."

"Just a smidge," I say.

She piles the white powder onto a mirror and pulls a razor

blade through it, chopping, cutting, and slicing it into perfect lines. She rolls up a dollar, sticks it up her nose and bends over the glass. In a snap, she sucks a pile up a nostril and hands the bill to me. "Here, you try."

I bend over, taking care not to blow out her lines, and inhale deep. Nasty chemicals burn my sinuses, penetrate my throat, leaving a bitter taste in my mouth. Regret hits me like lightning, rocking the peace I've carried for months. Jess takes another line and offers the dollar to me, again.

I shake my head.

"One is enough for me," I say.

She hands me her weed pipe, with the same white dust peppering the screen, and says, "You can smoke it, too."

"Nah," I say, handing it back to her. She shrugs and lights it up. A putrid vapor fills the room, making me want to gag. *What the hell am I doing?* I wonder, feeling like a stranger in a place I used to call home.

I don't trek back to my house until after dark, and when I do, I'm thankful for my brown eyes. Maybe my parents won't notice my dilated pupils. I bounce upstairs to find Dad dozing in his recliner, Mom taking a shower. I tiptoe to my room with guilt chasing me like a ghost, slip on my pajamas, and hunker down under my comforter.

"It's amazing how one poor choice can gulp a year's worth of goodness," I say to nobody.

I lie awake until five a.m., hating the heart pounding drug racing through my body. As I silently vow to never touch meth again, my mind wanders over my friendship with Jess: her need for a darker high, my desire to know God more. I tried coaxing her toward the Lord, took her to church once. She was a nervous wreck the entire hour, bouncing her legs and chomping her gum like a cow. I'm not sure if it was God or the drugs getting to her. At the end of the service, she hissed at me, saying, "I'm not coming back here, and don't ever talk to me about God again." But Jesus leaks out of me like water. I can't forget Him, can't stop talking about Him, can't stop talking to

Him.

"Lord, I am so sorry for doing this stupid drug," I say. "Please help me sleep."

My eyes grow heavy, and I promise God: no more drugs.

I should know better than to promise God anything.

While Jess circles the drain, Dad also follows Satan down the mouth of the pit. He takes a job building houses, falls into cocaine, and walks away from the Lord. The devil's dust is a hungry beast, swallowing Dad's job, his money, and his sanity. The bank repossesses his car and threatens to take our house. He can't sleep and that means one thing. He sneaks into my room after dark. And it isn't long before he drags me down the rabbit hole of drugs.

One day after school, he ushers me to his room, pulls a glass pipe from under his dresser, along with a black film canister containing a crystal rock.

"Your mother cannot know about this," he says.

Mom and I share a hit of weed on rare occasions, but Momma can't do cocaine. She says it geeks out her multiple sclerosis. And even though lots of my friends are snorting coke, I try to steer clear of the silky, white powder. It doesn't light up my world as Jesus does. And to be honest, if drugs aren't set before me, I don't go looking for them. Not even weed. Not anymore.

Dad sets the crack in the bowl and lights it up. I watch ribbons of white smoke float up the clear stem. He inhales, holds his breath, allows the drug to penetrate his lungs, and then hands the pipe to me.

"It's called freebasing," he says, placing the lighter to the crystals as I breathe deep.

Of course, this little escapade into smoking crack isn't fun, and it isn't free. It comes with a price. How I keep stepping in the same pile of shit is beyond me. I don't solicit my father for drugs or alcohol or any of the crap he gives me. I just don't see the abuse coming, and then I don't know how to say no when it happens. I just freeze, like a deer in the headlights of a tractor-trailer before it gets smashed. It's as if I'm stuck in the idea that if I don't comply, if I rock the boat at all, my whole world will collapse. My voice is stuck, and I don't have a will of my own. If I had my way, my family would be sane, sober, and normal. But my way is not an option, so I roll with the devil to keep my father happy and my mother safe in the lies we've always lived.

When Dad does this to me, and I don't fight back, I can't even look at my Bible. I can't talk to God about Dad or what he does to me. I can't talk to Jesus at all. It's like I slip into a place God can't find, a dark place He can't go into because He's holy. It's as if He's in heaven and I'm in hell.

And I don't know how to get out.

♥

Snorting blow shifts the tides of Dad's moods without notice, making him even more unpredictable. The entire family, even our animals, is at risk of his anger. Buttons is Momma's baby, and Bo, our sweet ole Lab, joined the family after following Stacy to the house. The stray refused to leave, sleeping on the deck night after night until we finally let him inside.

I come home one day to find scratch marks and an enormous hole in Mom and Dad's bedroom door. "Oh, no," I say, looking into Bo's giant cocoa eyes. *Shoot!* "Did you claw a hole in the door?" I ask, glancing at his paws. They are crusty with dry blood. I know why he did it. Buttons is in heat, and he wants to mount her. But he's a big boy and she's a little dog. He'd kill her if he got hold of her. "Dude, I can't fix this," I say.

The slam of Dad's car door makes me jump. I run to my room, beg Bo to follow me. Stupid dog stays behind to greet the monster. *Maybe I can smooth this over.* I wander toward the kitchen and find Dad leaning into the fridge for a beer.

"How was your day?" I ask, testing his mood.

"Not bad," he says, then follows my small talk for several

minutes.

When I feel safe enough to bring it up, I say, "Bo-Bo tried getting Buttons today."

Dad stops mid-chug, drops his gaze and glares at me under the brim of his cap. "What do you mean, he tried to get Buttons?"

He looks at Bo, cowering beside me, and asks, "Bo-Bo, were you a naughty boy?" Dad slams his drink on the counter, stomps to the bedroom, looks at the door, and booms, "Bad dog!" Bo rushes under the dining room table as Dad races through the kitchen, screaming. "You get your ass over here, now!"

Bo refuses to budge. He trembles as my dad knocks a chair back and reaches for his scruff, then slips between the table legs and scrambles past my father. I make for my room, unable to watch my dad chase our defenseless pup. When Dad's palm lands on Bo's hip, the sound of him squealing pushes me to slam my door, wedge my fingers in my ears, and rock back and forth, saying, "I hate you. I effing hate you."

Yelping echoes down the hall, and I repeat the words. "I hate you. I hate you. I hate you."

When Dad is done dumping his rage on our dog and the house quiets, I find Bo on the back deck and wrap my arms around him. Our sweet dog plops his head on my shoulder as I seethe. *How is this Bo's fault? He's just a dog.*

Jesus's words from Matthew 5:43–46 tumble into my mind: "Love your enemies and pray for those who persecute you, that you may be children of your Father in heaven. He causes his sun to rise on the evil and the good, and sends rain on the righteous and the unrighteous. If you love those who love you, what reward will you get?" (NIV).

Puppy howls ring in my heart.

I hate him, God. I'm so sorry, but I hate him.

Those embers of hatred spark a flame when Dad comes home a few days later, slamming the front door and stomping up the stairs. "Get your crap off the table," he says. "And wash the damn dishes!"

What is his problem? I slap my books shut and haul my backpack to my room. I was doing homework, and the dishes don't need to be done for another two hours. But I don't question him as I turn on the faucet to fill the sink.

"I told your brother to mow the grass after school! Where the hell is he?" Dad asks.

"Wrestling practice," I say.

"Chores come first," he says with a boom.

I turn away, squeeze soap on a dishrag, and scrub the silverware, doing my best to ignore him.

"Lazy ass kids, both of you! What have you ever done for me or your mother?"

I drop the spoons, grab a towel, and walk toward the dining room.

"You have something to say?" he asks.

I spin around, furrow my brows, and ask, "What have you ever done for me and Stacy?"

Red heat washes over his face. "Don't get smart with me, young lady."

"Or what?" I ask with a hiss.

The man who terrorizes my life steps back.

"I'm tired of your bullying, Dad," I say.

"Oh, yeah? What are you going to do about it?" he asks.

I narrow my eyes into tiny slits. "Well, I could tell the world our little secret," I say, tilting my head to the side.

Evil rumbles from deep inside him, contorting his face and turning his cocoa irises midnight black. He steps forward, shakes his head before thrusting a finger at my face. "Don't you ever threaten me again. You think you can just bring that up and throw it out at me?"

A chill runs up my spine as he slides closer, rage pounding the veins in his neck.

"You think you can scare me?" he asks, mocking my stare.

Fear petrifies my vocal cords, leaving me speechless, but I stand my ground and hold his gaze. Silence covers the room for one, two, three seconds before Dad spins on his heel, stomps downstairs, and slams the front door on his way out.

I release my breath. *Holy cow. What just happened?*

♥

The next day, I hear Dad's car door slam, the windows rattle as he tosses the front door shut, his booted feet marching up the stairs. The hairs on my arms prick when he pads down the carpet toward my room. Mom should be home any minute, but that doesn't mean I'm safe.

He knocks on my bedroom door.

"Come in," I say.

"Melissa," he says in his creepy Dad tone. "Can we talk?"

I give him a blank stare and say, "Um, okay."

"Come join me in the dining room, honey."

Bile rolls up my belly as I follow him down the hall, through the kitchen. He ushers me to take the chair across from him.

"Missy, my life has been tough. Many of the things I've put you through happened to *me* when I was a boy."

I stare at him and pray he'll be done soon.

"A woman molested me when I was little."

Gross.

"When I was seven, one of my foster fathers accused me of touching his daughter. I didn't do it, but that man refused to believe me." Dad's eyes fix in a daze as he says, "He punished me by hanging me over a well."

"What do you mean, he hung you over a well?" I ask.

"He took me outside, bound my legs, and hung me upside down . . . over a dark, black hole in the ground. It was hundreds of feet deep."

I gasp.

"How long did you hang there?"

He slumps, puts his head in his hands, and says, "Quite a while."

I shake my head in horror.

143

"The only genuine love I've ever had comes from your mother. I can't live without her." He sits forward with pleading eyes. "I battle so many demons. Being orphaned, having abusive parents, drugs, alcohol, Vietnam."

Silence looms as I watch him struggle for words. He leans back and runs his hands over his face to catch his tears. "I have failed you, Melissa. Failed our family."

What's happening?

"I am sorry for the evil things I have done."

I don't understand what he's saying.

"I will never touch you again, I promise."

What—?

"Can you forgive your old man?"

I stare at him, slack jaw. I try to speak but can't dislodge the words.

Do I forgive him? Do I have a choice?

"Come here, darlin'," he says, holding out an arm.

I push my chair back like a robot and walk over to hug him.

"I promise to do better if you will give me a chance," he says.

Then he weeps. In my arms, my father weeps. But as grief tumbles out of him, I cannot move. Cannot cry. Cannot feel a thing.

9

Burger-Flipping Freedom

Something inside me changes as I move through the second half of my junior year. Mr. Thompson gives me the Most Improved award in US history when I go from a D to a B in his class. That little bump, and a smidge of recognition, gives me a taste of something delicious. Success! Suddenly good grades are better than crack, and I don't want to just pass. I want to fly!

So I work harder, meet with my guidance counselor, talk to my teachers, and form a plan to graduate. I'm going to be a second-year senior, but I don't care. All I want is more As and Bs on my report card. And these changes don't come from me. I didn't mature overnight or decide to make better choices. It's God who's healing me and planting new desires in my heart.

When summer arrives, Mom says, "You need a job."

"Yeah," I say. "Lots of kids at school are working this summer."

"Money is freedom," she says, folding laundry on a Saturday afternoon.

"I suppose," I reply. "My five-dollar allowance doesn't stretch as far as it used to."

"And you are seventeen years old," she says.

"Burger Barn is hiring," I say. "But I don't really want to flip burgers."

"You've got to start somewhere."

"Ugh," I say, stomach churning.

The thought of working in fast food unnerves me. I don't even eat fast food. Mom never taught me to cook anything except sugar donuts and grilled cheese. How am I supposed to make a hamburger?

And the people. Ever since I was a girl getting whacked in the head at daycare or bullied at school, I've had a fear of people. It's the same fear that keeps me from participating in sports, trying out for the cheer team, or the dance team. I'm just too shy to socialize with people I think are normal. I can handle dysfunctional misfits. I cannot handle high achievers, overachievers, or achievers in general.

I sigh and stare at the carpet. The thought of taking orders, serving food, and communicating with John Q. Public paralyzes me. If there's one thing I know, it's that I'm a ragamuffin, and normal people cannot tolerate me. They will be hateful and rude. And I don't have any space left in my heart for hateful people.

"Let's go get you an application," Mom says, tossing unfolded laundry back in the basket.

"Now?"

"Sure. Why not?"

I don't have the energy to tell her what I'm thinking, so I just nod. Fifteen minutes later, Mom parks our Volkswagen below the giant Burger Barn sign.

"You can do this." She nods toward the glass entry. "It's just an application."

I sigh, step onto the curb and glance back at Mom before walking into the smell of french fries. White Out machines buzz behind the cashier, blending vanilla soft serve with a smattering of candies; gummy worms, chocolate chunk, strawberry pie pieces. I approach the counter and ask for an application. A snide girl with frizz-permed hair struts to the back and returns with a clipboard and a pen.

Snapping her gum, she nods toward the lobby and says, "Fill it out here."

I slide into a booth and complete as much of the application as I can. Name, address, phone number, birth date, no job experience, no references. Yikes. Signing the bottom line, I take it to the snotty girl at the counter.

"Wait here," she says and disappears down the hall. Thirty seconds later, she reappears, saying, "Come with me. Laurel wants to talk to you."

After a short interview, I walk outside holding a white jersey emblazoned with a giant neon cheeseburger. I hop in the car and say, "I need polyester pants and black shoes."

"You got a job?" Mom asks, squeezing my hand.

"I got a job flipping burgers," I say with a smile.

♥

Three o'clock Monday finds me standing on the corner, a quarter mile from home, waiting for a C-Tran bus. I roll fifty cents over in my hand, eager to board for the short ride to work. My shift begins at four and ends at eleven. Dad has agreed to pick me up, even though it's past his bedtime.

As I scan the horizon for the bus, a brown-haired boy driving a '71 Camero pulls up to the curb. I lean down to look through the passenger window and stare into a familiar pair of ocean blue eyes.

"Brent!"

"Want a ride?"

"Sure," I say, gathering my bags off the sidewalk. He reaches across the seat and shoves my door open.

"Thank you!" I say with a sigh.

Over the last two years, Brent and I have become good friends. We've shared space in classrooms, on field trips, and at a party or two. Through all my wild antics and crazy escapades, Brent never ridiculed or made fun of me. He did leave me behind at Willow Creek Park the night I guzzled too much Jack.

It took me a while to reconcile that in my mind. But beyond that, Brent stayed true to himself and didn't let my emotions get to him when I was melting down over losing him. I will always love him for accepting me in all my broken glory.

I give him a sideways glance and a small grin.

"Where to?" he asks.

"Burger Barn," I say, fingering the coins in my hand.

"Did you get a job?"

"Yeah," I say, taking a deep breath.

"You nervous?" he asks.

"It's my first day."

"You'll do fine," he says. "I have faith in you."

I toss the quarters in my purse and whisper, "Thanks," wishing I had faith in myself.

The parking lot is full when Brent drops me off. I approach a locked door marked Employees Only and pull in a deep breath before punching in the key code Laurel gave me. Nothing happens. I try again, making sure each silver button clicks when pressed. Three, five, four, four. Silence. The numbers don't work. I try one more time. Nope. Before I rap on the door, it swings wide and fast, just missing my face. A tall girl in her twenties lets me in.

"Hey, you must be Melissa."

I contemplate asking her to call me Missy. Before I can decide, she says, "I'm Cammie."

"Nice to meet you," I say.

I'm not sure why, but I don't give her my nickname. Maybe I'm hoping to hide tattered Missy under the rug, so she won't screw everything up. All the bullies, preppies, and misfits in my life know me as Missy. Maybe Melissa has a shot at normalcy or even success.

Cammie holds her cigarette high as I squeeze between her and the shelves housing a mishmash of boxes. "Here's your name tag. You can change in here," she says, leading me around the corner to a single-seat bathroom. I take my bags inside, press the lock, and dress into the ugliest clothes I've ever put on my body. I pin a plastic *Melissa* over my left boob and head out the door.

"Come on, I'll show you the kitchen," she says.

A tall blonde looks up from the grill, gives me a small wave.

"This is Milo," Cammie says.

As I peek into Milo's work area, I note the lettuce fragments, pickles, and other remnants freckling the countertop. There are two fryers crisping fries to golden perfection. The area is clean, except the floor, which is covered in smashed potato pieces, bacon bits, and other crumbles. Black chunks of grease make the beige linoleum slippery under my soles.

Cammie spins on her heel and leads me to the front counter. "This is Kelly. She will train you," Cammie says, walking away.

I recognize Snide Kelly as the girl who took my application. The smirk on her face tells me I fall short of her expectations. *Great, a bully.*

Kelly smacks her gum, slaps the vinyl countertop in front of her, and says, "Come on, let's do this. This is your till," she says, leading me to register number 1. Kelly's voice fades in and out as she walks me through the dozens of buttons covering the face of the register, saying, "This is how you add cheese, minus tomato; add malt to a shake; choose large, medium, small; combo meal, kid's meal; for here, to go."

The options are endless.

I spend the first three hours traipsing after Kelly, watching her punch orders in the machine and fill them, amazed by the sheer volume of product she produces in a matter of minutes. There are dozens of concoctions to master. Banana splits have three small balls of vanilla, split the banana lengthwise, place half on each side of the oblong dish. Add a squirt of hot fudge, a drizzle of pineapple, a scoop of strawberries. Flip the whipped cream can over and dollop on two dots. Finish with maraschino cherries. How about a peanut fudge parfait? A pump of hot fudge on the bottom, a ladle of peanuts, dash of ice cream, repeat, repeat. Don't forget the curlicue on top!

By the time I help my first customer, I am overwhelmed.

Most people greet me with kind eyes and a tolerant smile, especially after I say, "It's my first day. Thank you for your patience."

Around 9:30, the Jerk arrives, barking his order and glaring at me as I fumble over buttons on the till. I repeat it back to him, saying, "Three large M&M White Outs, one with a pump of chocolate, a peanut fudge parfait, a medium caramel shake, two cheeseburger combo meals, with a coffee and a lemonade." When he nods, I print his ticket, give him a plastic number, and move to help the next person in line. After punching in a third order, I stop to make the ice cream.

"Now, where do I begin?" I ask myself.

I fumble and stumble through M&M White Outs, forget the chocolate sauce, stop midgrind to add chocolate sauce, take forever. After fifteen minutes, the guy comes to the counter and yells, "What the hell is taking so long?" Kelly steps in to assist, huffing and sneering at me, like I'm a dumbass. Tears form behind my eyes, but I refuse to let them fall.

Standing at the shake machine, I reach for a medium cup, slap the metal collar on top, and pull the handle to release ice milk. I glance up to find Milo hovering over me. She whispers, "Don't worry, I dropped his hamburger on the floor."

What?! I stare at her, as Milo dangles his to-go bag in front of me, a grin spreading over her face. She's not kidding. Giggles form inside me as she slides over to the counter and hands him the sack. "Here are your burgers, sir." She winks at me as she heads back to the kitchen. Memories of grease chunks and smashed fries fill my mind. I imagine the Jerk taking a juicy bite of his contaminated burger. *Gag!* I personally couldn't imagine doing that to another human being. But I *am* happy to know someone here has my back.

The week wears on with me, dropping, spilling, tipping things over. I mess up order after order, frustrating patrons and peers, leaving my emotions raw. At seven o'clock Thursday night, Cammie tells me to call my ride.

"Why?" I ask.

"It's slow tonight. Clock out and go home." A small frown sets over her lips as she spins and walks away.

I walk back to the kitchen, grab the phone off the wall, and call Mom to come get me. Plopping onto the curb outside, I hang my head and let the tears fall. Ice cream from the White Out machine lines the front of my chest, smelling like sour milk. My pants reek of stale french fries, the bottoms of my shoes are slick with grease. *I am so embarrassed! How hard is it to make freaking ice cream!?*

As Mom buzzes up beside me in the Volkswagen, I pick myself up, dust off my behind, and climb inside.

"Hey, Dolly! How was your shift?" she asks.

"Awful! I made a mess of everything!"

"I think you are being dramatic, Missy."

The name Missy drags across my heart like a dirty rag. Missy equals failure. Missy equals filthy . . . weird . . . ragamuffin.

I yank the plastic *Melissa* off my shirt and toss it in my bag. I don't want to taint her with Missy's shortcomings and rotten attitude.

"Mom," I say with a huff, "I can't even make coffee! How was I to know you don't add water to the pot first? I didn't know that!" I say, slapping my thighs. "I scoop the grounds into the filter, slide the pot of water into place, and push the start button. Next thing I know, coffee is spilling all over the counter and onto the floor!"

Mom chuckles, glancing my way as she backs out of the parking space. "Umm. You don't put water in the pot first," she says, clearing her throat.

I moan. "No, duh, Mom! That doesn't help me now."

She laughs harder, putting one hand on her tummy and the other on the stick shift before cramming a foot into the clutch.

"Mom?!" I glance at her and wipe the tears off my cheeks.

"I can't believe you put water in the pot," she says, her body shaking in peals of hilarity.

"It's not nice to laugh at me, Mom."

My eyes bore into her as water runs from her eyes. Soon

enough, I catch her giggles and wipe my nose on my grease-laden shirt. We laugh all the way home and by night's end, my coffee snafu is nothing more than the joke of the day. Mom's lighthearted response helps me walk into my Saturday shift with a teaspoon of confidence. Unfortunately, the weekend is nothing but a blunder-filled mess. Sunday night, Cammie calls me to the break table.

"Melissa, we are putting you in the kitchen," she says.

"You are?"

"You train with Milo tomorrow," she says, tossing a towel over her shoulder. "Oh, and you can go home early again, clock out and call your parents." Relief melts over me like hot caramel. I am going to the kitchen! No more patrons glaring at me, no more talking to John Q. Public, no more curlicues on ice cream cones. Just flipping burgers and dipping fries.

♥

I adored Milo the instant she dropped the Jerk's burger on the floor. I like her even more when I catch her playing "Back in Black" on the air guitar. When she sees me waiting in the doorway for my first shift, she says, "Hey, girl! Let me show you the ropes," and my face breaks into a giant grin when she curls her upper lip like Billy Idol and pounds out the last few beats of the song.

"AC/DC is freaking awesome," she says, tying her blonde hair up in a scrunchie.

"One of my favorite bands," I say, following her into the kitchen.

"We keep the meat drawer stocked until eight p.m.," she says, pulling a pile of sticky pink patties out of the fridge. I watch her brown them on the grill before stacking them, half cooked into the warmer. "Keep them rare, then reheat them when you fill an order."

Gross! Who wants a rewarmed patty?

"Buns go through the toaster," she says, heaping them open

152

faced on a large metal roller. I watch them disappear into the hot oven as she continues. "Slather on the mayo and relish, top with lettuce, tomato, and pickle. Do not add onion unless they ask for it. People get pissed off when you put onions on their burgers." She takes me through the burger line, then shows me how to fry chicken strips, cod fillets, tater tots, and french fries.

"Hot dogs are simple," she says, folding a cold wiener into a bun. She tucks it in a paper tray and tosses it in the microwave, slamming the door shut. The printer taps one, two, three orders from the drive thru. I watch her snatch the sheets loose and tack them on the rounder above our heads, then I do my best to keep up the pace.

Three weeks into my new job, I work the burger bar alone while Milo is on break. She and Cammie sit at the two-seater break table, sipping soda pop and smoking Marlboros. I hear giggles and glance their direction.

"What?" I ask when I find them staring.

"We were just watching you smack that gum, girl," Cammie yells over the fan. I blow a ginormous pink bubble, suck it back between my lips, toss a greasy burger onto foiled paper, and fold it closed with precision and speed.

"You're doing an awesome job," Milo says.

"Thanks," I say.

"I'm glad you like it back there," Cammie says. "Laurel wanted to fire you until I suggested moving you to the kitchen."

Wow. Good to know.

♥

I hand the teller my check for one hundred dollars and thirteen cents and grin in delight as she slides a pile of twenties into my hand. At three dollars and thirty-five cents per hour, it took a lot of ice cream cones and burgers to rack up this chunk of change.

"Want to go to lunch?" I ask Momma.

"What?"

"I'd like to buy you a sandwich with my own money."

"I would love to go," Momma says.

So the first thing I buy is a sandwich and a cookie for my mother. I can't think of a better way to spend my hard-earned cash.

"How much is a plane ticket to Louisiana?" I ask Mom between bites.

"You'd have to call the airlines and ask," she says.

"I think I will."

"Going to see Grandma J?" she asks.

"I think she'd like a visit from her granddaughter," I say with a wink.

"I think she would, too."

So I buy a plane ticket and fly off to visit Grandma J for a week. When I get home, I quit Burger Barn to focus on school. Cammie says, "If you change your mind, your spot is open." Two weeks later, my wallet is empty, and I return to work. Turns out, earning my own money does bring freedom. I am free to buy designer jeans or two bags of Cheetos or my father's respect. When I work, I am neither home to be a pain in his butt nor am I a financial burden.

Working at Burger Barn also shows me I am not just a bumbling failure. I can get good grades, hold a job, and let the real me shine through. The real Melissa. I chuck Missy, the nickname, the person, the ragamuffin girl, out the door like yesterday's trash. From now on, Mom, Dad, Stacy, and everyone else I know can call me Melissa.

Honeybee.

♥

I sit with Jess in the stands of Mackenzie Stadium. Bugs dance in the spotlights shining over the field as we watch fellow classmates walk across the stage to collect diplomas. Tears threaten to trudge lines through the foundation caking my cheeks. I should be sitting with my graduating class, tassel swinging over decorated cap, gown swishing over heeled shoes. But I am not. I am 1.5 credits short of graduating, and so is Jess.

"I'm glad you came with me," I say to Jessica without making eye contact.

Neither of us has a driver's license or a car, so we spent senior year sitting at the back of the bus, just like in middle school. On the days Jess attended class, that is. Some of our friends have dropped out, addicted to drugs, having babies, or just falling off the radar. I thought for sure Jess was on the same path until she reappeared one day, high on meth, but ready for school. I love Jess, but we still don't spend time together outside the bus. So it took some prodding to get her here tonight.

"I want this," I say, looking at the proud families around us.

"You want what?" she asks.

"I want to graduate, walk the stage. Don't you?" I ask her, marveling at the strong desire blooming inside me.

"Maybe." She shrugs, shoving her index finger into the wad of gum in her mouth.

"I think I'll go to college," I say.

"What do you want to do?" she asks, winding the gum around her finger.

"I don't know. Be a legal secretary like Mom?"

"You mean you don't want to work at Burger Barn forever?"

"Well, I could. I am a supervisor now."

"I think Cammie would keep you forever," she says.

"No way," I say. "I want more out of life than Burger Barn."

♥

I graduate from high school four months before my twentieth birthday, walking the stage with Jess and a few other late-blooming friends. Then I make an appointment to register for classes at Clark College.

"You need a placement test," the career counselor says.

I complete an exam to measure my aptitude in math, science, and English. My scores in mathematics and science are lower than low, proof I paid zero attention during high school. English comes easy, allowing me to score a smidge higher.

"Looks like you're starting at rock bottom," the counselor says.

"That's no surprise," I say.

"This is the list of classes you'll need to graduate from the Paralegal Program," she says, circling ninety credits in blue pen.

"Wow," I say. "That's a lot of work."

"Two years," she says, pointing me to registration.

I chisel away at community college, learn about family law, corporate law (snore!), and estate planning (double snore!). I spend hours and hours at the typewriter, tapping out legal papers, research papers, and English papers. After working all week at Burger Barn and attending night classes, I'm pooped. And on this night, I'm awake until midnight, cramming for finals.

"Holy cow, I didn't know I could ever be this tired," I say, climbing under the covers of my snuggly bed. I'm out before my head hits the pillow. Minutes later, maybe hours later, the sound of rustling pulls my eyes open. I glance at the yellow haze of moonlight crossing my carpet, follow its warm glow over my walls, and catch my breath when a shadowy figure appears inside my door.

What the . . . ?

I bolt upright. It's my dad. My ears recognize his heavy breathing, and my spirit knows why he's here. He hasn't laid a hand on me since his apology. And his promise.

"*Get* your ass *out* of my room." I don't whisper and I don't say it quietly.

"Shh," he says, stooping like an enemy in the brush.

I raise my voice even louder.

"Get your *effing ass* out of my room, and don't you ever come back in here."

"Okay, okay," he says in a whisper.

"I mean it!" I say, "Don't you ever come in here again. Understand?"

He disappears into the hall, and I jump up to close my door, shoving my thumb into the lock. I lean against it, fight the tears brewing, and work to catch my breath.

"Holy cow," I say in a whisper and wipe at the salty rain covering my cheeks.

"I have to get out of here."

PART 3

The Escape

10

The Man With Espresso Eyes

I shuffle through the student center at Clark College, fanning my face with a spiral-bound notebook. The signs to the Employment Center point me upstairs and to the right, but I don't need their guidance. I know where I'm going. The job center has provided plenty of part-time work for me over the past few years.

I snap my gum, waltz up to the corkboard, and toss my hands on my hips.

"This is it?" I mutter, yanking the only index card off the board. I blow a giant pink bubble, suck it back with a pop, and say, "A trucking company?"

With a sneer, I tack the card back on the board, thinking I'll give it a week. I root through the classified ads, call a few friends, check the unemployment office. No luck. Seven days later, I wander back to Clark and find that same stupid card hanging in wait. I snatch it down with a huff and knock on the job counselor's door.

"Come in," she says.

"Is this the only job you have available?" I ask, fighting the whine in my voice.

"Can you believe it? They've been looking for a month! What's your major?"

"Dental hygiene, but I also have a paralegal degree," I say.

"Perfect! Oh, my gosh. They will be so happy to have you. Let me call them."

Before I can say a word, she plasters the phone to her ear, and taps out the number.

"Can you be there in an hour?" she asks, tucking the receiver under her chin.

"Today?"

"Yes, in an hour?"

"I don't have a résumé put together," I say, wanting to slip out the door and run.

"Can you throw one together? They really need help," she says.

I blow out a long sigh and nod my head.

"Awesome," she says, turning her mouth to the phone. "She'll be there in an hour."

The counselor jots down the address, phone number, person to contact, and shoves the sticky note at me, saying, "Ask for Meg, she seems super nice." I stare at the card for two seconds before jogging down the stairs, careful not to slip across the linoleum floor in my huarache sandals, and hightail it to my apartment across the street.

"Crap, where is my résumé?" I whisper, poking around my computer files. When I find the document, I click it open, update my job information. Tell them I worked at Burger Barn for three years, a dry cleaner for three weeks (no lie; that place was nasty), a daycare for three months (lest I lose the desire to bear children), a telemarketing company (that was not fun), a magnetics company, a bank, and an attorney's office. That's a whole lotta jobs for a twenty-five-year-old. I hit print, snatch the paper up, and run to the laundry hamper to dig out my black nylons. I pull them up for a sniff. Goodness only knows how many days they've been soaking up the rank scent of wet towels and dirty underwear.

"Good enough," I say, dousing them in White Diamonds perfume.

I toss on a sundress, pull my hair into a messy bun, and race out the door.

"Great day for August rain," I say, turning on my windshield wipers.

I follow the directions given. If I'm right, the trucking company is ten minutes from my apartment complex. Only I can't find it. So I circle back, make my way down Fruit Valley Road one more time. All I see are industrial buildings. No signs, and no trucks.

Grr. I glance at my watch. "Shoot, I'm late." I pull up to a convenience store, cover my head with an umbrella, dig a quarter out of my purse, and run to the payphone. Meg tells me to relax, drive north a quarter mile, and take a left at the yellow building. Five minutes later, I park in a gravel parking lot, hobble in high-heels over rain-filled potholes, careful not to twist an ankle, and find all the shop doors locked.

"Oh, my gosh!" I say circling the building twice. At last knock, a greasy guy in orange coveralls pulls up a ginormous garage door.

"Yeah?" he asks, eyeballing my fancy shoes.

I tell him I'm here to see Meg, and he ushers me upstairs to a small office. The room is long, narrow, and cramped with desks, filing cabinets, cardboard storage boxes, and stacks of paper everywhere. Like, I cannot find a bare surface in the place. Dena, the owner, and Meg, her assistant, clear off a spot for me to sit.

"Can you use a computer?" Dena asks.

"Yes, I know Word Perfect and Windows, Microsoft Word and Excel," I say.

"When can you start?"

I blink twice and stare between them. I don't tell them I have no desire to start. Instead, I stumble over my words, and we agree on two weeks.

"Um, what should I wear?" I ask glancing at the black smudges covering the carpet.

"Office attire," Meg says. "Only the guys wear jeans."

Well, that's a little old school. I hold my tongue and think, *Strike one!*

On my first day, Meg walks me to a typewriter from 1983, asking, "Do you know how to use this?"

"Of course," I say.

"Good, type the paychecks," she says, clearing a space on the desk.

"Can I have a chair?" I ask.

"Umm," she says, glancing around the office, "use this."

I stare down at the odd-looking contraption, purse my lips, and look up at her.

Meg says, "Rest your knees on this pad and lean your butt on the seat."

I gawk at the thing, and think, *Strike two!*

"It's called an ergonomic knee chair," she says. "We'll get you a real chair tomorrow."

I drop onto the ergo-bench, roll toward the desk, and try to stay awake while I type one hundred paychecks. At lunchtime, Meg invites me downstairs to join Dena's birthday celebration. "We ordered Mexican," she says.

I jog down behind her, grab a plate, and pile it high with chips, salsa, a burrito, and rice. Just as I shovel the first bite in my mouth, a deliciously tanned, fully muscled, scrumptious man steps up beside me. I gulp, cover my mouth with a napkin, and drink him in. He's dressed in a snug white t-shirt, blue jeans, and a smile that melts over me like chocolate.

"This is Darin," Dena says. "He's my younger brother."

I stare into his luscious brown eyes, swallow the wad of food in my mouth and mumble hello.

"Hello," he says with a twinkle in his eye.

I inhale deep, hold my breath, and think, *Homerun!*

♥

The warmth of his chest pricks the hairs on my body. I want to look up, want to melt into his eyes, but I am not this kind of girl. The kiss is coming. I can taste it on my lips. My heart pounds in my ears. Breath freezes in my lungs. I'm too shy, too timid for this physical game. His hands lock around my waist, pulling me so close, my head is forced skyward. My eyes lock on his cocoa browns, and I study him from a place I've never been. From feet away, I can drink in the whiskers shadowing his cheeks, the velvet texture of his dark brows, the way his lashes fan above his lids, sultry and thick. But from here, from this angle, I see the pearl of his teeth, the pink tint of his lips, and the streaks of auburn in his moustache.

"Have pizza with me tonight," Darin says, his voice thick.

I part my lips to say something, but no words come out. Does he want me the way I want him? Or is this just a game of tag with my heart? We've been doing this for weeks. Exchanging glances, sharing flirty giggles, brushing past each other in the office. But he hasn't pulled me close enough to smell the laundry soap on his white t-shirt or savor the sweetness of his breath.

I wriggle out of his grip.

"I love pizza," I say, walking toward my desk.

"Then go out with me," he says.

"I like how you wait until I'm quitting to ask me out," I say.

"Well, it's unprofessional to date girls at the office," he says.

"You make a habit of dating office girls when they give two weeks' notice?"

"Only you."

My cheeks flush crimson as I swallow hard, cast my eyes down.

"Pick you up at seven?" he asks.

I nod, drop into my chair, and sort through the invoices scattered atop my desk. As he walks out the door, I inhale deep, fight to focus on work, and douse the flame burning inside me. This feeling, this endless swell of yearning for another human being, is completely foreign. I've had boyfriends and felt love and longing for companionship. But this sensation, this fierce, suffocating, smoldering desire, is brand new.

I fan my face with a notepad, lean back in my seat, and say, "What is going on inside me?!"

♥

"Why are you staring at me?" I ask, sliding a cheesy bite of pizza between my glossed lips.

"I like watching you," Darin says, his eyes shimmering like stars in a midnight sky.

I pull the fork between my lips and peer at him through mascaraed lashes.

"Tell me about your life," he says, taking a sip of soda.

I narrow my eyes and tilt my mouth into a sly smile. I don't want to tell him anything. I just want to bask in this heartbeat, with him planted in front of me, dazzling me with his smile, his sexy eyes.

"I'm going to miss you," he says.

"No, your sister is going to miss me," I say, thinking of Dena.

"Dena hired your replacement. Did she tell you?" he asks.

I nod, and ask, "Is she as cute as I am?"

"Hardly," he says with a laugh.

I wink at him, stab another bite of pizza.

"Are you sure about leaving? We could keep you on part time."

"I can't work during clinicals," I say, popping the bite in my mouth.

"Sad," he says.

I take my time chewing, consider my short year at his company, how I fell in love with Meg and Dena. How I discovered the treasure of truck drivers, their servant hearts, and willing attitudes. My heart spawned a new kind of grit in my time with these blue-collar workers. I show up at eight in the morning, six hours after their shift starts. I clock out at five, when they are pulling in for the night. I shuffle papers in a warm office while they tarp and strap in the rain.

They come home dirty and tired after exerting every

measure of patience known to man when smaller vehicles cut into their lane, brake-check them, or honk as they scurry by. Truckers are the reason we have milk on the table, shoes on our feet, and movies at Blockbuster. And nobody ever gives them a blue ribbon, the Nobel Peace Prize, or any recognition whatsoever, except the multitude of motorists who thrust a middle finger out the window along with and an *eff you* when the truck gets in their way.

Where I anticipated harassment and jeering (because they are men and I'm a young woman who likes to dress cute), they delivered respect, loyalty, and kindness. Not once have I been hit on, cat-called, or sexually harassed. The law offices I've worked in could take a course on professionalism from the truck drivers I've come to know and appreciate.

"I'm going to miss all of you," I say.

He holds my gaze for a heartbeat, making me blush.

"But what's really sad," I say with a grin, "is moving back in with my parents to finish dental hygiene. Or maybe that's pathetic."

"Need help moving your stuff?"

"You want to help me move back home?"

"Sure, I've got time."

My heart skips a beat at the idea of another day with him.

"It's a date," I say. "I move home in two weeks."

"I'll put it on my calendar," he says with a wink.

"I like the idea of being on your calendar," I say.

He leans back, crosses his thick arms, and bores into me with those penetrating eyes.

"Tell me about Melissa," he says.

I grin and shake my head.

"You are halfway through dental hygiene, and you have a paralegal degree that you never used?" he asks.

"I interned for an attorney. She tried billing her clients for my time. Fifty dollars per hour." I shake my head side to side, and say, "I couldn't even use a copy machine."

He chuckles.

"She and her partner specialized in family law, but also took court appointed criminal cases. When her partner defended an accused rapist, I was done."

He shakes his head.

"I'd rather poke my eyes out with a stick than stand arm in arm with a rapist."

"So, you'd rather clean teeth?" he asks.

"Any day," I say.

He leans forward and grabs a slice of pizza off the pan.

"Tell me a secret," he says.

I grin, narrow my eyes at him, and work my fork around the plate.

What's he fishing for?

"I graduated from high school a year late," I say, popping a pepperoni in my mouth.

"No way!"

"Yep, I was a total failure in high school."

"That's a shocker," he says.

"I had a jacked-up childhood, my mom has MS, and I was a rebel," I say.

"And now you aren't?"

"God changed me," I say.

"You're a Christian?"

"Go to church every Sunday."

"Me, too," he says, "raised Catholic."

"Hmm, that's a more organized religion," I say, watching him through narrowed eyes.

"It's the same God," he says.

"Well, I don't know enough about religion to argue with you."

"Good," he says with a wink. "Come with me Sunday."

"To your Catholic church?"

He shakes his head. "No. A Christian church. Come with me. You might like it."

I grin, chew my food slowly, and consider this man who'd take me to church.

"Okay. I'll go to church with you."

"It's a date," he says, playing with his fork.

I pull a long swig from my cup and stare at him over the rim.

"How is your mom?" he asks.

"Shitty. MS is an evil beast," I say, crunching an ice cube. "It's eating her alive."

Darin watches me without words as my mind wanders back to the Moody Blues concert Mom and I attended last Mother's Day. It was my treat. I picked her up, drove us into Portland, and prayed for a parking spot near the door of the newly built Rose Garden stadium. God provided the perfect space, and I helped Mom from the car. We meandered inside to find our seats situated in an excellent viewing position—on the ground floor.

"You know," I say, "she couldn't walk down the steps at the Rose Garden."

"I'm sorry," Darin says.

"I argued with her over her ability to walk down the stairs, and she wept," I say, catching the one tear trailing down my cheek.

Darin puts his fork down and folds his hands.

"I had no idea she couldn't walk down all those stairs. We found the service elevator and that made it easier," I say, voice trailing.

I look up and lock eyes with him.

"You know, one of the reasons I believe in God is because of how He answers my prayers," I say.

"How's that?"

"Mom tires easily. I mean, I still thought she could go down the stairs," I say shaking my head to clear my thoughts. "She refuses to get a handicap permit, so I pray for a front parking space every place we go. And do you know what I get every single time? A front parking space."

Darin chuckles and leans back in his chair.

"Mom was a legal assistant for the Multnomah County District Attorney's office. She rode the city bus into downtown

Portland, traveling an hour each way, Monday through Friday, for fifteen years. And then they made her retire. Two weeks ago. Just like that."

"I'm so sorry," he says again, leaning forward.

"Me, too," I say, dropping my eyes. "Now she's home every day. Alone. She was just fine, and then she wasn't."

"Then maybe your move home is a good thing?" He asks, tipping his chin to catch my gaze.

I shrug and say, "My father's an ogre, so it's going to be tough."

"Are your parents still married?"

I nod.

"Does your dad work?"

"Yep. He's the breadwinner now," I say, thinking of all the years Momma worked while Dad struggled with drugs.

"Do you have siblings?" he asks, picking up his fork.

"A younger brother."

"Is he at home with your parents or in college?"

I cough, shove a palm to my face, and say, "My father caught Stacy cutting classes and using meth, so Dad packed a duffel bag full of Stacy's clothes and tossed it onto the porch. Told him, 'You can finish high school, or you can get out.'"

I glance up at Darin and say, "So Stacy moved out. He was seventeen."

"Wow," he says.

"My mom snuck him groceries for months so he wouldn't starve."

"That's tough," he says. "But I don't blame your dad."

"Well, it's not all my brother's fault."

I take another long drink of soda, muster the courage to open the door to my scary life.

"My father is an addict," I say, gauging Darin's reaction.

He returns my stare with soft eyes.

"And abusive," I say, dropping another crumb.

Darin watches me work to find the words.

"He spanked us both, and a well-earned butt-whipping

never hurt a kid. But my dad was over the top. He left bruises on my brother's back and thighs. Dad used to beat Stacy pretty hard," I say.

We eat in silence while Darin processes the ugly parts of my life.

"How many boyfriends have you had?" he asks, a sly grin working up his cheeks.

This time I almost choke.

"What?!"

"Come on," he says, tapping my toes under the table. "How many?"

I roll my eyes, take a long drink, wipe my mouth and stare into his cocoa browns.

"One in middle school, one in high school, and one in college," I say.

He chuckles.

"I shacked up with the last one," I say, digging an ice cube out of my cup.

"Living in sin, huh?"

"Until I could afford a place of my own," I say, staring at him. "It was the only way to escape my dad."

He nods and leans back in his chair.

"What about your love life?" I ask.

"Just one girlfriend," he says. "Long term. Didn't work out."

"Sorry," I say.

He nods, takes a sip of soda.

"I don't bed-hop, if that's what you're asking," I say.

"Neither do I."

I grin at him and kick his toes. "Glad we got that out in the open."

He smiles, grabs another slice of pizza, flops it onto his plate, then stares at me again with those luscious eyes. I hold his gaze and time stops. I lean forward, rest my chin in the palm of my hand, and melt into him. *Yum.*

"How's it going over here?" the waiter asks, breaking the spell.

"Fine," I say and shoo him away.

"You turned out pretty amazing," Darin says with a grin.

"You think?"

"Oh, I definitely think so," he says.

We devour the rest of the pizza and visit for another two hours before Darin drives me back to my apartment, walks me to the door, kisses me good night.

And good morning.

♥

I finger the syringe in my palm.

"We practice on fruit because it feels like human flesh," the nurse says.

I glance at Mom. She fell going up the porch steps and broke a rib. The doctor prescribed interferon injections to slow the MS. So here I am with a needle in my hand. I look at Dad, the orange in front of me, and the other people in the room. *Blech!*

"Let gravity do the work," the nurse says.

Double yuck. I swallow hard and rub the goosebumps off my arms.

"We inject the thigh," she says.

I glance at my mother's bony legs and wonder which one to poke.

Mom catches my stare and says, "Dad is giving me the shots."

"I'm okay," I lie. "I give shots in dental hygiene, too."

"That's different," Mom says.

A young mother sits across the table from us, her three little boys clamoring for attention. *How does she care for them with a crutch on each arm?* I wonder. I lean to Mom and say in a whisper, "She's young."

"I bet she has progressive MS," Mom says. "That's worse than mine."

"I'm glad you were healthy when I was little," I say.

"Me, too," she says.

♥

Darin and I sandwich together like peanut butter and jelly, a blend of salty sweetness all sticky with adoration, affection, and lust. It's the clingy kind of smothering that makes sane people shudder. But I'm lost in it, pickling like pigs' feet in a Mason jar. I've never been so consumed by a man before. His mysterious allure baffles me, but I am like a moth to a flame, getting sucked into the fire without realizing the risk.

Maybe moving home is propelling me into Darin's arms? Watching Momma slip away and lose her battle with multiple sclerosis, pokes holes in my heart. Mom's the good parent. How do I live without her? How do I watch her life float away like a mist?

Maybe it's Dad? He's moody as ever, watching his wife suffer in the clutches of a relentless disease. There's not enough alcohol, not enough smoke to kill the pain of waiting for his wife to die. Because that's what's coming. That is the future on the horizon. Misery and death for the only person who's ever loved my father. The loss, the unknown, makes Dad volatile, unpredictable, unmanageable. And I live in his presence. He sets curfews on my time, nags at me for not helping enough, talks crap about Darin, makes me want to leap off a bridge.

Maybe it's dental hygiene? I worked like a mad dog to get into a program that only accepts twenty-three students per year. My instructors treat the profession like it's rocket science or brain surgery. Their expectation is perfection, and that is unattainable. I spend my days competing with twenty-two other girls for the perfect patient, the favor of an instructor, and time with our clinical dentist. It's insane, and I loathe every minute of it. But this career offers an excellent wage for a three-year education. I can't quit unless I want to shuffle back to my minimum wage position at Burger Barn or tuck my tail and suck up to some unethical attorney.

In a nutshell, I'm stuck. Life is like quicksand, sucking me into an insidious, merciless pit. And Darin is my cool drink of water in a dry and weary land.

I watch Darin's chest rise and fall, my heart ballooned with a passion I can't define—as if fear married hope and birthed a wart-covered, sin-infested toad. And that toad is me. Because God is not my prince, Darin is. A man is my hope, my future, and I capture him like a prisoner. There's an itch inside me the man can't scratch, but he's happy to try, as if God created him to satisfy my every desire, loving me, spilling his passion into me like tequila into an empty flask. And I drink him, drink him in long, starving for his love. I fly high on him, drunk on his affection. Then I am thirsty, and we try again. We shop together, cook together, eat together, sleep together. Erase the world together. We are sick and living in a dangerous place.

He rolls over, catches me staring, kisses me long.

"Let's take your parents out for dinner," he says.

"Why?" I ask, moving away from him.

"I'd like to get to know them."

"You met them when I moved home."

"Yeah, but I want to *know* them," he says.

I sigh, roll out of bed, and say, "Fine."

Darin invites my parents to dinner at a local brew pub, and we all yak like old pals over burgers and fries. The guys talk music, fishing, and work, while Mom and I people watch, chatter about my days at school and her days at home. Families pile into the restaurant, filling the booths surrounding our table. The sound of their chatter awakens a longing inside me. I stare at Darin, wonder if he is the one to make my babies with. And for a second, just a tick on the clock, I relish the thought of being a mother. Until a tiny girl dolled in a rainbow tutu trots our way, squealing as she dives under our table. Dad giggles like a goofy old man until the mother pries the girl off his legs. I swallow hard, remember my past, remember who I am, who my father is.

And what he's done to me.

My heart sinks. How do I balance a normal life with the jacked-up lie I live? What do I tell Darin if we get married and have a daughter? My father can never be around our children, or anyone's kids, for that matter. I take a long draw off my strawberry margarita, glance around the table, thankful to keep that skeleton tucked away.

But dry bones rattle and clink when you move their trunk.

"That little girl was stuck on your dad like glue," Darin says when we leave.

Goosebumps prick the hairs on my arms.

"You should invite your parents to our summer barbecue."

I inhale sharp.

"Dena hosts a giant picnic every summer."

"I don't think so," I say.

"Why not?" he asks.

Silence.

Darin stops at a red light and stares in my direction.

"What's up, Melissa?"

I shake my head, fight the tears brewing in my eyes. The ghoul pokes its face out, and I work to shove it back inside. But I can't. I can't lie to this man, this person I've given my heart to. But I can't tell him the truth either. How do I look him in the eye and say, "My Dad molested me"?

"Melissa?"

"I can't—"

"Okay," he says with a sigh.

We drive in silence as tears cascade down my face. When we pull up to his house, he turns off the car, like nothing happened. I follow him inside. He tosses his keys on the counter and asks, "Want some ice cream?"

"Sure," I say.

Fear bounces around my heart like a pinball. What do I say if he asks again? How do I shield him from the horror of my father? How can we have a future without the truth?

He dishes out two scoops of mocha for me, three for him, and points to the couch.

"Let's pick out a movie."

An enormous sigh escapes my lips as I spin toward the

family room. We collapse on the sofa, nibble dessert, and get lost in the television until the grandfather clock chimes midnight.

"Dang it! I'm late," I say, remembering my father's ridiculous curfew.

Thrusting my arm into the wrong hole of my Levi jacket, I grab my purse and race for the door. And just like Cinderella, my glittery white dress turns to filthy rags as the clock rings its final bell and Darin steps in front of me.

"So what's going on, Melissa?"

Staring at the floor, I fix my coat and ignore his question.

"Tell me."

I pinch my eyes shut to hold back the tears and shake my head side to side.

"Tell me."

His hand holds me back as I crack open the door.

"Why do you hate your dad?"

My tongue sticks to the roof of my mouth.

"I know you hate him," he says.

"Yes, you are right! I hate him! But I need to go!"

"Did he abuse you?"

I gasp, tears coming faster than I can catch them.

"Did he touch you?" Darin asks.

I tremble at the force of his question.

How does he know? How can this man see what the whole world has missed my entire life?

Sobbing, I drop my head in a shameful nod.

He steps in closer, grabs my chin, and tries to hold my gaze, but I can't even look at him.

"I'm sorry," he says, pulling me tight against his chest. "I want to beat his ass."

"You can't do that," I say.

"I know. Your mom needs you—"

"Wait," he says, "does she know?"

"No!" I gasp. "Absolutely not!"

He holds me another minute, pulls away, and stares at me

with furrowed brows.

"You are an incredible woman," he says. "Thank you for telling me the truth."

Then he kisses me long and walks me out the door.

11

Tattle Tale

Mom's health spirals out of control, forcing her to retire, use a cane, and stick herself with interferon needles, but she and Dad won't change how they live. She's still puffing her Vantage cigarettes, hitting the weed pipe at night. An argument could be made that marijuana abates the spasms and nerve pain that come with multiple sclerosis. But she's not just looking for pain relief. She's appeasing my father.

Every weekend, he lugs Momma, along with her cane or her walker, up the Columbia River Gorge to camp or sleep over with friends. And what do they do during their adult time away? They drink. Like fish. Bender after bender. Either my parents are in denial, or they don't give a hoot about Momma's future. I never question their behavior. I don't dare poke my nose into their business, lest I give my father a reason to boot me out. He's never been a fan of nosy neighbors. Or bossy children.

During the week, Mom sits home alone, watching *Perry Mason* reruns. Sometimes she rides a bus for the physically disabled to an adult daycare where she socializes with people thirty years her senior, playing games and eating lunch with them. At night, Dad goes to the bar, leaving me to care for Mom. I eat dinner with her, wash the dishes, hold her slippery body upright in the shower, and shuffle her to the potty. On the weekends, I take her grocery shopping and clean the house.

It doesn't take long for Mom to toss the interferon, saying, "The side effects are worse than my MS." Now she needs a urine catheter. But she can't insert it on her own, so our trips to the bathroom morph into me putting petroleum jelly on the tip of a long, red tube, before sliding it into Mom's urethra to relieve the pressure on her bladder. It feels wrong, looking at my mom's naked body in the shower. But it feels especially wrong to look at her lady parts.

"I'm sorry," she says when only a thimble of pee trickles into the pot.

"It's okay," I say.

"My daughter isn't supposed to see me like this," she says.

Maybe if you made better choices, I wouldn't have to, I think to myself. I can't say that aloud, so I lift her off the toilet, pull up her diaper, and kiss her cheek.

"This ain't no big thing, Momma. I'm in healthcare, remember?"

She gives me a small grin, and I shuffle her back to the couch.

The hard things in life continue to drive me into the arms of my lover as days, then weeks, then months tick off the calendar. A full year later, Dad still doesn't approve of my relationship with Darin, but I don't care. My interest in my father's opinion died when I realized he is no more than a cheap imitation of a man. So I keep up the pace at school and at home, because I love my mom, and because I have no other choice. But her ever increasing needs wear on me, leaving my heart raw and fractured.

"I don't know how long I can keep this up," I say to Darin one night over dinner.

"What do you mean?" he asks.

"Taking care of Mom, dental hygiene, living under Dad's roof."

"It's not your responsibility to take care of your mom, Melissa."

"Yes, it is. I'm her daughter."

"No, it's your father's job. You are there to help him."

"That's what I'm doing," I say.

"Babysitting your mom while your dad stops at the bar after work?"

I stop and remember Dad smashing his Z28 into a guardrail on the interstate bridge. He's crashed twice since I've been home. Both times, he walked away without a scratch, or a DUI. I shake my head in wonder. I won't even drive after sipping a glass of wine or popping a Benadryl.

"Okay, maybe babysitting Mom so Dad can drink is inappropriate," I say, picking at my salad.

"Talk to Pastor Greg," he says.

"You think?" I ask.

"Yep," he says, shoving a bite of fettucine in his mouth.

How am I supposed to talk to a pastor when I'm sleeping with Darin? We aren't married. We go to church every Sunday and pretend like we are, but God knows we are a couple of fakes. I'm sure He's not happy with our fornicating.

"I'm not sure I can talk to a pastor," I say.

"Why not?" Darin asks.

I stare at him and roll the ice cubes around in my glass.

"He's not going to judge you, Melissa. Just go talk to him."

♥

I walk into the church building on a blustery fall morning, with sweaty palms and a pounding heart. The lady at the front desk ushers me to Pastor Greg's office, offers me a beverage, then departs with a smile when I decline. Pastor steps out from behind his extra-large desk, offers me his hand, and laughs when I wipe my palm on my jeans before completing the handshake.

"What can I do for you, young lady?" he asks.

Darin and I attend a large church. And we sit in the back. Even though I'm here every Sunday, I don't know this man standing across from me. I've never met him. That makes our conversation both easy and challenging.

"I need some advice" I say.

He nods and ushers me to sit.

I exhale, rub my palms over my thighs, and say, "This is hard for me."

"Take your time," he says.

"I'm in dental hygiene, and I'm living with my parents while I finish clinicals. I can't work because school is full time. My mom has MS, so I help take care of her."

"She's disabled?" he asks.

"Yes, she is. I'm a grown woman, so I contribute to earn my keep."

He nods.

"I clean the house, take her shopping, do laundry. And I'm happy to help. But I also give her a bath and a catheter. My dad goes to the bar after work and leaves me alone to tend to her at night."

I blow out a long sigh, pinch my lids shut to escape the pastor's gaze.

"And my father is abusive."

Several seconds pass before I find the courage to open my eyes, and my mouth.

"He molested me, starting when I was little. He stopped when I was in high school. Living with him is traumatic, but my real struggle is caring for Mom. I think my dad should be there after work to bathe her, help her to the toilet, and take care of her. But I live in his house, so I follow his rules. I want to obey the Lord, but I am conflicted. What is my responsibility, and what is his?"

Pastor rubs his palms together.

"Well, you did an excellent job of spitting it out," he says.

I nod and sit on my hands.

He sits for a minute, rubbing a palm over his jaw. "First of all, I'm sorry for what your dad did to you. God does not author child abuse. He doesn't like it, doesn't condone it, and one day your father will answer to God for his actions," he says, giving me a firm stare.

179

"Does your mother know?"

I shake my head and say, "I never told her."

He leans back, folds his arms, and says, "The Lord teaches us to honor our mother and father, and I commend you for stepping up to help them. But your mother's care is your father's responsibility, not yours. It is your job to fulfill God's call on your own life."

The burden lifts with each syllable he utters, leaving me speechless. I swallow hard and work to respond. "Really?" I ask, grabbing a tissue to catch the tears running down my face.

"You need to step back and let the consequences of your daddy's actions fall on him, and your mother. They made their choices, now you make yours."

My mouth falls open.

"Stop saving him," he says.

I stare at him and wonder how to do that.

"Go in peace, young lady. You are going to be fine. God will see to that."

"Thank you, Pastor," I say, standing to shake his hand.

Thank you for setting me free.

♥

Darin and I sip hot mochas, dodging the hustle and bustle of the mall crowd, when my phone rings. D-A-D blinks at me in black pixelated letters. I let out a sigh, rein in my sinking heart, and open the phone.

"Hello?"

"Where are you?" Dad barks.

"Shopping with Darin."

"You need to get your ass home. Now!"

Darin leans in to eavesdrop on our conversation and watches my composure change from happy-go-lucky to isolated and anxious. I turn away from him and cup a hand over my ear to block out the noisy mall.

"Why?" I ask.

"You need to contribute to this family a little more."

"It's Saturday, Dad."

A long silence fills the receiver as I wait for him to explain.

"Come home now or get your ass out of my house."

Click.

"Dad hung up on me."

"What?" Darin asks.

"He said, 'Come home or get out.'"

I fix my eyes in a daze. "He says I'm not helping enough around the house."

Darin shakes his head and lets out a long sigh.

"I can't believe he'd kick me out," I say.

"You are not going back there," Darin says.

I just stand there, working my lips between my teeth.

"Call him right now. Tell him you are coming to pick up your things."

I take a deep breath and dial his number.

"Dad," I say, "I'm coming to pick up my stuff."

I click my phone shut and stare at Darin.

"Want me to come with you?" he asks.

"No," I say, walking toward the mall exit.

"I need to do this alone."

My heart races as I park in Mom and Dad's driveway, make my way up the walk. I finger through keys on my key ring, slip one in the deadbolt, turn the knob, and step inside. The television is off, lights are off.

"Mom?"

Silence.

"Mom!"

No answer.

I pop open the garage door. Dad's Camaro is gone.

I wonder how long I have. I jog to my bedroom, slide the closet door open with a bang, grab my suitcase and duffel bag. I race to empty my dresser, stuffing shirts, underwear, sweaters, and jeans into the case, zip it tight. Run to the kitchen for garbage bags, shake one open. My hands fumble over jackets, coats, and the afghan Mom gave me when I started college. Breathing comes hard and fast as I work to tie the bags, run them to the car, toss them in the backseat, dash back to the house.

"Makeup," I say, darting across the hall to collect shampoo, conditioner, mascara. In haste, I drop a bottle of Cetaphil into the tub. The crash echoes into the room, making my nerves hairpin tight. I pull three large boxes of books from my closet, haul them to the car, huff them inside. The Bible that Pastor Drew gave me for high school graduation slips into a crevice deep inside the trunk. I resist the urge to pick it up and leave it wedged where it landed. Within minutes, I collect every item I own and load it all into the car. I race back up the walk, stuff my key in the door, and secure the house before scampering away like a filthy church mouse.

As I drive away, I want to feel guilty for bailing on my mom. But the truth is, my parents live the life they choose, they always have. Without regard for me or my brother or Mom's health. And if they've never cared, why should I?

♥

I secure an apartment in an older, affordable complex and fill my pantry with Top Ramen and Quaker oatmeal. Between savings, grants, student loans, and hand-me-down furnishings, I make it on my own. After a short stint building houses in sweaty Las Vegas, Stacy moves in with my parents to care for Mom and keep her company while Dad works. Don't ask me how this happened. Stacy's been the black sheep for the past five years, dabbling in cocaine, meth, LSD, and any other drug he can use to escape reality.

Mom and Dad offer my brother free room and board in exchange for his lofty nursing skills—not. But again, I don't complain or question. I love my family. My brother needs help and so does Momma. And I'm thankful Stacy, drunk, stoned, or stupid, is with our mother. He's the only other person in the world who loves her as much as I do. Mom is the tie binding us together. And who knows? Maybe God will intervene and work a miracle in Stacy's life.

Weeks pass before I muster the courage to return home. When I do, Momma acts as if I never left. Drawing me in for a long hug, she says, "I missed you, Dolly." We don't talk about my leaving. I think she understands that a girl can only take so much abuse. Instead, I update her on school as I prepare to graduate, and she tells me she's proud of me.

Dad remains stony and distant, harboring a stiff, cold anger whenever I'm around. He makes me uncomfortable, but I don't let him shake me. Over time, my confidence makes him suspicious. One day, when I stop by to visit, he says, "Melissa, I'd like to speak with you outside."

He pulls out his pack of smokes and disappears out the back door.

"I'll be right back, Momma," I say, kissing her soft cheek.

"Hey, darlin'," Dad says, "sit here."

I dip into the chair opposite him, watch the ash grow on his cigarette as white tendrils of smoke weave around his hand.

"Baby, I have to ask you something," he says, picking his nails.

Why is he nervous?

Dad leans forward and asks, "Does Darin know?"

I give him a puzzled look.

"Did you tell him what I did to you?"

Ah! So that's why he's nervous. An odd sense of betrayal lurks around me, but I don't let fear or guilt dominate my answer. Holding my breath in tight, I say, "Yes."

That word is like a bomb exploding into Dad's world, and time stops as shards of truth lodge into his reality. His olive skin turns ashen gray, beads of sweat break out on his face. Silence rests between us for several seconds before Dad nods his head and crushes his cigarette in the ashtray. His Adam's apple jumps up and down as he swallows hard and fast.

"He has known for a while," I say.

"Who else knows?"

"Stacy."

"Your brother knows?"

"I told him when we were kids. Not sure he remembers," I say.

Dad nods, eyes fixed in a daze, as the monster he created grows like a beanstalk in his soul.

♥

Grandma and Granddad drive up from Las Vegas to attend my graduation. I pull into Mom and Dad's driveway, park beside my grandparents' Corolla, and skip to the door with glee.

"Missy," Granddad says, giving me a peck on the cheek and a long hug. I smell the sweet tobacco of the pipe he hasn't smoked in years. It lingers in my heart, if not in the air. I hug my skinny Grandma, resist the urge to cradle the silky, crepey skin hanging from her triceps. When I was a girl and she carried me around, I'd cup her baggy arms in my hands and let the soft texture of her love minister to my heart.

"Hello, Melissa," she says, holding me tight.

This visit isn't like those of years past. Instead of basting a hot turkey breast in a steamy oven, Mom sits tucked on the couch with a walker at her feet. Her eyes shake from nystagmus, and her speech spills out like the tiles of a Scrabble game, all mixed up and flipped over. The whole scene makes me sad. My grandparents already lost one daughter—my aunt Kathy when I was just five.

Grandma cuts into my thoughts, studies me with delicate eyes, and says, "I think Granddad and I are the only ones attending your graduation tonight, honey."

"What?" I ask, glancing over her shoulder.

"Your dad isn't feeling well, and Granddad isn't strong enough to help your mom navigate the school gymnasium," she says.

"Where is Dad?" I ask, swallowing the word bastard as I step around her.

"He's on the patio," she says, eyeing the sliding glass door.

I know the minute I peek outside and find him sitting in his bathrobe, his skin clammy and ashen, that he is not sick. He's having a nervous breakdown.

Selfish, son-of-a . . .

I stare at him with hard eyes and fight the urge to scream in his face. He's falling apart because I told Darin. That's what this is all about.

I look back at Mom.

"I'm sorry, Dolly. We are sitting this one out," she says with a stammer.

I glance between my parents, nod at Momma, and wrap my arm around Grandma's waist. She leans in to kiss my hair and says, "Don't worry, honey. We will be there." Of course, they will. Because they are the sane people in this jacked-up family.

Stacy walks up with a beer in hand, and says, "Hey, Mis."

I glance at my brother and fight the urge to stare at him. His gaunt frame, along with the purple shadows draping his face, tells me he's still using drugs. A smattering of tattoos decorates his five-foot-four frame. I know without looking that *Melissa*, along with *Mom* and *Dad*, lies inked on a scroll across his chest. My name, forever stitched over his heart in black ink, tells me he loves me no matter what. And we may not be close, but we are forever knit together in the wordless pain of our childhood.

Stacy nods toward the front door and I follow him outside. When we are out of earshot, he asks, "What's up with Dad?"

I swallow hard.

"Do you remember what I told you in front of Jessie's house when we were kids?" I ask.

His brown eyes fix on mine, then roam around my face. He knows the answer, even though he doesn't want to. A joyless chuckle escapes him as he fishes in his pocket for a cigarette. My eyes never leave his. I want him to know. He must know.

"Seriously?" he asks, lighting his smoke.

"Yes."

"I thought you were lying," he says, inhaling deep.

"I was not lying," I say without a blink.

"What am I supposed to do with that?"

"Nothing," I say, "But Darin knows. And Dad knows Darin knows. And that's what's eating our father right now."

Realization settles in Stacy's eyes as the puzzle pieces fall into place.

"Holy cow. Dad's afraid you'll tell Mom," Stacy says.

I nod.

"Are you? Going to tell Mom?"

"Hell, no," I say. "Why would I wreck her world?"

He nods and says, "I understand."

I drop my eyes to watch ants trail up and down the warm concrete driveway.

"I'm sorry, Mis. That he did that to you," Stacy says.

"I know," I say.

"I should have protected you," he says.

"Don't do that to yourself, Stacy. I was never yours to protect."

"But I'm your brother. That's my job," he says, catching a tear before it falls.

I pull my baby brother, my fiercest protector, into my arms. We hold each other long, then I look him in the eye and say, "Thank you for believing me."

"I love you, Mis," he says.

"I love you, too."

Dad's cowardice dies down after my grandparents leave. And a few months later, he packs up Momma and says, "I'm selling the house and cashing out my 401K to care for your mother at home. We are moving to Arkansas."

It makes sense to my rational mind. The cost of living in Arkansas is a quarter what it is here. They can sell the house, use the equity and Dad's retirement to be together day after day. But he can't lie to me. I know what he's doing. He's running. Running from the truth. Escaping before I find the nerve to tell my mother and melt his world to ashes.

♥

Around the time my parents leave, I take a job at a dental office, pack up the apartment I never sleep at, and move my things into the new house Darin buys for us. Darin suggests moving Stacy into my apartment, since my brother's got no place to land. I offer to pay his rent until the lease is up. Stacy still struggles with drugs and can't hold a job outside the flaky construction companies that let him come and go at his leisure. Mom and Dad are gone, so it's up to me to support him anyway I can.

My affection for Darin grows when he cares for my brother. Maybe that's why I move in with my lover, no questions asked. Darin and I both have a history of romantic commitments that bit the dust, so to speak. So rather than discussing marriage or a future commitment, we just skip that step and get busy shacking up. I, for one, don't want to jinx the good thing we've got going. So we buy furniture, hang wallpaper, plant flowers in the yard. And we ignore God. I just assume Darin will propose soon enough. And I can't focus too far ahead with all the life change happening around me.

So much life change!

One day after work, I settle into making dinner when the phone rings. I grab the receiver off the wall, tuck it under my chin, and say, "Hello."

"Melissa? It's your father."

"What's up?"

"I have some news, honey. Can you talk a moment?"

I turn off the burner, pull out a chair, and cram the phone to my ear.

"Sure," I say.

"Your brother found us."

"Did something happen with Stacy I don't know about?"

"No," Dad says. "Not that brother. Your older brother, Timothy."

Time stops. Goosebumps pull the hairs rigid on my forearms. I want to speak, but my tongue sticks to the roof of my mouth. Too many questions race through my mind. Like, where? And how? And oh, my gosh!

"You mean, Mom's baby?"

"Yes. He contacted us several months ago," Dad says.

Hold the phone! Several *months* ago?

"What do you mean, several months ago?"

"Well, about six months ago," Dad says.

"You've known about him for six months, and you didn't call me?!"

"We didn't want to upset you," he says.

I close my eyes, breathe deeply, and work to still my raging pulse. It upsets me when my father treats me like a child. Goodness knows I've handled *him* all my life! *Grr!* "When can I meet him?" I ask.

"He is coming here first," Dad says.

Happiness pours out of my heart, radiating an indescribable joy down through my bones. Momma gets to meet her baby! I am so excited for her! And him!

"He'd like to speak with you. Can I give him your number?" Dad asks.

"Yes!"

An hour later, my phone rings again. I snatch it off the wall, collapse into a chair, and let the sound of my older brother's voice melt my heart. He rattles off his story, but I'm so overwhelmed, I can't comprehend his words. His parents renamed him Brian. He is married. He grew up in the same town as Momma and even went to her high school. His parents are amazing, and they love Jesus!

Joy, laughter, love, and light all spill from me as we talk for more than an hour, sharing childhood stories, memories, asking questions. And when we hang up, tears trickle down my cheeks as I savor the enormous blessing of having this man in my life. God gave me another piece to the puzzle of my heart. And God gave Momma her baby.

♥

To reward myself for five years of college and landing a well-paying job, I splurge and buy a new car. When I clean out the nooks and crannies of my old Chevy, I discover the Bible Pastor Drew gave me, still wedged down in the corner of the trunk. It's been riding in the dark for over a year, like a stowaway on the ship of my life. I pull it free from the crevice and inspect the damage. The gold foil decorating the edge of each feathery page is worn to a crusty silver. Mold covers the upper right corner of the leather binding. The pages are stuck together, wrinkled, and shrunk from moisture. It looks like the well-worn Bible that church attendees carry, only I've never even opened it. My heart sinks. How could I treat God's Word so poorly?

I drop to the curb, open the book at random, and read the words, beginning in John, chapter 4. The story of the Samaritan woman at the well jumps off the page and into my conscience. I turn my eyes toward heaven and think, *How convenient that my Bible would just plop open to this page.*

This is where Jesus tells the woman "everything" she's "ever done," including having five husbands and cohabitating with a man she's not married to. I close the Bible and take a deep breath. It feels like God just punched me in the chest. Because I've been here before, with a man who wouldn't marry me or didn't care to.

I met Jason in college, and I loved him to the moon and back. So we shacked up, but he didn't want to get married. Every time I prayed and asked God what to do, I would encounter some random stranger or long-lost friend who would ask me if I was married yet. When I told them no, they'd say, "Young lady, you need to leave that man if he won't marry you." Or they'd say, "He's sampling the milk without buying the cow, and that is not acceptable."

I wanted to stay with Jason, get married, and have babies. But the dude wouldn't budge. And God told me to leave the guy every time I prayed. When Jason finally told me he was never marrying anyone, for any reason, and that included me, I packed my bags and left.

That was a lifetime ago.

Darin and I have been together for three years now and cohabitating for twelve solid months. He's never mentioned marriage. I don't want to be the wet blanket or the needy girlfriend, so I don't bring it up either. But what started as me pursuing my own life now feels like me discarding my God-given family to chase a man who's not my husband. And I wonder. Did I put Darin and college and money ahead of God, thinking the Lord would hang in there while I disobeyed Him? Was I supposed to have stayed behind and taken care of Mom?

Life feels good, with a new job paying the bills and a terrific man on my arm. But the Lord is telling me that without Him at the center of my life, I'm on shaky ground.

"I think I need to start over," I say, folding the Bible into my arms.

The next morning over breakfast, I say to Darin, "I think I'll talk to a counselor."

"Whatever works for you, honey," he says, snapping the newspaper open. "I'm sure a therapist will help you deal with the past."

I don't tell him it's our present living situation rubbing my heart raw.

"Call the church and ask them for a name," he says.

"I already did," I say, sipping whipped cream off my mocha.

He glances at me over the paper.

"I have an appointment tomorrow," I say.

During my first visit with Michelle Banks, I tell her about Momma's illness, my parents' move to Arkansas, and my current living situation.

"I love Darin so much, but I want to honor God," I say.

"Pray about it," she says.

"I don't need to pray," I say. "I've been down this road before."

"How's that?"

"During college, I moved in with a boyfriend. I wanted to get married so I could pursue a relationship with Jesus."

"And?"

"He didn't want to pursue a relationship with me or Jesus, so I moved out. I figured Darin was a good choice, since we go to church. But here I am, shacking up in sin, just like I did before."

"So, you already know the answer."

"I guess I do," I say.

"Get an apartment," she says. "Can you afford to live on your own?"

I nod.

"Just put a little space and time between you," she says. "And see what happens."

"Okay," I say.

Michelle studies me for a few seconds. "Do you have something else you want to tell me?"

My heart pounds in my ears as I consider telling Michelle about my dad. She's a therapist, and I should feel safe spilling my beans, but I hesitate.

"I'm not sure I can say it out loud," I say, glancing at the door.

Muffled voices ribbon under it like smoke. Michelle's office sits in the center of a busy commercial building. If I can hear the people outside the door, can't they hear me, too?

Somewhere in my illogical mind, I've always believed if I say the words out loud, my dad will know. And Mom will die. Even though that is impossible, my little girl spirit can't think outside the fear. And every time I've ever told, shame has covered me like a soggy blanket.

Michelle watches me as I inhale deeply. I remember I am a grown woman. I remember my parents are thousands of miles away. I try to be rational. I drop my voice to a whisper and say, "My dad molested me."

"I'm sorry," she says. "How old were you when it started?"

I curl long strands of hair around my finger, keep my eyes on the shadows passing under her office door, and say, "I don't know. I was little."

"Three? Four?" she asks.

My face heats up with memories of the june-bug house. I nod, saying, "Yeah, maybe four or six? I'm not sure. I just know he told me that Momma would die if she found out."

I hear voices outside her door and my tongue freezes. Michelle waits for me to finish, but my heart is done.

"I can't do this," I say, reaching for my purse.

"Wait," she says.

"I'm sorry," I say, yanking open her door.

I hear the word *coward* echo in my heart as I run down the stairs and out the door.

"I am a coward," I say as I jump in the car, throw it in drive, and speed away. As I turn onto the freeway, I tuck the memories of my childhood back inside my musty heart and focus on what hurts now.

A life without God.

When I get home, I walk inside to find Darin washing dishes. I grab his arm, look him in the eye and say, "I'm moving out."

"What?" he asks, dropping a pan in the sink. "Why?"

"Because I've done this, 'living in sin' thing before, and it doesn't work out. I want a relationship with the Lord, and I want a man who loves me enough to marry me."

"You got all this from your counselor?" he asks, drying his hands on a towel.

"No, I got all this from God. And my counselor," I say.

"I thought you were going to talk about your past."

"I did," I say with a shrug. "And my future."

"Don't leave," he says, grabbing my hand.

"I'm not leaving you. I'm leaving this house," I say.

"Please, don't."

I fall into his arms and let the tears come.

"I have to," I say, pulling back to look in his eyes.

"Just stay another week," he says.

I shake my head side to side.

"Please. Give me a chance, Melissa."

"One week," I say and fall into his arms again.

12

Kisses From Heaven

I step into a long, white gown, with simple scallops along the bust. Darin's mother pulls the zipper up my back, buttons the collar at the nape of my neck, and secures my veil over a messy bun. With a pair of vintage diamonds in my lobes, a new sixpence in my shoe, a blue garter wrapped around my thigh, and Darin's father on my arm, I walk down the twenty-foot aisle to Canon in D. Darin takes my hand, and we say, "I do," on the balcony overlooking the pool at Disney's Wilderness Lodge.

It's a perfect day. Except I'm missing my family. Not one of them attends the wedding, which is fine, but I yearn for my mother. A girl's momma should be there to fuss and fawn over her daughter on the wedding day. Darin and I chose Florida for its proximity to Mom, but Dad has refused to make the journey. According to my father, flying would be hard on Mom, but I think the trip would be harder on him.

Darin and I spend the next seven days riding Big Thunder Mountain Railroad and Splash Mountain, eating at MGM's Prime Time Café, and coasting the slides at Blizzard Beach. We sleep in every morning, suntan by the pool in the afternoon, and sip sweet Moscato before bed. It's a slice of heaven, and I savor every moment away from the normal stresses of life. Plus we discontinued all birth control before the wedding.

We'd like to make a baby.

When we get home, I pick up a pregnancy test, just in case. And on the day my period is due, I slip out of bed, open the package, and pee on the stick. I wait on the cold, hard toilet as urine creeps up the prize window. A pink line appears to the far right, prompting me to check the diagram on the box. One line means negative. I lean back, let out a sigh, and pop on the cap. Standing to wash my hands, I lay the test on the edge of the sink and eyeball it every few seconds. And just as disappointment settles in for the day, a pink shadow appears to the left.

"Is that another line?"

I toss on a robe, hold the stick in the sunlight pouring through the bedroom window and watch, mouth agape, as another pink line forms.

"Oh, my gosh! Oh, my gosh!"

Palming the test, I run from the room, down the stairs, to find my husband watching television on the couch. I shove the pee stick in his face.

"Do you see two lines? *Do you*?"

He pushes my hand back to focus, squints his eyes and says yes.

"Oh, my gosh! Darin! We are pregnant!"

Tears fill my eyes as I cup my hand over my mouth, shocked to think there is a tiny egg implanted in my uterus. An egg growing into a baby! Our baby! Darin laughs, pulls me down for a hug, and whispers in my ear, "Congratulations, Momma."

As salty tears trickle down my cheeks, my mother's face fills my mind. Her soft gray eyes, her bright smile, her tender heart. I want to be just like her.

"I have to call my mom," I say. "She's going to be a grandma!"

♥

I pick up a copy of *What to Expect When You're Expecting* and follow it like a religion. No lunch meat, no tuna, no caffeine.

At work, I take extra precautions to protect my baby. No nitrous for my patients and no ultrasonic scaler, lest those high frequency waves run amuck in my womb. My pregnancy follows a normal trajectory through the first trimester with plenty of morning sickness, fatigue, and sore breasts.

At the start of my second trimester, I book a flight to Arkansas. Stacy agrees to join me, although I hesitate to take him along. Darin wants my brother with me "to keep me safe," which is hilarious since Stacy is still using drugs. The morning of our flight, Darin pounds on the picture window of the house my brother's crashing at. No answer. I ring the doorbell. No answer. Call his cell. No answer.

"Damn it, Stacy! Wake up!" I yell outside the door.

Ten minutes later, my groggy brother answers the door, his face shadowed in stubble, eyes bloodshot red, clothes wrinkled from sleep.

"Shoot, I slept through my alarm," he says, jogging back inside to get his bag.

I narrow my eyes at him as he hops out the door, hocks a wad of spit in the bushes, and gives me a cheesy grin.

"Ready?" he asks.

I spin on my heel with a humph and climb into the cab of Darin's pickup. My husband doesn't say a word on our fifteen-minute drive across the bridge to PDX. He doesn't have to, because I can't hold my tongue for five minutes.

"We're late," I say, glaring at Stacy over my shoulder.

"I told you, I slept through my alarm," he says.

"Looks like you slept off a bender," I mutter.

"What's that?" he asks, craning his neck toward me.

"You heard me," I say.

I whip around and seethe at him. "You are almost thirty years old. Get your shit together!"

He chuckles in dismay and holds his words until we get to the airport. Smart man, holding his tongue in front of my ginormous husband. Darin's got bones to pick with my brother after Stacy abandoned my apartment, leaving it in shambles without so much as a thank you. My husband volunteered to clean it out so I could get my deposit back. I never saw the mess. Stacy left that for Darin's eyes only.

At the airport, I kiss Darin long and follow my brother to the door. My husband shouts, "Stacy," and points at him, saying, "you take care of your sister."

My brother nods, then lets out a long sigh as we step through the revolving door. He doesn't say much as we board the plane, except that he wants the window seat.

"No way," I say. "I bought the tickets."

"Come on, Mis," he says.

"When you buy the tickets, you can have the window," I say, buckling my seatbelt. And with that, Stacy hunkers into the middle seat, puts his head back, and closes his eyes as the plane takes off.

I stare outside as the plane climbs higher and the sun rises over the city of Portland. The blue sky, puffy white clouds, and majestic views take my breath away. Pockets of snow rest in the crooks and crannies of Mt. Hood, Mt. Jefferson, and the Three Sisters. Bodies of water glisten like tiny diamonds among layers of dark evergreens. I crane my neck to drink in the fading Cascade Mountain range and fight the homesick feeling lurking in my heart. I hate leaving Darin.

As clouds roll in to obstruct my view, I turn to watch Stacy sleep. My heart melts at the sight of him as a grown man. In my mind's eye, my brother is still a little boy, flexing his muscles and fighting bad guys. In the make-believe worlds of our childhood, during our tumultuous years as teenagers, over the rocky paths of young adulthood, Stacy was my fiercest protector. He might be a little messed up, but I know he'd fight to the death to save me. Even now.

I should have given him the window seat.

Regret gnaws at my heart. I don't know when this snooty attitude slithered onto me. I don't think for one second I'm better than Stacy, but his choices frustrate me. He was the smart, sweet, charismatic child. Part of the gifted program in elementary school. Everyone loved my brother, and all his druggie friends still do. But he threw it all away, for what? My brother could have been an astronaut, and he chose drugs instead.

Just like our father.

We land in Little Rock several hours later, pile into the rental car, and make the drive south to Monticello. When we park in the driveway, the side door opens and Dad wheels Mom down a long metal ramp to greet us with hugs and kisses. Dad carries in our luggage, then gets busy frying fish and potatoes. My mouth waters in anticipation. Fresh fish is on my pregnancy menu, my nausea is gone, and 90 percent of the day I'm hungry as a bear out of hibernation. We devour dinner. I clean up the table and wash the dishes while Dad and Stacy step out for a smoke.

"Are you sure I can't help?" Momma asks from her wheelchair.

"Stop," I say. "I can handle a few dishes on my own."

She sighs, watches the boys sitting on the porch, puffing away.

"Are you still smoking, Momma?"

She shakes her head. "Nope. Cigarettes geek me out."

"What about weed?"

"Doesn't help anymore, so why bother?"

"Good," I say. "It's about time you quit."

The next morning, Dad and Stacy pack up their fishing poles and a case of beer, then head to the lake, leaving me to care for Mom. I cannot sit still, cannot bear to look at Mom for too long, with her shaking eyes, pale skin, and bone-thin limbs. My heart aches for her, and if I'm honest, being in Dad's house creeps me out. So I use my nervous energy to scrub Mom's floors, vacuum, wash sinks, toilets, and clothes.

When I run out of chores, I sink onto the couch, and rest my head on Mom's shoulder.

"How are you doing, Momma?"

She lifts a shaky hand to scratch her head and says, "Fine, I guess."

"How do you pass the time?" I ask.

"This," she says, fixing her eyes on *Perry Mason*.

"How many times have you watched this episode?"

She shrugs.

"Does Dad take you out?"

"Sometimes he drops me off at Aunt Shellie's grocery store, so he can cruise town in his Camaro. Or go fishing."

"He doesn't leave you alone?"

"Not for long, no," she says.

"Do you enjoy your time with Aunt Shellie?"

She nods with a smile, saying, "She feeds me lunch."

"I love her. She is such a sweet person," I say.

"And sometimes Dad takes me cruising in the car, too," she says.

"And you haven't had another incident?" I ask.

Momma gives me a blank stare.

"With Dad taking pills?"

The lightbulb comes on as Mom remembers the day Dad passed out on the couch, with his head in her lap. Right after they moved to Arkansas, he took some Oxy, washed it down with vodka, and lost consciousness. Momma couldn't wake him up. And she can't walk, she can't drive. So she called me, and I called the local fire department. They sent a medic over to make sure Dad was breathing.

"No more incidents," she says.

"Are you happy?"

"I am as happy as I can be," she says.

I wonder how. How is she happy living in this tiny house, with multiple sclerosis and a drug addict as her only companions?

I lean over, kiss her cheek, and grab her hand before laying my head on her shoulder for a snooze. Several snores later, a slam of the screen door propels me off the couch.

"Caught some dinner," Dad says, holding up a string of fish.

Dad fillets the trout, lays it in foil, tops it with onion slices, fresh garlic, and his custom lemon sauce, then pops it in the oven to bake while I toss a bag of peas in the microwave. I set the table. Stacy transfers Mom from the couch to her wheelchair, and Dad says grace before we all dig into his delicious cooking. As Stacy, Dad and I devour our meal, slicing, knifing, and scooping, I watch Mom's arm shake to work the peas into her mouth. By the time the spoon reaches her face, most of the vegetables are on the table or in her lap. She furrows her brows, pushes her spoon in for another pile, and repeats the messy process. All that work for a few peas.

"Momma, can I help you?"

"No," she says.

"She can feed herself," Dad says. "It just takes her a little longer. Right, Momma?"

She nods, stabs a bite of fish, scowls at me, and shoves it in her mouth. She then picks up her spoon and digs into those obnoxious peas again. It's hard to sit and watch her drop food all over the floor. Poor woman can't even enjoy a meal. I stare at her, and as she pulls those peas to her mouth, I say, "You're an ornery old coot." Mom bursts out laughing and dumps her peas all over the table.

♥

I bask in the sunshine behind the dental clinic, with my feet propped on a picnic table, and my hand over my belly. My tummy thickens every day, from the pregnancy and all the food I scarf down. Darin is the guilty party here, packing my lunchbox with two sandwiches, chips, fruit, and a cookie.

I toss a banana peel into the garbage, unwrap my second PB-n-J, and sink my teeth into the squishy white bread for a bite when I feel a jump in my stomach. *Gas. That's just what I need. A rumbly tummy in my patients' ears.* When it happens again, I stop chewing. It feels like a butterfly hatched inside me. Then it dawns on me . . .

It's the baby!

I dial Darin on my cell phone and shriek, "The baby is kicking!"

Days later, an ultrasound technician says, "It's a boy."

"A boy?" I whisper as warmth climbs from the umbilical cord to my heart.

"What should we name him?"

"Well, we talked about naming him Austin or Addison," Darin says. "You pick."

"Addison," I say as a smile creeps up my cheeks.

The technician takes a long time, clicking buttons and moving the contraption side to side. When she furrows her brows, and excuses herself to find my doctor, I glance at Darin. Before we can speak, a female obstetrician appears. She repeats the process, applying a little gel, pressing the wand against my abdomen. With a sigh, her eyes meet mine.

"You have what we call a placenta previa," Doctor says.

I narrow my gaze.

"The baby is fine," she says.

"Okay," I say with a long exhale.

"But the placenta is attached low, covering the opening of your cervix."

"That sounds bad," I say.

"It means we need to schedule a C-section. And if you bleed, get to an emergency room."

I don't give much weight to her worry. God created this life, and if He plans to keep my son tucked away inside me, He will. And if He doesn't? Well, I don't think like that. So I just do what the doctor says. I check for blood whenever I use the restroom

♥

Addison's kicks and wriggles tickle my heart. I talk to him nonstop, sing to him, and dance around the house cradling my swollen belly in my hand. He's my buddy, my partner in all things mysterious and funny and charming. I am smitten, feeling as if I know him already.

Six weeks pass with only one trip to the emergency room. I had a little bleeding, but it stopped before we arrived, and the doctor sent me home with no concerns or limitations. So, I carry on at work and home like normal. I listen to my body and try to rest when the tugging pain inside me draws me to the couch. I've never been pregnant, so I assume this pinching and pulling is round ligament pain . . . Until I wake up at three a.m. to a gush of warm fluid running down my thighs.

"Oh shit," I say, flicking on the bedside lamp.

I toss the covers aside. It looks like someone dumped a pitcher of cherry Kool Aid in our bed. My nightgown, my legs, the sheets, and the mattress, are covered in watery pink fluid.

Blood.

"Oh shit," Darin says and jumps out of bed.

"Don't move!" he commands, tossing on a shirt and jeans. I hear the jangle of his belt, doors opening and closing, keys in his hand. As I stare at the bloody mess, a sharp pain fillets my insides.

"O God, it hurts!"

My husband lifts me from bed and cradles me against his chest. My body rocks against his as we descend the stairs and hustle out the door to his pickup. He props me inside, fastens the seatbelt around me, and hops behind the wheel. Tossing it in reverse, he dials his mom, who calls 9-1-1.

"He's driving a hundred down the freeway," she tells the dispatcher. "Please notify Washington State Patrol." Her voice echoes through the phone. "His wife is hemorrhaging." I draw in a deep breath. "She's pregnant," I hear her say.

As we cross under the scaffolding of the interstate bridge, Darin hands the phone to me.

His mom says, "Are you going to OHSU or Emanuel?"

Darin asks me the same question. My doctors are at OHSU, but Emanuel is closer.

"Emanuel," I say.

"Why do I hurt so much?" I ask her.

"Honey, you are in labor."

"I can't be in labor! I'm only twenty-eight weeks along! Oh, God! That hurts." I howl, pulling my legs into my belly.

"Stay calm. Breathe. Deep breaths," she says. "They have a team waiting for you."

Darin stops outside a tall, brick building, and, sure enough, a group of people dressed in scrubs stand at the door, gurney in tow. My husband yanks open my door, gathers me in his arms, and lays me on the bed. The group rushes me into bright lights, up an elevator to a spacious room where they grab the sheets of my gurney and haul my pregnant body onto another bed. Lights and cords hang from the ceiling. I hear a helicopter singing, *whop, whop, whop*, outside my window. Life Flight. My heart sinks for the person arriving in that propelled contraption.

Then it dawns on me. We are on the same floor.

An intravenous line comes first. Nurses attach a bag of magnesium sulfate. It slows my contractions, but makes my arm burn like fire. A nurse gives me a bag of ice to cool the blaze running into my vein while an obstetrician props my feet in stirrups. Warm gel covers my belly. A grainy picture of Addison appears on a small black-and-white screen. The whooshing rhythm of his heartbeat fills the room.

"We are going to give you a steroid shot in the thigh," a nurse says, prepping the syringe. "This will help your baby's lungs mature."

"Is he okay?" I ask between gasps.

Time moves in seconds and hours, with people rushing, poking, prodding, imaging, examining me and Addison. And like a storm pulsing by, the waters still and the sun comes out.

"Baby looks good," the doctor says, wheeling up beside me on his gray stool. "You abrupted. There is a partial tear between the placenta and your uterus. The bleeding throws you into labor. We thought your water broke, but it was plasma. Looks like you've been bleeding for days."

I stare at him, try to understand his words.

"You are stable, the baby is fine. We'll keep you in the

ICU another forty-eight hours, then transfer you to a normal room," he says. "You'll be on bedrest until this little guy is ready for the world."

The ICU? Abruption? Hemorrhage? Bedrest?

I remember the tugging, pinching pain in my belly the past few weeks. The myriad of patients who failed to show for their appointments at the dental office and the dentist insisting I lie down to rest during those canceled appointment times. God knew this was coming. God was already protecting us. Addison and I are not alone. Sleep steals me away as Darin phones my parents, the dental office, and his family. Darin's mom calls the church. They add me to their prayer list.

This day melts into the next and melts into the next, until I am in a room with a window seat, ordering double for breakfast, and watching *Sponge Bob* on Nickelodeon. I can't walk the halls or sit up in bed, not without bleeding and labor pains. I'm allowed to shower, use the restroom, sit up to eat, then it's back to resting. When I bleed, the nurses inject medications in my arms, my hips, my thighs. A phlebotomist comes every third night to draw blood from the vein of my left arm. It's a good thing God answered that first prayer during my appendicitis. If He hadn't, I don't know how I'd survive all these jabs.

A nurse wheels me around the neonatal intensive care unit —the NICU, they call it. Behind two sets of steel doors lie God's most fragile creations. Tiny babies, measured in ounces, rest in warm plastic incubators. Rubber tubes hang from their noses, mouths, and bellies. As he pushes me along, explaining gavage feeding versus gastrostomy tubes, I get the sense my baby will not need the NICU. A radiant peace settles over me, and as we cruise past each little babe, I say a prayer over them.

I listen when the nurse says, "Premature babies risk blindness, cerebral palsy, learning disabilities, delayed development, and sudden infant death syndrome." I dismiss all his words. God created this life inside me. He's going to knit Addison together however He sees fit and give me the strength to be his mother.

A barrage of visitors eats up my hospital time. Stacy and his girlfriend, Dawn, Darin's family, and co-workers from the dental clinic take turns keeping me company day after day. And my parents call from Arkansas to check on us every afternoon.

"We pray for you and little Addison all the time," Mom says.

"Thank you, Momma," I say. "God is listening." I know He is because I am not suffering in the long days, or the longer moments, of waiting. Patience rests on me like a dove. I'm not bored or stir-crazy, even though I have only five channels on my ceiling television—and it's election season. I just lie and wait, as any good mother does when her bun is baking. I want Addison healthy, so this downtime feels like a blessing, not a sacrifice.

I get lonely, though, even with all the visitors. I miss Darin. He stops by after work, brings me dinner, and dessert. But he never spends the night. I guess eight hours in a stiff recliner doesn't offer him a good night's rest. And again, I don't complain. I just close my eyes in the dark of night, tell the Lord thank You, and remember I'm not alone. God is with me. And He's baking my sweet little baby to golden perfection.

♥

I lie on my left side, working a needle and thread over a baby blanket, when pain slices through my belly. I draw in a sharp breath. Warm fluid gushes down my thigh. I shove my thumb into the red call button. The speaker crackles to life.

"Nurses station."

"*Help!*"

Two nurses burst through the door and drop the metal rails on my bed. One straps a fetal monitor on my belly. Addison's heartbeat whooshes into the room with a thump, thump, thump as the other nurse wraps a blood pressure cuff around my bicep.

"You're having a baby tonight," she says, popping the chilly cup of a stethoscope against my arm.

"I'm only thirty-three weeks," I say.

"Honey, thirty-two weeks was the goal. It's safer to take him now than leave him inside you."

"The doctor is on his way," someone says.

They lift me from bed to gurney, wheel me through two sets of double doors, and leave me in the care of another stranger.

"I'm Doctor Turner," says a woman with spikey, brown hair. "Your anesthesiologist."

Doctor Turner props me on my side and rubs antiseptic on my back.

"We have to do a spinal block," she says.

Great. More needles.

"You get to be awake when Doctor Stein delivers your baby."

I smile. Under any other circumstance, I'd tremble in fear, beg them to put me to sleep before slicing me open. But this is for Addison. All the pokes and jabs, the long days, and longer nights. All the heart-racing, arm-burning, nauseating medications. All the pain and suffering are worth it to have him born healthy. Because my choices impact his life, his future, not just mine.

"I am going to inject a local anesthetic into your spinal fluid," she says.

She doesn't need to tell me the rest. I aced anatomy and physiology.

"First let's numb your skin," she says. Those tiny pokes burn, but I don't move.

"I need you to roll up like a shrimp," she says.

I curl my pelvis down, stretch my back toward her.

"Slight pressure," she says.

I hold my breath, freeze in place.

"You are so calm," she whispers.

It's not me, it's the Lord, I think.

"Done," she says. "I'm impressed. You didn't even flinch."

"That's the power of prayer," I say as she rolls me onto my

back.

Clutching the cross around my neck, I tell the Lord, *Thank You.*

She gives me a sip of something pink.

"This will help you relax."

As she turns away, Darin appears, wearing blue scrubs two sizes too small. I giggle at the thin fabric hugging his hips, thighs, and biceps.

"They didn't have your size?" I ask with a belly laugh.

"Ha, ha," he says, grabbing my hand.

They hang a drape between my face and belly, obstructing my view. Darin leans down and says, "How are you doing, Beautiful?"

"Fine," I say. "We are having a baby tonight."

He squeezes my hand, kisses the back of it, and peeks over the drape.

"Are you comfortable?" Doctor Turner asks.

I nod.

Darin leans over me. "I love you," he says.

"I love you, too. Thanks for coming in," I say as he peeks over the drape. "For a guy who doesn't like blood, you're awfully curious."

"It's amazing how clean your insides are," he says, likely expecting my guts to fall out like a smashed raccoon.

"Maybe you can tell me all about it later."

"No, really, it's amazing," Darin says.

"The baby's out," someone says.

Addison's faint howl reaches my ears. "Oh, my gosh," I say, tears pooling in my hair.

A nurse leans into view, holds up our sweet bundle, and says, "We'll examine him and clean him up while they staple you shut."

The resident who performed my surgery takes his sweet time with the staple gun. Click . . . click . . . click . . . My toes tingle and the arches of my feet itch.

"I can feel my feet," I say, wondering how much longer the

spinal block will last.

I hear Dr. Stein say, "Let me take over for you."

When the senior physician steps in and the clicking picks up the pace, I sigh in relief.

The nurse peeks over the drape again.

"Addison is huge for a preemie! He weighs five pounds, eleven ounces, and he's twenty and a half inches long," she says.

"Wow, just imagine if you had carried him to term," Darin says.

"He's a miracle," I whisper.

"Here you go, Momma." The nurse places a tiny bundle beside my head. I relish the sight of my son. Feathery peach fuzz covers his forehead, cheeks, and chin. I slide my finger into his hand. He grabs hold, makes a fist, and squeezes until his paper-thin nails blanch. Globs of silver nitrate cling to his spindly eyelashes as he works to open his cloudy, blue-gray eyes.

"He can rest in the NICU while you're in recovery," a nurse says, plucking him up.

"I'll walk Addison to the NICU," Darin says. "I'll be back."

I want to call out and tell them to stay. I want to hold my baby. But a fire is smoldering under the railroad tracks crossing my belly, and I'm so exhausted. They inject morphine into my IV and wheel me into recovery. I'm hurting like heck and fully loaded with drugs when Darin returns to make the standard phone calls. When he calls Mom and Dad, I can't talk long with the pain zipping through my abdomen.

As I close my eyes and try to sleep, a pediatrician steps up to my bed.

"Addison is the king of the NICU," he says. "He's doing great! Suckles a bottle. Doesn't need a ventilator or feeding tube. His skin is a little yellow. We'd like to keep him a week for observation."

My heart sinks. Addison and I are connected at the heart, not just the womb. I don't want to leave him here.

"Seven days, and you can take him home," Doctor says.

I nod and say, "Okay, thank you."

My gratitude outweighs my sadness. I'm so thankful. Thankful God carried us through a long six weeks in this place, thankful for the doctors and nurses who cared for us, thankful for the janitor who visited with me when she mopped the floor in my room, thankful for the church who prayed over us, and thankful for my loved ones. And I have no words to express how grateful I am that my ginormous preemie isn't hardwired to his incubator.

Seven days. I think with a smile. I can do seven more days.

♥

The hospital releases me four days later, keeping Addison for observation as promised. Darin works long hours and I can't drive, so I spend the next two days wandering the house alone, missing my baby, and wondering if he's okay in that giant brick building without his momma. When the day arrives to bring Addison home, Darin's mom takes me to Toys R Us to grab a car seat, then drops me at the hospital doors. I toss a diaper bag over my shoulder and drag the box with the car seat onto the elevator. I'm not supposed to carry anything heavy, but I'm alone. What's a mother to do but slip on her big girl panties and get on with it? I ride to the second floor, drop the box at the nurses' station, scrub in at the sink, and push the security button.

"Hello?"

"This is Melissa Olson. Addison's mom."

It feels weird to say those words: Addison's mom. But they settle onto me like royalty. I am a mother. The staff buzzes me in, escorts me to his plastic cradle. I lift a swaddled Addison into my arms, stare into his hazy eyes, and my heart blooms like the petals of a rose into an inexpressible, gut-wrenching, soul-aching love. A terrifying love, it is.

"Do you have a ride home?" the nurse asks.

"In a few hours," I say, glancing at the clock on the wall. "My husband is at work."

"You can rest in here," she says, leading me down the hall. She opens the door to a room full of recliners. "Let me get you a pillow."

I shuffle to a chair and sink my aching body into the cushions. Every move jars the crusty incision tucked in the folds of my shrinking belly. I wince as I position Addison in the crook of my arm. The doctor prescribed Vicodin for the pain, but I can't take pills. What happens if the sedative leaches into my breast milk? The doctors and nurses swear it won't hurt Addison, but they don't care about my baby as I do.

The nurse props a pillow under my elbow.

"Thank you," I say.

"We just fed him, so he should sleep for you," she says, dimming the lights.

I stare into Addison's sleeping face, marvel over his miraculous birth. The fact that he weighs so much more than doctors anticipated. He sucks eagerly on a bottle nipple, even though he can't latch onto my breast. Olive, robust color replaces the sickly yellow tint that covered his skin. Without Jesus, and the miracle of modern medicine, we'd be dead. The both of us.

"What shall I do with you, little one?"

His rosebud lips pucker, mouth suckling as he dreams. "I missed you, baby boy." I peel back his blue blanket, peek at his veiny body. Tears fill my eyes as I cuddle him to my breast. "Oh, my goodness, you are beautiful," I say, closing my eyes to snooze until Darin arrives to pick us up.

♥

Mixing bottles, pumping milk, and swaddling my little critter, all the while with staples folded into my baggy belly and ankles the size of tree stumps, leaves me brimming with tears every heartbeat of every day. Breast milk is best. I read it on the Similac can, hear it on television, read it in my parenting books. But when I pump my milk, tears and snot pour out of my face like Niagara Falls. I can't do it. The hormones racing through my body make me want to jump off a bridge. So I do the best I can. With formula.

Addison cries for hours every night. I try everything to calm him. Warm showers for colic, car rides in the dark, endless rocking, cooing, swaying, more formula, less formula, a binky. The endless wailing may be challenging, but doing it alone is heart wrenching. Mom lives in Arkansas. And she's disabled. Darin works too much, so he's little help. No one from his family, work, or the church reaches out to help. So at night, I walk circles around our house with silent tears streaming down my face and a miserable baby folded into my arms. On those long, dark, nights, all I can do is pray, cry, and wait.

Despite the purple crying, Addison gains weight like a prize fighter. He is always hungry.

"Sneak some rice cereal into his bottle," someone says.

My parenting books say it's not good on his digestion to eat solid food before six months of age. After much consideration, I decide to heck with the parenting experts! Let them come console my baby when he sobs himself blue! So I mix a little rice cereal with warm formula and sneak a taste into his mouth. He sucks it off the spoon, grabs my hand in his drooly fist, and drops his jaw open for another bite. I feed him the whole serving. Then I feed him another. And he sleeps. For the first time in four months, we all sleep five consecutive hours.

Hallelujah.

13

Momma Come Home

I unbuckle Addison from his highchair, careful to pull his thick legs out of the holes. He nestles into my chest, his head lulling as sleep tugs his lids down. The kitchen phone rings, making me jump. Addison's eyes pop open as I snatch the receiver off the wall.

"Hello?"

"Melissa?"

"Dad," I say, collapsing into a chair, "what's up?"

"Honey," he says, sighing deep, "I hate to bother you with this."

"With what?"

"I can't take care of Momma at home anymore," he says.

Addison plucks out his binky to nibble on the phone cord.

"What do you mean?" I ask.

"There's a nice facility five minutes from the house," Dad says.

"Okay?"

"I can't bathe her anymore," he says. "She can't bear weight on her legs."

I blow out a sigh. I knew this day was coming. We all did. And here it is. Momma is fifty-one. Fifty-one years old, and Dad's committing her to full-time care. Away from home, away from normal, away from the man she's loved for thirty years.

"I understand, Dad. Do what you need to do," I say.

After we hang up, I call Stacy.

"Hey, baby brother," I say through tears, "Dad's putting Mom in a home."

"I know," he says. "He already called me."

"Should we fly down? Addison needs to meet his grandma."

"I think we should," he says. "Except I can't pay for my ticket. Dawn and I just bought our wedding package. I don't have the money."

"I'll pay your way," I say with a smile, catching tears on my sleeve.

"Are you sure? I can't pay you back," he says.

His integrity strikes my heart. That miracle I hoped and prayed God would do in my brother's life? Well, He is smack dab in the middle of answering that request. I smile big, glance toward the ceiling, and whisper, "Thank you, God."

"Mis, are you sure you want to cover me? Like I said. I can't pay you back," Stacy says again, interrupting my thoughts.

"I'm sure," I say. "I'll even give you the window seat."

♥

Stacy, Addison, and I arrive in the sultry south a week after Dad moves Momma out of the house. Grandma and Granddad greet us outside the nursing home.

"When did you get here?" I ask, wrapping my arms around Grandma's bony shoulders.

"Yesterday," she says, reaching out to touch Addison's hair. Grandma and Granddad are just a short flight from Portland, so they've already had the blessing of meeting their great-grandson.

"Hello, Addison," she coos. "Remember me?"

I glance between them and savor the way my son studies my grandmother's soft eyes. "Your dad seems pretty heartbroken over leaving your mother in here, so we are staying with him," she says.

"We are staying at the Best Western," I say. There is no way I'm sleeping in my father's house again.

"Are you prepared for this?" Grandma asks as I tuck Addison into his stroller.

"Do I have a choice?"

"I suppose not," she says with a sigh.

My grandmother's stoic nature disappears behind a curtain of uncertain trepidation. I'm not used to seeing her fragile like this, so I inhale, stand up tall, and put one foot in front of the other. Someone's got to be strong in this place. Guess it will be me.

The sting of ammonia wafts up my nose as we cross through the automatic doors. I try not to gag. Ten steps inside, and the pungent odor mixes with the salty smell of stale cafeteria food and the hustle and bustle of Momma's new world. Addison balls up tight as we pass a menagerie of fragile people, all stretching out their wrinkled hands to touch his fresh skin. I smile and say hello to them, encouraging my son to loosen up by relaxing my body and my attitude in this foreign environment.

These are Momma's roommates now, these relics wandering the halls. The agile shuffle around with tennis balls covering the feet of their walkers. Some babble or call me the name of a loved one as their vacant eyes work to match my face with the images haunting their memory. The most delicate are parked in wheelchairs, heads lilting sideways, foamy spit crusting the corners of their lips. These sweet oldies wait for someone to dignify them with a hug, a hello, or a wipe of the nose.

My heart wrenches at Mom's incarceration in this place. Gone is the fragrance of her Forever Krystle perfume, the scent of Head and Shoulders in her hair, the aroma of fish, and potatoes in the deep fryer. There is no linger of stale smoke in the air or warm beer in the sink.

Life is so unfair. Momma is the good parent, a dependable person, a woman of mercy and grace. When she worked downtown Portland, she carried a pocket of change to share with the "less fortunate" sleeping on the sidewalks. If she had leftovers from lunch, she'd rest her sandwich bag atop the dumpster, "So they don't have to dig for food," she'd say. Daddy deserves this suffering, not Momma. And she's at my father's mercy. A fact that buzzes like a bee in my grandmother's bonnet.

"I hope Clint doesn't park her in here and get on with his life," Grandma says.

Grandma and Granddad don't like my dad, they never have. They've bailed him out too many times and could never see the benefit of Mom marrying such a louse. But Mom was pregnant with me before they wed and plum smitten with my dad. Grandma and Granddad had already encouraged Momma to give up one baby. They couldn't very well ask her to give up another. Not when the daddy was willing to step up. Regardless, I'm sure they didn't want her marrying Dad then, and they don't want her in this nursing home now. But what can they do when they have no legal recourse, no ethical means to declare my father unfit to decide for Mom? Once again, Mom's choices shackle my grandparents and leave them powerless to do anything except watch her die in this place.

"We're so glad you came," Granddad says, kissing my cheek.

"Me, too."

"Wish it were under different circumstances," he says with watery eyes.

"I know," I say, snuggling into him.

We walk arm in arm while Stacy pushes Addison's stroller.

"She's in here," Grandma says.

We round the corner to find Mom tucked into a bed guarded by high metal rails.

"It's like jail," I say to Stacy.

Momma can't see well, with her eyeballs wriggling back and forth, so Grandma hollers, "Jodie, the kids are here." This makes me laugh since Mom isn't deaf.

Momma looks confused until Stacy leans over her and says, "Mom." Then she beams like a Christmas star. Stacy hugs her tight, kisses her cheek, coos in her ear, and steps back.

"Momma," I say, balancing Addison on my hip.

"Hello, Dolly" she says with a smile.

"Look who came with us," I say.

She gasps and says, "Ad-di-son," in her breathy, broken speech.

"Want to hold him?" Stacy asks.

"Yes," she says, smiling wide as Stacy slides him into the crook of her arm.

"Wow," she says, "he-is-so-big!"

I laugh and say, "I know!"

"He's-a-pre-emie?"

I chuckle again. "He's a hearty preemie."

"Hel-lo, Ad-di-son," she says, planting a clumsy kiss on his head.

Addison babbles, blows spit bubbles in her face, and tries to eat his socks. He doesn't whine or squirm or pitch a fit. She looks at him, and he slides back into her arms, as if he's been there since the day he was born.

"That's amazing," Stacy says, watching them coo back and forth.

I swipe at the tears running down my cheeks and nod.

"He loves her," he says.

"He sure does," I say. "And he can feel our love for her, too."

We make ourselves comfortable, and for the next few days the four of us tend to Momma, helping her out of bed, pushing her to the dining room, helping her to the bathroom, helping her into bed. Momma can't keep up with our chatter, so she watches us, keeping her eyes on Addison until her lids drop.

When it's time to fly home, we are exhausted.

"I wish she lived in Washington," I say to Stacy as we board the plane.

"I think she'd miss Dad, don't you?" he asks.

"I suppose if he visits, she'll be okay," I say.

Addison blows spit bubbles in my face as I strap him into his car seat. I collapse down beside him and blow out a sigh, thankful Darin encouraged me to purchase a separate seat for our baby.

"I meant to ask you," I say, glancing at my brother, "how's sobriety?"

"Amazing," he says. "Thirty days in jail is better than detox."

Stacy had done a little time in the slammer before moving in with Dawn. Upon his release, Dawn rented him a room in her house, told him to keep the drugs out, and more than a friendship blossomed.

"And you're still clean?"

"Yep," he says. "Dad offered me some weed and I said no."

I smile and pat his hand. "I'm super proud of you."

"Having Dawn in my life helps," he says with a grin.

"Dawn's an answer to Mom's prayers," I say.

"And mine," he says with a wink.

♥

"Hi, Miss Jilly," I say through the phone to the nurse in charge of Mom's care. "Can I speak with Jodie, please?"

"Hold on, honey. Let me check on her," she says.

The phone clicks and pops while I wait one, two, three minutes. It screeches to life when she picks up, saying, "Honey, Miss Jodie cain't come to da phone. She ain't got it in her today. I'm sorry."

"Is she doing all right?" I ask.

"She just tired," she says.

"Okay, thank you."

Momma's been cooped up in that home for four years while MS whittles her brain's gray matter into Swiss cheese. She can't hold the phone in her hand anymore, so a compassionate nurse holds the receiver to Mom's ear while I jabber. In recent months, Momma's tongue won't give up a single word either, but I keep calling, so she can hear my voice.

"You know, honey," Jilly says, interrupting my thoughts, "Mista Clint ain't never come up here and see yo momma.

217

Maybe 'bout once a month he show up. He got his new girlfriend come see Miss Jodie, but he ain't neva show up."

"Dad hasn't been there in a month?"

"No, ma'am," she says.

"Thank you, Miss Jilly. You take good care of her," I say, dropping the cell phone in my lap.

I sigh as Darin sets breakfast in front of me.

"My illustrious father hasn't been there in a month," I say, biting into a piece of bacon.

"Why don't you move her home?" he asks.

"Here?"

"To Washington. Yes," he says.

"How?"

"We could rent an RV and drive her back."

"That would be a long road trip for her," I tell him.

"We could fly her home," he says.

"Not commercial," I say.

"What about a medical plane?"

"Is there such a thing?"

"Look it up," he says, shoving his laptop toward me.

I call three companies. They all quote me at least twenty-thousand dollars to move her. Far more than we can afford. And I cannot find a nursing home to take her; not one with a Medicaid bed that scores well on inspection. So I say to God, "If you want her here, make a way," and I let it go.

I arrive home months later to find the red light on our answering machine blinking. I set my groceries down, open a pack of fruit snacks for Addison and push the play button.

"Hello, Melissa?" A male voice echoes in my kitchen.

I grab a jar of spaghetti sauce and head for the pantry as he continues talking.

"This is Rick from Air Med."

I stop midstride, put the jar on the counter and walk to the phone.

"Our rates have dropped."

I jot down his number and call him back.

"I can fly Jodie into PDX, with two nurses on board for fourteen thousand dollars."

"Make it twelve," I say.

"Deal," he says.

I call Grandma and Granddad.

"You are what?" Grandma asks.

"Moving her home."

"Oh, yes! Thank you," Grandma says, her voice thick with tears.

Granddad picks up the line in Kathy's old room.

"Missy!"

"Hi, Granddad!"

"We will split the cost with you," he says.

"I didn't tell you how much—"

"We don't care," he says. "We just want her home with you kids."

Tears fill my eyes at my grandparents' relief and generosity. Their reaction confirms we are doing the right thing.

"How'd this come about?" Grandma asks.

"God," I say. "This was all God."

"Will your father let her go?" Granddad asks.

"He already has," I say, recounting the conversation I had with Dad months ago. He agreed to let me have Mom *if*, and only *if*, Oregon allowed him to keep her retirement. By God's grace, the state transferred Mom's PERS money to my father, so he agreed to give me power of attorney and release her into my full custody as soon as I moved her to Washington. "So, here we are," I tell my grandparents. "Moving her home. With my father's blessing."

Their relief is palpable through the phone line as they send me their love and promise to visit soon. I hang up, let out a long sigh, and my heart stops when I remember: Mom needs a place to live.

"O Lord," I say to God, "I don't know where to put her."

The Yellow Pages. It's a random idea that just pops into my head. I pull out our five-year-old phonebook, flop its thick pages open to nursing homes, and drop my finger on Westfield Care Center.

"That's only fifteen minutes from my house. How did I not see that before?"

A quick internet search tells me their inspection score is excellent. I call the facility. One Medicaid bed is available. Addison and I pile in the car and race to Westfield for a quick look at Momma's new room. The halls smell like lavender, the staff is smiling, and the residents are clean. We give the place two thumbs up.

♥

Momma's body looks like a mangled skeleton. Her muscles, in permanent spasm, pull her arms in like chicken wings and her legs into a fetal position. Her wrists fold into her forearms, fingers pinch into her palms. Hand towels, rolled and taped, nestle in her hands to keep her nails from digging into her soft, veiny skin. I want to pull her limbs straight, relieve her from the invisible coffin ravaging her body, but I can't. She's been contorted so long her limbs might snap like a rotten rubber band if I tried.

"Momma," I say.

Medics lift the rails on her gurney, drop an IV bag onto her lap, and wheel her up next to me. She peers at me with her sparkling gray eyes.

"Hel-lo," she says with a croak.

I bend to kiss her head and study her up close. Her auburn curls are gone, replaced with layers of short, silver hair cropped close to her scalp. Her face looks gaunt, with jutting cheekbones, sunken eyes, and hollow spaces around her temples. Her teeth are extra-large, covered in sticky, yellow plaque. Long, troll-like nails, caked with white, smelly debris, punctuate her digits. Her elbows poke out at sharp angles and her pelvis contorts to the right forcing her hip skyward.

I run a hand down her side and fight the urge to cry when

all I feel is silky, baggy skin. And bones. My mother is a bag of bones. She is starving to death. I swallow hard and take a deep breath. *How is she even alive?*

"Welcome home," I say.

Her mouth opens in glee, but no words come out.

"I know, you are glad to see me," I say.

Her cheeks lift into a grin as she nods her head. Stacy, Dawn, and their baby girl scoot up beside us. "Momma. Meet your granddaughter, Roselyn." Stacy says. "We call her Roz, for short."

Mom lights up like a firefly when Stacy lays Roselyn on her pillow. Mom works to plant a kiss on Roselyn's head as Addison races up beside me and vrooms a Hot Wheel over the rail of her bed. I bend over, gather him in my arms, and say, "Addison, this is your grandma Jodie. She is my momma."

Mom stares at him, mouth agape.

"Can you say hi?" I ask him.

My four-year-old son leans his ginormous head down toward my mother and lays his face on her cheek. She puckers up, plants a smooch on him, scrunches her nose, and locks eyes with me. Words are not needed. I can read her heart. She is happy to be here. With her family.

Addison wriggles out of my arms and races to grab Darin's hand.

"We're going to grab something from the vending machine," Darin says, whisking my son from the room. Dawn swaddles Roselyn and follows them out, leaving me and Stacy alone with Mom. We take turns hugging her, cooing to her, and smooching on her until a nurse walks in.

"Hey, Miss Jodie. I'm Linda," she says, leaning over Momma.

Mother's gray eyes study Linda. If she could, she'd pull Linda in for a hug. But her arms are locked up, so Mom bathes Linda's face with adoration, fixing her eyes on her nurse like a baby does its momma.

"She's a jewel," Linda says, staring into my mother's eyes.

"I know," I say.

Linda slides a cuff onto Mom's arm to take her blood pressure. Then she begins assessing Mom's overall condition. When she rolls Mom to the side and pulls down her paper diaper, she waves us over. "We'll have that gone in a jiff," she says.

I glance at the wound on Mom's butt, exchange glances with Stacy. The tender spot looks like a rotten, melting apple, complete with a red raspberry center, ragged, frothy edges, and a blue-gray border.

"That's disgusting," my brother says, walking toward the door.

"Is that a bedsore?" I ask.

Linda nods. "The staff at her old home didn't move her enough."

Stacy shakes his head and says, "I'll be back."

I nod at him. This examination is not for the faint of heart. I walk over to face Momma.

"Hey Mom, can you open your mouth?"

She drops her jaw open.

"She has thrush," I say, looking at the white patches covering Mom's tongue. I know if I wipe it, her tissue will bleed like a wet sponge.

"From the antibiotics," Linda says. "Let me take care of that." She pops a nystatin swab between Mom's lips. I look away, unable to watch my mother grimace and gag. "We need to change her diaper, put some fresh clothes on her, and get her some food," Linda says, eyeing the door.

"This is probably a good time for us to go," I say, studying Mom.

As I watch Mom's eyes roam the room, an unexpected fear rolls over my heart like a misty fog. The Enemy of my soul whispers, "Look at her just lying there. I can do all kinds of bad things to her, and you'd never, ever know. God didn't protect you, so why would He protect your fragile mother?"

I draw in a sharp breath and freeze in my tracks. He's right. I would never know if someone hurt my mom. It's my job to protect her. The beast of control claws its way up my back. My heart pounds in my ears, my face flushes bright red. I can't spill my panic on anyone else, can't tell Darin or Stacy or anyone. They'll think I'm crazy. Maybe I am?! Fear clutches me until my blood runs cold and I can't catch a breath. No one notices my angst. Nobody hears the voice in my head telling me something bad will happen the minute I walk out the door.

I inhale deep, blow out slow, inhale deep, blow out slow. It's true. I don't want to leave Momma in this place. What if someone is mean to her? What if someone violates her? She can't tell me when bad things happen. I want to insulate her, wrap her in a bubble, and watch her like a hawk.

"You ready?" Darin asks from the doorway.

I close my eyes, inhale, exhale, and whisper a prayer. I bend down to kiss Mom's face. As I drink in her smile and study her glowing eyes, I remember how God brought her home. This was His idea, not mine. Tears trickle down my cheeks and my heart swells with the good, great, amazing love of our Lord. I inhale again and blow out slowly. "Resist the devil, and he will flee from you," God's Word says (James 4:7 NIV).

"You are going to be just fine," I say to my beautiful mother.

"I'll see you tomorrow, Momma."

♥

The staff at WCC shower my mother in love and affection. Her bedsore heals fast, leaving a soft, blue spot to remind us of the pain she endured in Arkansas.

"Her body must hurt," I say to Linda.

"She doesn't complain," Linda says.

"Do you, Miss Jodie?" She hollers at Mom.

Momma just grins and grins.

"Can we stretch her limbs? Maybe a little every day?"

"No," Linda says. "It's too painful."

Well, it's killing me to watch her live like a tangled ball of string. So we visit a neurologist in Portland. The doctor assures me nothing can be done, "except maybe a little Botox, but she'd have to come weekly." Momma cannot travel to the hospital for injections once a week. The benefit does not outweigh the risk, so she is stuck. Twisted up like a human pretzel.

Then one day Linda says, "We ordered Jodie a custom wheelchair."

"You did?"

"Your mother is so tiny, she needs the chair to fit her body," Linda says. "It will hold her in place, so she's comfortable sitting."

I didn't even know it was possible to have a custom wheelchair made.

"Thank you," I say.

The Lord is good. He is oh, so good.

The nursing assistants spoon feed Mom pureed meat and potatoes, hydrate her with thickened water and protein shakes. I feed the nursing assistants Jolly Ranchers and Hershey's kisses by leaving a stocked candy jar in Mom's room. I want the staff to know I appreciate them. What's more, if they sneak in for a candy, they can sneak a peek at Momma, too.

One day, Linda says, "Your mother is always happy."

I chuckle.

"I'm serious," she says. "All the time. She's never sad or angry or fussy."

I study my mother as she watches the old people shuffle by her wheelchair. If she were well, Mom would grab their hands, listen to their stories, and bring them in a batch of Toll House cookies. Instead, she does what she can.

She smiles.

"Only at bath time and wheelchair transfers," Linda says. "Those are painful times. Otherwise, she is happy every moment. It's quite remarkable. Makes me wish I had known her when she was healthy."

I lean over to kiss Mom's head. She smiles at me with her big teeth and shiny eyes.

"It's Jesus," I say in a whisper only Mom can hear.

How do I make Linda, the medical assistants, or the rest of the world understand? Even I can't fathom how she finds peace, tranquility, and joy in a body ravaged by MS. How is she so happy living like this? In a care facility? Away from her home, her husband, and her family? I think Momma knows she is just passing through this world, that Jesus is her home. God says so in His Word. But to see it with my own eyes, to witness the radiance of her skin, the light in her countenance. It's like she's seeing angels or heaven, while the rest of us are blind.

"I wish our other residents had what your mother has," Linda says.

"Me, too," I say as the nurse walks away.

Me, too.

♥

"Hey, Momma," I say, walking in to see her on a balmy July afternoon.

"It's roasting in here. Doesn't this place have air conditioning?"

I drop my purse and plant a kiss on her forehead.

"You are burning up! Let me open a window," I say, scampering across the room.

When I turn back, Mom's face pulls to a frown, her eyes fix in a daze, and she shakes. Not a tremor or the rattly eyeballs I'm used to. This is a full-on convulsion. Like she could shimmy out of her chair and land on the floor.

"Nurse!" I run into the hallway. "Help!"

Linda rushes in, glances at Mom, and pushes a button on the wall. Another woman runs into the room. "Call an ambulance," Linda says to her.

"Your mom's having a seizure," she says, pressing her fingers into Mom's wrist. "Was she shaking when you came in?"

I nod. "She looks terrified," I say.

"She's okay, honey. It's the heat."

"There's no air in this facility?" I ask, kicking myself for not remembering this essential detail.

"No," she says, "you can install a window unit, though."

I glance at the window, grab my phone, and call Darin.

"Mom needs an air conditioner installed in her room," I say through tears. "She's having a seizure as we speak."

"Oh, honey, I'm sorry," he says. "I'm on it."

"I should have known," I say.

"This isn't your fault, Melissa."

"It is. I should have known."

"Stop," he says. "I'll get one installed tonight. She's going to be fine."

Medics walk in and ask, "Do you want to transport her?"

"Yes," I say, staring at my mother's haunted expression.

"You ride with her, honey," Linda says.

"I'm riding with Mom," I say to Darin. I tell him I love him and drop my phone into my purse. As I follow Mom to the ambulance, my body feels heavy, burdened by sickness and guilt, knowing, and not knowing. I'm so tired. So very tired.

We pull into Peace Health, the medics unload Momma, and wheel her into an examination room. The doctor confirms the seizures. A nurse feeds IV fluids and mystery drugs through the tube in Mom's arm. The shaking stops. Mom falls asleep, and I take a deep breath.

"Why don't you go home and rest," says the nurse.

I nod, kiss Mom on the cheek, and meander down the hall, averting my eyes from the rooms with open doors. Bells, beeps, and chimes of all kinds ring out the melody of infirmity in this place. The sounds trigger me, pulling me back to my days lying in bed, waiting for Addison to be born.

I find the gift shop on the second floor and relief washes over me when the fragrance of merchandise masks the smell of sickness. When the clerk offers a kind hello, I find the strength to gather my emotions and smile back at her. My whole body relaxes, and I fight the urge to cry, distracting my aching heart with the trinkets and goodies lining the shelves. Magnets and cards offer comfort and laughter. I spin a rounder of coffee cups; each one pouring out words of hope and inspiration. I stop to finger scarves for chilled necks and beanies for bald heads. The magnitude of loss haunting this building steals my breath.

A rack of stuffed animals beckons me to touch soft fur, stare into glass eyes, and ponder the small hands that will hold each critter. A shaggy black dog catches my eye, reminding me of Buttons. I pick him up, pay his "adoption fee", tuck him into my purse, and call Darin for a ride home.

When I arrive the next day, Mom's wide awake.

"I got you something," I say, tucking the scraggly pup into her hands.

"Oh! He is so cute! I think I'll call him Scrappy," she says.

I freeze, gawk at her, and drop my jaw.

"Thank you, honey!" she rattles on.

Wait . . . What? What's happening?

"Momma?"

"Yes?"

"You can talk?"

"I can!" She beams at me with a toothy grin.

I glance up at the drip going into her arm.

"Come, and sit down," she says. "Tell me how you are doing."

I want to talk, ramble on about my life, but I can't say much. All I can do is stare at her in wonder. How is this happening? I glance up at the drip again. The fluids and medication must be reducing the inflammation in her brain. Soon enough, these medical interventions will disappear, as will she, back into the clutches of an uncontrollable disease and the advanced directives dictating her future. Mom's orders are specific. No intravenous fluids, no feeding tube, no ventilator to sustain her long term. When her body fails, she wants to go home to Jesus.

It's hard for me to reconcile and excruciating to watch her wither away by choice. I collapse into the chair beside her and fight the lie of control. The truth is, I am powerless. Love respects the other person. Love respects my mother's faith in God, her decision to wait for Him to deliver her. Love does not meddle, does not bicker, argue, or fight for self.

Love lets go.

I stare at her and ponder how the MS sneaks in like a thief to steal a gem at a time, until the vault is empty. For the past five years, I thought there were no treasures left. But here she sits, coherent and capable. Resurrected for a day? An hour? A minute?

I can't explain this miracle, don't know how long we have together. So I relish a blessing the world takes for granted. The ability to communicate. I talk, and she listens. Then she talks! My mother talks to me! About her, Addison, Darin. My dad and Stacy. I savor every word, as she jabbers on and on, with time slipping by like sand between my fingers. When the nurse comes in to unhook the IV, I want to make her stop. But I can't. All I can do is tell God thank You for this rainbow in the storm and wait for the cocoon of silence to swallow Momma up again.

When we return to WCC, an icy blast cools her room. My amazing husband snuck in while we were away and mounted an air conditioning unit in her window. And just as I predicted, Mom's speech never returns. But neither do her seizures, thanks to God's love and Darin's thoughtfulness.

14

A Sacred Good-bye

Living in Washington means lots of family time for Momma. Grandma, Granddad, and her siblings come to visit in August. Stacy, Dawn, and their baby girl visit every Saturday. Addison and I spend afternoons wheeling her around the garden. We stop to admire the daisies and watch finches gather seed from the bird feeders. My heart toward Dad softens as I care for Momma. She is not a burden, but I feel helpless, as if all I can do is watch God steal her away, molecule by molecule. Six years of doing this alone had to crush my father's heart.

When the sun lingers further south and the leaves change from green to a menagerie of yellow, orange, and red, Dad comes to visit us. All the way from Arkansas. This is his first time back since they moved south. Stacy is happy to see him. I am not. But I am grateful for his guidance when WCC calls us in to sit down and talk about Mom.

We gather around a cafeteria-style table. Me, Dad, Stacy, a WCC administrator and Linda.

"She is losing weight," Linda says, tapping her ballpoint pen on the table.

We all nod.

"I'd be shocked if she lives until Christmas," she says.

I inhale deeply. Dad picks his nails, and Stacy crosses his

arms.

"When her body shuts down," Linda says with her eyes fixed on mine, "it's important to withhold her water."

"You mean, dehydrate her?" I ask.

"Yes," she says, "because if you don't, she will drown."

I furrow my brows and stare at her.

"Her lungs will fill with fluid." She shakes her head side to side, pulls her mouth into a frown, and says, "It's a painful way to die. Trust me."

I purse my lips and stare into space as Linda, Stacy, and Dad talk about Mom's advanced directives.

"She wants to be cremated," Dad says.

I hear him, but their conversation is muffled, like I'm listening from the bottom of a swimming pool. *Which is worse? Drowning or dying of thirst?* I wonder.

We all agree to honor Mom's wishes, keep her as comfortable as possible, and relish the days we have left with her. When the chatter stops, we walk outside, and I drop my head on Stacy's shoulder. Dad folds his arms around us, and together, we cry. Our hearts beat with the same rhythmic pain, the ache of suffering and loss. The center of our family—the glue holding us together, our shining light—is dying. We know it, of course we do. But it hurts to plan for it.

As we sniffle, bodies shaking with tears, I momentarily understand my father. For just a blink, just one tick of the clock, I peek into the pain of Daddy's world. The infinite loss defining his life. Losing his momma at age five, his daddy forever. Losing the purity of his childhood, his innocence to molesters in orphanages and foster care. Losing his sanity in Vietnam.

And now losing the love of his life.

No wonder Dad couldn't care for Momma in Arkansas. No person ever took the time to equip him with love, integrity, or the faithfulness needed to complete the task. But they equipped me. Dad and Momma and Jesus. They equipped me to handle her care. I swear the only reason I ended up in dental hygiene is because the Lord knew what I needed. I stopped picking teeth when Addison was born. But I use those critical thinking skills every day.

♥

"Momma, do you want me to baptize you?" I ask, holding a Styrofoam cup in my hand.

She nods.

It feels a little superstitious, but to my knowledge, Momma's never been baptized. "Is Jesus Christ your Lord and Savior?"

"Yes," she says in a whisper.

"Are you a sinner in need of His grace?"

She furrows her bushy brows and says yes.

"Do you love Jesus with all your heart?"

She nods and gives me a toothy grin.

"I baptize you in the name of the Father, the Son, and the Holy Spirit."

I dip my finger in the cup, put a smidge on her forehead and smile down at her.

"I hope I'm doing this right," I say with a chuckle.

"M-e, to-o," she says.

My cup of water and Momma's statement about Jesus doesn't save her. She's already saved by His grace. That is apparent in her shiny eyes, constant smile, and peaceful demeanor. Our little ceremony serves to remind her whom she belongs to. God's bus is picking her up soon; she needs to be packed and ready when He arrives.

I'm not sure how religion works, exactly. So to be sure we've sealed the deal, I ask a pastor from church to do the same thing. Pastor Janice walks into Mom's room, asks her the same questions, dips her finger in a foam cup, and draws a wet cross on Momma's forehead.

Now Mom is good to go.

When I tell Grandma about baptizing Mom, she says, "Melissa, we baptized her as a baby in the Methodist church."

"Well, twice more won't hurt," I say with a giggle.

We prep Mom for heaven and our hearts for good-bye. Then my birthday arrives, then Addison's birthday, then Thanksgiving, Christmas, Stacy's birthday, Easter. Of course, the Lord makes liars out of us. He's the Author of life and death. Not me. Not Linda. Not even Momma herself.

Mother's Day arrives and I am tickled to spend the afternoon at WCC with Momma.

"That's good Jell-O, huh?" I ask, scooping a thick bite of raspberry goop into Mom's eager mouth.

She nods before dropping a glob down her bib.

"Don't waste that," I say, making her chuckle. "Don't choke," I say, wiping her mouth.

She frowns at me.

"Want a scoop of beef and potatoes?"

"N-o," she croaks.

"Squash?"

"Uh-uh." She squirms in her chair.

"Drink your Ensure," I say, working the straw between her lips.

She pulls a thick swig from the straw, then another, before moving her head to the side.

"More?"

She shakes her head no.

"Momma, you need food to keep you strong," I say, thrusting the straw at her.

"N-o."

I sigh, remove her bib, and wheel her out to the garden. She closes her eyes for a snooze in the patchy sunshine. I run my fingers over the soft veins on her hand, savor her deep breathing, and the smile crossing her face when she wakes to find me staring at her.

"Happy Mother's Day," I say.

"Hap . . . Moths . . . Da."

"I know, Momma." I pat her hand. "I understand."

♥

On Memorial Day, Linda calls, saying, "Jodie has a fever. Probably a bladder infection."

"Keep me posted," I say.

I don't think much of Linda's phone call. Urinary tract infections are a constant battle for Mom. I'm sure it's nothing. We just got home from the beach, and I have a million things to do. I make Addison lunch while Darin mows the lawn. I wash the dishes, toss a load of laundry in the washer, put Addison's toys away. When I sit to gobble a sandwich, a thought drops into my head, along with a strange urgency.

Mom is dying.

"I have to go," I say to Addison, grabbing his hand. "Let's take you outside to mow with Daddy."

"Are you going to Grandma Jodie's?"

"Yes, baby. I think Grandma might be sick."

"I'll pray for her," he says, hopping onto Darin's lap.

"Going to Mom's," I holler at my husband over the noisy mower.

Darin nods, turns the machine around, and rumbles off with Addison on his knee.

When I walk into Mom's room fifteen minutes later, I find her resting alone in the dark. Her roommate is nowhere to be found, the television is off, and the blinds are drawn.

"Mom," I say, clicking on her bedside lamp.

She doesn't move.

"Momma?" I kiss her forehead. "You are burning up!"

She lays motionless.

"Mom!"

No response. I sink into a chair, flip open my phone, and dial Stacy.

"Hey, Mis. What's up?"

I swallow my tears and say, "It's Mom."

"I'm on my way," he says.

I snap my phone shut, slide her drapes open, draw the sheet off her body. She doesn't twitch, roll, or stir. The cadence of her breathing remains steady. I press my cheek against her wet forehead.

I'm not ready for this, Lord.

Linda's footsteps pull me to sit. "Hey," she says. "We added another antibiotic. It's not working."

I nod and reach for a tissue.

"I think we should call hospice," she says.

I nod again.

"I'm sorry, honey," Linda says, laying a palm on my shoulder.

I give her hand a squeeze.

"If she wakes up thirsty, give her a straw-full," she says.

When Linda shuffles out, I lean back to study Mom, her soft breaths, relaxed face, deep slumber. God's taking her home soon. Then what? Every heartbeat of my life, Momma's been here. Even in her sad estate, she's here, with me, in this place. When God takes her, what do I do? I've never even been to a funeral. Not one. I've seen them on television, the movie screen, but never real life. Maybe God can tell me what to do. What's that Bible verse people read at funerals? *Yea though I walk through the valley of the shadow of death . . .?*

That's the one.

I wander to the television room, wade through wheelchairs and walkers to reach the bookcase, and pull a Bible off the shelf. I don't understand Psalm 23 and funerals. Why do people quote these verses when someone dies?

I plop down beside Mom, flip open the feathery pages, and read aloud. "The Lord is my Shepherd, I lack nothing. He makes me to lie down in green pastures, He leads me beside quiet waters, He refreshes my soul." (Psalm 23:1–3 NIV).

I read about the valley of the shadow of death. Read about fearing no evil. I still don't get why people read this in the cemetery. Like evil is coming to get Mom . . .? Evil isn't taking my mom. She's been living in the shadow of death for ten years, and God's been here all along. And God's coming to get her, to take her to heaven.

I snap the book shut as Stacy walks in.

"Hey," he says.

"She won't wake up," I say.

I offer him my chair.

"Momma," he says with his face hovering over hers.

"Has she been like this the whole time?"

"Yeah."

"Not awake at all?" he asks again.

"I couldn't wake her up," I say.

"Do you think she's dying?"

"Yeah," I say.

"Can she hear us?" he asks.

"I don't know. If she can, her body is too weak to respond."

"I hate this," he says.

"Me, too," I say, grabbing a tissue from the box on Mom's table.

My brother shakes his head and pulls up his t-shirt to wipe his cheeks.

"I don't know how to watch her die," he says.

"Me neither."

We spend the day resting beside her, watching her breathe, watching her sleep, wiping sweat from her brow. When night falls, it's late.

"We need to rest, Mis," he says.

"What if she dies after we go?" I ask.

"Then it's God's will," he says.

"I wonder if she sees heaven," I say. "You know, like the stoning of Stephen in the book of Acts?"

"I don't know, Mis. You know more about the Bible than I do."

"I think she is already with Jesus," I say. "Here and there at the same time."

♥

I wake up at seven a.m., fumble with my cell, and dial the nursing home.

"How is she?" I ask, rubbing my eyes.

"Same as yesterday."

I drop Addison with a sitter, stop by Target to pick up snacks for the nurses and a CD player and music for Mom's room. At WCC, I arrive to find sunshine streaming through her windows, her sheets pulled aside to cool her body. She lies on her back today, with pillows holding her twisted legs in position, her bony hip jutting skyward. A sheen of sweat wicks her skin, saturating her satiny nightgown. Her breathing is soft and rhythmic, just like yesterday.

I rattle the glass candy dish, toss in suckers, peppermints, and lemon drops with a thud, thud, thud. Glance at Mom. Nothing. I make a ruckus setting up the CD player, popping in the disc titled *Gentle Harp*. Glance at Mom. Still nothing. I turn up the volume, lean over her face, and say, "Momma."

Her brows twitch.

"Momma!"

Her lids flutter open.

I hover inches from her face and say, "Momma!" I say it again and again, pulling her awake. When her beautiful eyes meet mine, I say, "Oh, Mom! I missed you!" I plant a kiss on her cheek. "Are you thirsty?"

She nods. I prop her up, grab the straw, and drain thick liquid into Mom's dry mouth. She swallows it down. I watch her sticky tongue run over her parched lips and dab some petroleum jelly on them. She offers me a weak smile, gulps another straw of water, then closes her eyes. I whisper "I love you" in her ear. She props her eyes open, smiles at me, and nods her head before slipping into another deep, rhythmic sleep.

This day melts into the next as we wait on the angel of God to collect her. I call Dad, lay the phone to her ear. He says, "I love you, Jodie." She doesn't stir or move. I call Grandma and Granddad, lay the phone to her ear, and listen to her parents' chatter, with Grandma on the kitchen phone and Granddad on my aunt Kathy's old phone. This is the way they've always communicated via telephone, with Granddad on a receiver in the other room so we could all talk together. Tears roll down my cheeks as their tender voices serenade kind words in her lifeless ear.

Around the end of the third day, weariness settles in like a cold mist.

"Why is she still here?" I ask with a sigh.

"I don't know," Stacy says, shaking his head.

"Maybe she can't leave with us in the room?"

"Want some food?"

"Sure," I say, my stomach gurgling from a three-day hunger.

"Momma, we are going out for a burger," Stacy says. "We love you." We meander out the door toward the car. "McDonald's?" he asks.

"Yes!"

Over quarter pounders and salty fries, Stacy and I ponder Mom's struggle to leave this earth.

"Maybe she needs Dad's permission," I say.

"We've been calling him every day."

"Yeah, but maybe he needs to tell her she can go," I say.

"It's worth a try," he says, stuffing the last bite of cheeseburger into his mouth.

When we get back to her room, the hiss of oxygen joins *Gentle Harp* and her rhythmic breathing. A nasal cannula hangs across her face. Linda walks in and says, "We added some oxygen. Just for comfort."

I nod, knowing this tiny bit of oxygen cannot sustain Mom's life.

"She's still here," I say with a sigh and dial Dad.

"Hey, honey, how's Momma?" he asks.

"The same. We think she needs your permission to go."

"Let me talk to her," he says.

I put Dad's voice to Mom's ear and listen to him coo, telling her she's a good wife, a good momma, a good friend.

"Jodie. You have my blessing to leave. Go to Jesus, honey."

"Thanks, Dad," I say before hanging up. Then we wait. And wait. And wait.

The sun sets, the moon rises, and we head home for a little rest.

In the wee hours of the night, I wake with a sudden urgency to check on Mom. I slip on fresh clothes, pop Dixie Chicks in the CD player, and drive extra slow to the nursing home. I drag my weary bones from the car, shuffle up to the door, and ring the bell. The girl at the desk recognizes my name, my tired voice, and unlocks the door.

"Momma, why are you still here?" I ask when I walk into her dimly lit room.

I lean back in the chair beside her bed, prop my feet on the nightstand, and crack open a frosty soda. Sweet, brown syrup fizzes over my tongue, and down my esophagus. Opening the Bible on her nightstand, I read Psalm 23 and pause to repeat the last verse. "Surely goodness and mercy shall follow me all the days of my life, and I shall dwell in the house of the Lord forever and ever."

I watch Mom sleep and I think about her life. Her gentle smile, tender touch, contagious laugh. Goodness and mercy have followed her all the days of her life. Even through this awful disease. I've never prayed for God to heal Mom. Some people might wonder why a Christian, a person who believes in miracles, wouldn't ask for one. I know the answer all the way to my bones. I know it better than I know the skin on my body or the room I'm sitting in. Momma said the words in her letter. The words that solidified my faith, even as God worked to help me believe:

> You can be aware of Faith as easily as you can be aware of earth. Faith is as certain as is the existence of water. Faith is as sure as the taste of an apple, the smell of a rose, the sound of thunder, the sight of the sun, the feel of a loving touch. Hope is a wish, a longing for something you don't yet have—but with the expectation

of getting it. Faith adds surety to the expectation of hope.

Because of Jesus, and my mother, I have faith. And I have hope. Just like the end of the psalm says, Mom will dwell in the house of the Lord forever and ever. Jesus is better than this world, paradise is real, and that's where Mom is going. I read verse 5: "You prepare a table before me in the presence of my enemies; You anoint my head with oil; My cup overflows."

God is at work, preparing a table, even now, at this evil time on earth. And one day, I will sit at His table with Mom and Dad and Addison and Stacy and Darin. We have been anointed, and we will be with Jesus. I know this without pause, without hesitation. So I don't ask God to heal Mom. I ask Him to take her! Take her home. And take me, too. When my time comes.

And right now, my cup overflows.

"I'm so happy to be here, Mom," I say.

And I am. Because this moment, all these heartbeats, they are sacred. This space is holy. The Lord is near, I feel Him. And in this holy place, where Mom lingers between life and death, I witness God's kingdom in Jesus taking my sick Mom to heaven. Where there is no more pain, no more weeping, no more MS, and no more death. This hallowed place, this time we sit in right now, is both excruciating and beautiful.

♥

Jesus takes Momma home several hours later, with Stacy and I sitting beside her. We whisper our love into her ears one final time, then walk outside to breathe in the scent of fresh cut grass and bask in the sunshine peeking through the billowy clouds overhead. I stare up at the heavens, pull out my cell and call Darin for a ride home. I'm in no condition to drive.

The sound of my husband's voice melts over my heart, pulling me to tears.

"She's gone," I whisper through sobs, "Can you come and get

me?"

"I'm sorry honey," he says. "I'm on my way."

"I have to call my grandparents," I say, then hang up the phone.

Sitting on the curb outside a place I'll never return to, I take a deep breath and dial Grandma and Granddad. I've never heard a more painful sound than my momma's momma dropping the phone in shock, her stoic voice reduced to a whimper. My last call is to Dad, who shares my relief at her passing.

When we get home, I climb into bed and fall into a fitful sleep. Darin orders Olive Garden and a white calla lily. I rouse for a breadstick and pasta, then crash again. Around midnight, I awake to my husband snoring next to me. Restless, I tiptoe to the kitchen, click on the light, and long for human connection. In the wee hours, there are no phone calls, no visitors, no conversations. Just me and the memories of Mom dying. Gentle Harp, the cadence of her breathing, and the oxygen machine ring in my ears. The smell of sickness, and her color fading to gray, haunt my mind. This grief after hours buries me in sadness.

"God, what now? What do I do with this?" I pray.

An idea strikes. I pull out pictures of Momma in her youth, line them across the table, and study them one at a time. I remember what she was like when I was a girl, a tween, a teen, a young adult. Before she needed a cane, a walker, a wheelchair, or a nursing home. Then, I pray, "Lord, take the memories of death and replace them with life."

Fatigue drags my lids down. I tiptoe back to bed and sink into the covers. And just as sleep pulls me into the land of lucid dreams, I hear my mother's voice say, *I love you.*

I hear it as surely as I hear Darin snoring beside me. My eyes pop open and I inhale deeply. I heard her! I heard my mom's voice! I giggle and giggle as tears pool in my ears and hair.

"Thank You, Jesus," I say in a whisper.

When I wake up seven hours later, I can still hear Momma whispering in my ear. And in my memory, she is young, strong, and vibrant.

She is alive.

♥

We honor Mom's request for cremation and buy a plot in a local cemetery. Stacy and I split her ashes. He and Dad plan to scatter half of her remains on the Lewis River when Dad visits later this year. I plan to bury the other half to honor my grandparents. They buried their first daughter, my aunt Kathy, after she died. I figure we should bury Momma, too.

After I secure her remains and her plot, her family flies in to pay their respects. Because Mom lived between two states and spent so much time in a nursing home, her friends dwindle to two, so we don't plan a formal memorial. Just a gathering at her gravesite and brunch afterward. Grandma and Granddad, along with her brothers and sister-in-law, arrive on Wednesday.

"When will he be here?" Grandma asks, sipping tea at my kitchen table.

"Anytime now," I say, setting out glasses for our guests.

I stare at Grandma a moment and watch her fidget. She pulls the stray hairs at the nape of her neck, crosses her arms, runs fingers over the sweat on her glass. This is unlike her. My grandmother is stoic, strong, determined. Not fragile, not skittish.

"Grandma? Are you nervous?" I ask, sliding into the chair across from her.

"Wouldn't you be?" she asks. "We are about to meet the baby we gave away. What if we didn't do the right thing? What if he hates us?"

I laugh and say, "He doesn't hate you! Don't be silly, Grandma."

She gives me a stern look.

"He has awesome parents, people who love him. He grew up on a farm, for crying out loud. And he didn't have to grow up with our father, so that's saying something," I say.

The doorbell rings, silencing the room. We've talked to Brian on the phone, every one of us. But not one of us has met him in person. I stand and meander toward the door with a pounding heart. I can see him through the glass entry. He's tall, like Granddad, with thick, dark hair. He smiles at me through the glass. He has my mom's beautiful teeth. I pop open the door and hold my breath as I peer right into my mother's gray eyes. Tears burst to life in my heart, but I don't let them fall. I can't freak this poor guy out. I'm sure he's as nervous as the rest of the family.

"Brian?"

"Melissa?"

"You have my mother's eyes," I say.

He steps inside and says, "I do?"

"Oh, my goodness, you sure do," I say. Tears leak down my cheeks as I wrap my arms around Momma's baby and ponder how God cared for him, protected him, loved on him, then brought him home.

"Come meet the family."

Grandma and Granddad shower him with affection, hugging on him and asking him a million questions. Stacy and the rest of the family follow suit. We visit awhile before donning our jackets for a funeral in the rain. My tummy quakes as we pile into the car. This is the hard part for me. We don't have a minister or a formal speaker, so I'm doing the talking. Just me, God, and a Bible.

At the cemetery, we gather around her stone, and I open with verses from Revelation. I don't read or recite the Twenty-third Psalm. Instead, I read about heaven, and Jesus, and the Book of Life. I talk about Mom alive in heaven and I pray, thanking God for Momma and asking Him to comfort us as we mourn. And as I look around at the people Momma loved, I can't help but praise God for the glory of this moment. One day we will all be together, just like this, on the new earth. One day, there will be no good-byes, no death, no suffering. It will just be us and Jesus. And maybe some talking animals.

PART 4

The Truth

15

Rainbows And Skeletons

It's amazing how Mom's passing changes my perspective, as if God took my dirty glasses and gave me a fresh pair. A pair with rosy lenses. It sounds crazy, but my heart relaxes after Mom goes to heaven. Because she's alive and well. With Jesus. This sounds trite and easy, but it's not. The whole inside of me aches, I miss her so much.

Losing Mom is my first experience with death. And grief. I've been sad, had my heart broken, felt disappointment. But there's nothing like mourning the loss of a human. Cycles of emotion rock my heart like a song on repeat. Sorrow, anger, guilt, joy. Sorrow, anger, guilt, joy. Time stretches a little further between episodes, tricking me into thinking the worst is over. Then *bam*, grief sneaks up to zap me again, pulling me into a mess of tears. It strikes unexpectedly and in the oddest places. When I'm watching a movie, taking a walk in the park, sharing a meal with my family, or when a certain song comes on the radio.

Church is the worst. I can't walk into the building without a river of tears brimming my eyes. The Lord and I share a sacred connection through Mom. When I'm close to Him, I'm close to her. This odd mix of grief and hope births a deep well of sacred happiness inside my heart. A mysterious, indescribable joy that is found only in my link to heaven. I feel this joy even when I cry. This feeling reminds me of how it takes rain and sun to make a rainbow.

I love color in the sky. Sunsets and sunrises remind me that Jesus will return the same way He left after His resurrection. He ascended to heaven in front of the disciples, and He will descend from heaven in front of the whole world when He returns. I also love the rainbow because it reminds God of His promise to Noah in Genesis and His believers in Isaiah. A promise never again to flood the earth or punish those who are in Christ. And the rainbow isn't a bow. It's a full circle when viewed from heaven or a plane flying at thirty-thousand feet. God remembers His covenants through a halo of color.

The sightings begin right after Mom passes. I see dozens of them. Rainbows. And double rainbows. Arching over our barn following a late afternoon rain shower. In the road spray when I drive down the highway. Haloed around a full moon. As a sliver of color peeking through the cirrus clouds on a hot August day. In the sprinklers. Across my Bible when the sun arcs through my water glass on a winter morning. And best of all, in the pink hue of an early morning sunrise.

No joke. I see rainbows everywhere.

Every streak of color in the sky feels like a game of peek-a-boo between me and the Lord. God knows that anytime there is sun and rain, I will run outside and look at the sky. So I feel it's a personal and intimate gift when the Lord hits the heavens with His paintbrush. The more He woos me, the more I wonder: Who is this Creator? Who formed, not only the earth and all its amazing critters, but the galaxies, too? He knows the name of every star, guards the life of every sparrow, and counts the hairs on my head, at the same time. Who is He, this Person who carried my mother away to paradise?

When I try to understand, I'm overwhelmed. Because all I wanted was heaven instead of hell. And Jesus did so much more. He pulled me from drug abuse, alcohol abuse, and child abuse. Escorted me through college and a high-risk pregnancy.

He blessed me with a faithful, generous, loving husband. He walked with me through Mom's illness and death. He brought heaven to earth and planted hope in my heart. And I want to know Him more, want it more than anything.

But I'm afraid. What about the hellish monster in my closet? What about the wounds from the sexual abuse? They are still open and oozing inside me. Where was God when my dad slid his hands under my blankets? Where was He when I kept secrets from Momma? Where was He during all that pain? And how am I supposed to trust Him?

♥

I plop down in the sanctuary and fan my face with a trifold bulletin. Pacific Baptist Church isn't our home church, but I heard they offer an amazing kids' program. So while Addison's out back playing tug-o-war and water games, I'm sitting on a pew, waiting for the adult service to start.

I glance at the bulletin. They have a food pantry and a volunteer-staffed medical office on the grounds. "Impressive," I say.

And they have a full page of support groups. For addicts, alcoholics, victims of domestic violence, singles, widows, divorcees. My eyes freeze on the last group listed: *Hope for Survivors of Sexual Abuse.*

The words glare at me from the page. I shake my head, rub my eyes, and look again. Then I laugh.

God is talking to me. That is clear. I drop the bulletin, look at the ceiling and laugh again. Not the "you're-so-funny" kind of laugh. More like the mocking, "yeah-right" kind of laugh kids give their parents. I glance around the room at all the beautiful hearts in this place. People loving people. Just like the church I accepted Christ in. I listen to the conversations, watch the body language, drink in the worship music, learn from the sermon. When the service ends, I glance at the ceiling again.

"Really?" I ask Him. I can't hear God, but I know. I know what

He wants me to do. It's time to tackle the beast hiding in my closet.

♥

Like a good physician, God provides what I need to dress the wound. I call the church, meet with the support group facilitator, she invites me to join, and tells me to schedule an appointment with a Christian counselor. I call the counselor. Her name is Kate.

"Healing is a process," Kate says. "It takes time."

I'm scared but I'm also excited to slay this beast and be free. And who knows. Maybe it will be easier to say the words aloud now that Mom is in heaven. So I share my story with Kate. I tell her how and when Dad touched me. Tell her how I wanted to die, kill myself with drugs and alcohol. Tell her about my relationship with Darin and how I got lost in him. Tell her about Momma. How Momma never knew what happened to me. Not with her head, anyway. I suspect my mother knew with her heart, though.

Every session, every word, every syllable offers freedom and hope.

I join the support group. Wow. Words cannot express my gratitude to these courageous leaders. These women who sit with a small circle of fractured souls and let us share our tales of horror, cry with us, and pray with us. And the women who find the strength to tell. To peel the crusty, infected bandage off their hearts and let us all peer at the ulcer inside. My hat is off to them. They make me feel normal. They make me feel as if I'm at home with them, in their broken places.

And the most amazing part of the journey? The most fragrant, mysterious, eye-popping part of the whole story? Jesus walks among us, like another broken friend. He came to earth for the sick and the sinners as well as the righteous. Abuse makes us sick. But here, in this place, this church support group, we find salve to heal those gaping wounds.

God reminds us of His amazing love, especially in Psalm 56:8, where He says He keeps account of our wounds, collects our tears in a bottle, and keeps a record of them in His book.

The leader hands out a workbook. This bundle of pages asks stunning, personal, brutal questions. We are expected to spill all the beans. Every last one of them. Leave no stone unturned. So we do. Over a period of months, we find the courage to tell it all. The who, the what, the when, and the how of the abuse. Tell how it impacted our hearts and minds. We tell on the person who did it, and the person who ignored it. And when we are done telling and telling and telling, we pray. We lay those stinky, rotten, decaying, corpses in the light of Jesus Christ, and His truth. His love picks the death off us like a crow eating roadkill, one morsel at a time. That is a graphic analogy, but it's true. Listening to the atrocities perpetrated against other women isn't easy. It sucks. It's grueling. It's graphic.

Want to know what's harder? Remembering my own past. It's so awful. When it's my turn to puke it up, I talk about the june-bug house, the fear of Momma dying, and how she died anyway. I tell them how Dad snuck into my room at night, cornered me after school, taught me to trade my body for favors. How he medicated my broken heart with drugs and alcohol, then ran away with my mother when I told my husband the truth.

Most of the grotesque memories come back easy-peasy. But my preteen years slip through the cracks like a key down a storm drain. Fractured images float in and out of my mind, but I can't put the pictures together. I pray, pull out old photos, listen to music, but nothing works. The frustration boils inside me. I'm ready to be done, already.

Just give it to me, God. I beg and beg. There is nasty stuff inside me, tucked deep under my tender heart, like an infected sliver or a boil. It's stinky, painful, and I want it out of me! But God doesn't expose it all at once. He gives it up a piece at a time, or maybe a slice at a time, but never in large measure. I assume He knows it's too much, but I disagree. Because I don't want to come back into these memories ever again. I want to hurl them up and flush them. So I push it and push it.

Maybe seeing the old rental house on 67th Street will help me remember, I think.

I drive to my old neighborhood and park in front of the house. It's so much smaller than I remember. Sadly, it also sits in disarray, with tattered, moldy siding, moss on the roof, and weeds in the yard. This is what time does to things left unattended.

I recline on the leather seat of my SUV. Cherry blossoms rain a blanket of pink petals over my windshield. Sprinkles of rain flatten them into a red, clumpy mess on the glass. A bright yellow school bus pulls up and flicks out a stop sign. Kids roll out the door, scatter up driveways, swinging lunch pails and backpacks. The sound of their laughter carries me back twenty-five years.

I picture myself getting off bus number 79, my size 5 feet skipping up the drive. I see myself walking through the garage door, letting it drop shut with a bang. My fingers run over the smooth veneer of our dining room table, the scratchy tweed of our black and white couch. A crispy red stain lies hidden beneath the center cushion. I hear Dad yelling at me for spilling the nail polish, and Momma flipping that cushion over, saying, "It's no big deal."

My mind's eye takes me bare footed over the plush carpet of our formal living room. I stop to touch Mom's wicker furniture, breathe in its woody scent. I tiptoe past the bathroom toward my bedroom, then Dad's, and draw a blank. All I see is my canopy bed and my parent's dark walnut furniture.

No abuse comes to mind, not a stitch.

"Dang it," I say, slapping the steering wheel.

I sit for several minutes. Pray and pray. Nothing comes. Not one thing. The darkness is locked away, in the back of my mind, deep in the places God won't let me go.

Not yet anyway.

♥

I walk into an afternoon therapy appointment to songbirds tweeting, sunshine on my back, and hope in my heart. My months of therapy and group are wrapping up, and I'm ready to move on to freedom and the abundant life of Christ.

"Come in," Kate says, leading me to her office.

She clicks the door shut behind us, and I collapse on the couch, kick off my sandals, and tuck my feet into the maroon cushions. I've spent so much time here it feels like home. I catch Kate up on last week's homework. We talk about forgiveness, how letting go of the pain is for me, not my dad. My heart is confident I've forgiven him for the abuse. I don't wish him any harm. I don't hate him. I pray for him and want only the best for him. I still don't want to be around him, and that's okay.

When it's Kate's turn to talk, she says, "It's time to confront your father."

Gulp.

Bible verses about love covering a multitude of sins, turning the other cheek, and forgiving all things run through my mind.

"Forgiveness is critical," she says. "But so is accountability."

Maybe she's right. I've used Jesus's words to cover my dad's fanny for so long. I'm not sure if it was the devil or the church or my father who made me believe keeping his secret was the best choice. Maybe it was me.

I sigh.

"You need to hold him accountable," she says again.

"Dad has no idea I'm in therapy," I say, wondering how he will react.

"It will help you heal," she says.

I sit quietly for a minute or two.

"Can I write him a letter?"

"You bet you can."

A day later, I sit at my computer and stare at the blinking cursor.

"Dear Dad . . ."

My instinct is to begin slow and sweet. Sugar coat my words, cover my father's sins, protect him from my anger. But once I open my heart and start writing the truth, that desire drops dead. Angry words pour out of me, hot and sharp, like knives of hatred slicing into my father's soul. I say things like "I hate you. You've ruined me. You bastard." When I'm done writing, I want to drag the dagger free and watch him bleed!

"Dang it!" I say, tapping the delete button.

"Lord, help me speak the truth in love."

I breathe deeply and begin again.

> Dear Dad,
>
> This may be hard for you to read, for that I apologize. I am in therapy and my counselor suggested I put my thoughts in writing, so here goes.
>
> When I was a little girl, and a teenager, you did sexual things to me that were inappropriate, illegal, and inexcusable. You molested me and made me believe Mom would die if I told her. Well, Mom's in heaven, so it's time to pull the secrets out of the closet.
>
> Because of you and the abuse, I cannot live a normal life. My days are full of fear, anxiety, and anger. I have been the weird girl all my life. When you fed me drugs and alcohol, it compounded the problem. Shame on you.
>
> I know you were victimized, unloved, and abandoned as a boy, and I am sorry. You use those wounds to condone your behavior, which is not okay. I don't abuse my child, even though you abused me . . . so you have no excuse.
>
> I am in a support group at church to help me overcome what you did to me. Satan planned evil things against me, but Jesus is redeeming them all. God is the Father to me that you are not, and I love Him more than you can imagine. I have faith in

*His ability to heal me and bless me with the life He
desires.*

*Because I love the Lord so much, I forgive you—for
touching my body, making me lie to Mom, feeding me
drugs and alcohol. I forgive you for betraying me in
a way a dad never should. I release you to Jesus and
pray you allow Him to restore your spirit.*

*Remember, God works all things together for the
good of those who love Him. May you learn to love
Him with all your heart.*

Melissa

A week later, my phone rings.

D-A-D lights up the screen. I inhale deep and whisper a prayer for strength.

"Melissa?" Dad's voice is muffled.

"Yes," I say, swallowing hard.

"I got your letter."

I sit and wait for him to continue.

"I am so sorry. Thank you for forgiving me, I don't deserve it."

I wait for him to finish.

"You know, honey, after Vietnam, I started drinking and doing drugs. Those substances change a person, make them do things they wouldn't normally do."

Leaning back in my chair, I breathe in and stifle the urge to scream.

"Dad," I say, interrupting him.

"Yeah?"

I inhale deeply and blurt out the truth.

"You cannot blame your actions on narcotics and booze. Altering your mind removed your inhibitions. You enjoy exploiting little girls for sexual pleasure. You are a pedophile. Until you look that monster in the face and name it, you will never heal."

I'm not sure how those words spill from my mouth, but they

catch Dad off guard.

"You're right," he says.

Then he weeps. He cries his heart out, and I feel no sympathy, no need to remove his pain. No anger or rage or sorrow pummels my heart. All I feel is ice cold nothing. Because the monster has a name. Pedophilia. And the name is on the table.

After several minutes, I say, "Dad, I love you and I forgive you."

"Thank you," he says through sniffles.

"I want you to deal with this and heal."

"Okay, baby," he says, "I will."

♥

The shame of incest runs inky black roots into the heart of a family, leaving every person stained. Stacy is no exception. My brother knows Dad molested me, and he never chooses sides. His reluctance to confront or disown Dad is understandable. Mom raised us to love one another, to walk our talk, and I respect my brother's resolve.

My conflict is not Stacy's muted response to Dad abusing me. It's the secrecy. He refuses to tell his wife, and he doesn't want me telling her either. I never consider how his denial impacts my healing. I'm used to covering our family's shame. But my brother has a daughter. And that is a problem.

After Mom died, Dad flew back to Washington for a week and stayed in Stacy's house. I reminded Stacy to never, ever leave Roselyn alone with her papa.

"Not even while she sleeps," I told him.

When Dad left, I set aside my concern for Roselyn. Our father hates traveling and probably won't visit again. Problem solved! Until Stacy's wife wants Roselyn to see Papa in Arkansas.

"Seriously!" I say to the Lord.

"What am I supposed to do with this?" I ask Him.

Silence.

"You are going to have to protect Roselyn. Or show me what to do," I say.

I forget about Roselyn and Dad until the day I saunter out the front door to a harmony of lawn mowers and buzzing bees. Sunshine and sweet grass pull a smile to my face as I glance at my grocery list, snap open the car door, and climb inside.

"You have to tell Dawn." The Voice in my head stops me in my tracks. *Where did that come from,* I wonder. *I wasn't even thinking about Stacy.* I hear it again. "Tell Dawn."

My jaw drops. I think God is talking to me. This never happens. Not ever.

"Call Stacy," He says.

Now?

Silence.

My brother is at work, so I ignore the conviction and hope it will go away. But it pokes at me like a sliver, and I think when God grants me the luxury of hearing His voice, I should probably do what He says.

"This is going to be so hard," I say to the Lord.

After dinner, I dial Stacy.

"Hey, what's up?" he asks.

"Can you talk?"

"Sure."

"I'm sorry," I say.

Tears roll down my cheeks as I muster the courage to speak. My brother is going to hate me. Now that Mom's gone, we are precarious. What do we have to cling to? Our sickening, heartbreaking childhood? We don't have much in common, don't spend time together on the holidays. Plus, he hasn't forgiven me for slapping his cheek during a drunken stupor when I was fourteen years old. The night I tasted Jim Beam for the first time, drank until I puked, and refused to tote my brother down the same path. According to Stacy, I smacked his face a few other times, too. But I don't remember hitting him. Because I was wasted. And stupid. And I've been sorry ever since.

"Missy?" His voice cuts into my thoughts. "Sorry for what?"

I drop my head, pinch my eyes shut, and inhale.

"You have to tell Dawn."

"Tell her what?"

"That Dad molested me. She needs to know. To protect Roselyn."

Silence rolls in like a blanket of wet clouds.

"We've discussed this," he says.

"Either you tell Dawn, or I will," I say.

"Are you threatening me?"

"Yes, I am. No more lying to your wife."

"Telling Dawn should be my decision. Roselyn is my daughter, not yours."

"It is your decision. But if you don't tell her, I will. Because Roselyn is my niece, and I know our father in a way you don't. I promise you. He will hurt her. And I will sacrifice our relationship to protect your little girl."

"I can protect Roselyn," he says.

"Not if Dawn wants Roselyn to know her papa," I say.

Silence. Long, deafening silence.

"Damn," he says, breathing hard into the phone. "Damn it. I don't want to tell her. It's embarrassing."

"I understand and I'm sorry," I say.

"I would never let Dad hurt Roselyn. I'd kill him if he touched her, and he knows it." He sighs. More silence. "Okay, I'll talk to Dawn," he says.

"Promise?"

"Yes."

"I love you, Stacy."

"I love you, too," he says.

Days later, Dad calls and says, "Dawn knows."

I sit in silence a moment. *What's he talking about?* My mouth drops open. *Stacy told his wife.*

My heart pounds in my ears as I wait for Dad to speak.

"Your brother said you gave him an ultimatum," Dad says, his tone quiet.

"I did. She needed to know the truth."

"Stacy is pretty angry with you, darlin'," he says.

"I don't care how Stacy feels," I say, lying. It breaks my heart to hurt my brother, but I cannot allow my emotions to dictate my actions. What's right is right, and protecting my niece comes first. Period.

Dad waits in silence.

"God gave me instructions and I followed them," I say.

He sighs into the phone. "You've done the right thing. I'm glad your brother isn't keeping secrets from his wife."

I release stale breath from my lungs and say, "Me too, Dad."

"And guess what?" he asks with a chuckle. "Dawn doesn't hate me." Dad sniffles and blows his nose, his voice thick with tears as he says, "Stacy said she still loves me."

"Of course she loves you," I say.

"I'm not all bad, Missy," he says.

"I know you're not all bad. You've blessed me with so many good things. Wisdom and music and kindness. You are the first person to help a man down on his luck," I say.

More than once, Mom and Dad invited some random acquaintance to live in our downstairs basement while they kicked a bad habit, looked for work, or hid out from an estranged spouse.

"Remember Randy?" I ask.

"Yeah, I just talked to him a few weeks ago," he says.

"Remember how he lived downstairs for three months when I was fifteen? How he stole our car and went to jail?" I ask with a laugh.

"It took us weeks to find the Opel," he says.

"I used to write Randy letters in jail, telling him all about Jesus," I say. "And Momma and I would visit him."

Images of metal detectors and glass partitions spring to mind.

"You taught me so much about loving people, Dad. You

taught me respect, discipline, and mercy. You did good with what you had," I say.

"Thank you, Melissa. Your words mean a lot to me."

"You're welcome," I say.

"And Dawn still loves me," he says.

"We all love you, Dad." *We all love you.*

♥

I root through the white bookshelf decorating the wall of our small home office, yank a stack of books free and scatter them on the floor.

"No to King James Version," I say, putting a large, black book back on the shelf.

"Oh," I say with a coo, "I remember this." I finger the cover of an old Bible. Its white, leather face smothered in nicotine stains, black smudges, and green Crayola marker. I run my hand across its spine, let the dust of three decades layer against my skin. It's been in my possession forever, but I've paid it no mind, shuffling it from place to place. In this moment, for whatever reason, the weight of it sits heavy in my hands.

This is the Bible from my childhood.

I close my eyes and picture its insides. The dedication line reads: To Melissa, Love Mom, penned in my mother's silky script. The second line says: Missy Melissa Kay, in scratchy pencil. I chuckle, remembering Momma's cornflower blue crayon, and my compulsion to correct her by placing a *Missy* before her *Melissa* when we practiced my penmanship.

Opening my eyes, I unstick the pages of the book, peek inside to confirm my memory and smile to find it just as I pictured. Mom scrawled 1977 at the base of the page and I wrote *I love God and Jesus* just above it. I always had to have the last word, and if Momma was going to write in my Bible, then by golly, so was I.

"I was such a sassy pants," I say, squeezing my eyes shut to free the tears clouding my vision.

I read the words aloud, whispering, "I love God and Jesus."

I remember writing these words, telling the Lord inside my little-girl heart that I accepted His Son, even when I was just six years old. Momma told me then that I couldn't have God without Jesus, so I took them both at face value. Momma said Jesus died on a cross to save me and the whole world from our sins. And I took that at face value, too. Momma said He was resurrected and alive. Well, Jesus has always been alive to me, even when I couldn't see Him, didn't know Him, and didn't want Him.

And God is Jesus's Father.

"Wow," I whisper, considering the impact of those words. "Father?"

I flip through the pages yellowed by time and consider God as a Father. This Bible sat in a drawer of my room every night my earthly father put his hands on me. This Bible heard every foul utterance, every slap of the belt, every time my father filleted me with his hot temper and harsh words. Jesus's Father listened in while my father hurt me.

I shake my head and plop the book shut. Do I dare go here? To this place where I question almighty God? How is it that Jesus called Him Abba or Daddy? What did Jesus see that I cannot? I shake off this unsafe thought and put the Bible back on the shelf.

"Moving on," I say, remembering the task at hand. Glancing at the stack of books, I decide to run to the Christian bookstore. Addison needs a Bible for school, and he should have his own Good Book to refer to—just as I did.

The next morning, I pack Addison's backpack for his first day of elementary school.

"Can I bring Big Dog?" my sweet son asks, clutching his stuffed rottweiler.

I run my hand over his freshly buzzed hair and say, "Of course!"

He smiles at me with his eyes big as saucers. I kneel, pull him close, and ask, "Are you nervous?"

"Just a tiny bit," he says.

"This is the same school you went to last year. You loved kindergarten. Loved your teacher and your friends," I say, kissing his fat little cheek.

He wipes it off with his palm and says, "Quit kissing my face, Mom."

I chuckle, back out of his space, and hand him the backpack. "Ready?"

He nods, takes my hand, and leads me out to the car.

After a short drive, I walk Addison beyond the double doors of New Tides Christian, say hello to his teacher, smile at the other mothers, and resist the urge to smooch all over his face before I leave. Back outside, I sit in my car for several minutes, staring at the cross above the bell tower. New Tides is attached to our church, so I feel no fear in leaving my son here. What I can't get over is the fact that he gets to attend a private Christian school. He's never been in daycare, never been a day without me. And now he's here, with amazing staff, good friends, and Jesus.

"We are so blessed," I whisper, "So, very blessed."

When I pick my son up after school, he tells me all about his new buddies. I am so happy he has friends because I have none. Zero. Not one. I dumped any semblance of authentic friendship when I cannon-balled into the deep end of my husband nine years ago. I had a friend in college, but she moved. I had work friends when I cleaned teeth, but they disappeared after Addison was born. And honestly, I'm not a people person. I'm an introvert. I struggle to make friends with other women. Because I'm deep. And most of the girls I know are shallow. But now I'm lonely. So I do the only thing I can. I pray and ask God to send me a friend. A true friend.

The next day, the very next day, a mom stops me in the hallway at school, and asks, "Melissa, would you be interested in praying?"

I stare at the tall brunette. Her name is Marilyn. Her daughter is in Addison's class. I've chatted with Marilyn in the lunchroom, sat with her during field trips. But I've never had a coffee date, or an extended conversation with her.

"Pray?" She asks again. "Do you want to meet to pray? For the school?"

I try not to gush, because I know this is Jesus working.

"Yes," I say, "I'd love that."

I want to cry, jump up and down, and squeal in delight. But I refrain. I don't want to freak her out.

"Awesome," she says. "I'm forming a group."

A group sounds intimidating, and the thought of praying with a bunch of women makes me sweat, but more than one friend might be nice. And again, this is the Lord's invitation.

"Let's meet Tuesday mornings," she says.

"Perfect," I say.

When Tuesday arrives, I am nervous to pray out loud but exhilarated at the thought of spending time with other women. I still want to gush, cry, and tell Marilyn thank you. My spirit needs girls who love Jesus like I do.

Seven of us meet in the church sanctuary. I don't want to overwhelm anyone with my enthusiasm, so I sit quietly and study the mothers around me. Each seems kind, genuine, and concerned for the well-being of our kiddos and the school. Best of all, they all love Jesus. And since He is the anchor in our group, I don't give my past a second thought outside of His redemption.

Marilyn prays first, bowing her head and talking to God like an old friend. I hang onto her every word. She prays for teachers, students, office staff, and the school administration. Sarah does the same, only she calls God, Father God. Her candid conversation with Him as Father strikes me. Is she talking to God the same way Jesus does? I think back to my little-girl Bible, the one I had held in my palms just days before. And I wonder, *Could I ever call God Father? Could I ever call Him Daddy?* I shudder at the thought. So I call Him Lord Jesus, and I think He's okay with my reference.

We meet every week. At first, we focus our prayer on the

school. But after some time together, we pray for each other, too. It's not long before I tell them my story. I'm not thrilled to share the dirty parts of my life, but I want them to know Jesus is good, especially when life hurts. I want them to know He's near to the brokenhearted, He's faithful to help us out of the pit, and He gives us beauty for ashes. I want them to know Jesus the way I know Him.

I think my story helps in short order, because in the weeks that follow, the economy takes a major dump. The Great Recession, they call it. It's a scary time. Life changes for every one of us. Businesses fail, homes are lost, and marriages struggle. I'm glad I've gone ahead of my friends in trusting Jesus for healing, provision, and protection. My hard journey provides wisdom and hope to those seeking God in dark times.

And while I share my authentic self with them, my friends teach me about the God they know. They talk about praying over decisions, hearing God's confirmation. They seek His guidance and counsel in marriage, business, child rearing. Even finances. And they yield to Him. They teach me to pray about every decision I make. They also introduce me to a God who's loving and kind. In my mind, Jesus has always been the picture of mercy. But God has not.

Once again, I face the confusion of God being good. Of God being my Father. My Daddy. When I pray about it in my quiet time and tell the Lord I'm confused, he sends Marilyn to the rescue. Again.

"Have you ever done a Bible study?" she asks one day after prayer time.

"Nope," I say.

"Not one?"

"Well," I say with a sigh, "I did attend a women's study once. I got all the answers wrong. So I quit."

Marilyn laughs and says, "We can do a Beth Moore study. She's easy to follow."

We start with *Believing God*. It makes me grin to think of Jesus serving me this dish first. Because if I'm not believing

God, what's the point? We watch a lesson on the web, do a little homework every day, and meet over coffee to discuss. God gives me a nibble of Himself through this study, and He is so delicious, I can hardly wait to learn more. So when another friend from prayer group hosts a weekly study at the school, I jump at the chance to participate.

We follow Beth Moore through a bundle of lessons. God blows my mind in the book of Daniel, when He dances with Shadrach, Meshach, and Abednego in the fiery furnace. The three men walk out of the blaze without a singed hair or the smell of smoke on their bodies. God takes my breath away when He saves the Jewish nation through Esther. I find relief in His forgiving David after the king's atrocity with Bathsheba. I open my heart to the God of love in the book of John and then discover the fruit of obedience in James. God gives good things to His children, not just pain and suffering. And Jesus is the firstborn of all God's kids.

Including me.

Praying with the girls and learning about God the Father opens a bright, new, fascinating world for me to discover. I feel like Indiana Jones or a prospector searching for gold as my hunt for Jesus shifts from gentle seeking to hot pursuit. The rainbow tells me God remembers His promises, so those are what I cling to as I search for evidence of Him working in my daily life. I want so much to just trust Him. I long to hand my life over to Him and just let go. Instead, I tote around a thousand questions.

Will He break the generational curses and deliver me from the mental illness haunting my dad? Despite therapy, I still struggle with depression, anxiety, and posttraumatic stress. Will He break those chains? Will He protect Addison from the evil haunting my past? Or will my son end up like my dad, drug addicted and mentally ill? Will my life be abundant as Jesus promises? And what does that even look like? Lots of money, prosperity, success, and good health? Or is it something more?

I yearn to see the goodness of God in the land of the living. I want to see Him alive and active all around me. Will He show me the mystery of who He is? Will He reveal how wide and high and long and deep His love is?

I don't know. But I'm about to taste and see.

16

Haunted By A Holy Ghost

There is no bus to Addison's private school, so I drop him off and pick him up every day. He meets me outside the door of his second-grade class, grabs my hand, and drags me toward the car, eager to gulp down a snack and jump on the trampoline in our backyard.

One day, he asks, "Mom? Can I take guitar lessons?"

"Where did that come from?" I ask, walking him across the parking lot.

"I want to play guitar," he says.

"Are you old enough to play?" I tease. "A guitar is a large instrument."

"They make guitars for kids, too, Mom."

I laugh and say, "Buckle up child. We'll look into it when we get home."

I schedule lessons at a local music shop. Darin volunteers to take Addison to his first one.

"Don't buy him a guitar," I say. I know my husband's generous heart. If our son wants to invest in something, Darin is all in.

"Yep," Darin says.

"I mean it," I say. "Rent one first, please."

"Yep," he says, again.

When they get home, Addison marches in sporting a brand new, child-sized, acoustic.

"Listen, Mom," he says as I glare at Darin.

Addison props his foot on a kitchen chair, rests the guitar on his knee and picks out "Skip to My Lou" in perfect rhythm.

My jaw drops.

"Do that again," I say.

He giggles, places his fingers over the fret board, and plays the song again.

"I can't believe you play so easily," I say.

"Isn't that wild?" Darin asks.

"I learned this one, too," Addison says, strumming out "Mary Had a Little Lamb."

"Dude, you are so good!" I say with a laugh.

"Well, I did play drums in high school," Darin says with a wink.

I roll my eyes and say, "Sorry, honey, this talent didn't come from you."

"What do you mean?" Darin asks. But he knows the answer.

My father is a self-taught guitar prodigy. He didn't start playing until I was four, never read sheet music, but by the time I turned five, he could play Cat Stevens, Neil Young, Dan Fogelberg, and Fleetwood Mac by ear. He could also sing along in perfect pitch. That's why we joined the hippies in North Carolina. So my dad could focus on music.

"You know, Addison, my dad plays guitar," I say.

"He does?!" My son lets out a whoop. "Is he good?'

"He made a vinyl record when I was a little girl," I say. "It was a forty-five, with one song on the front and another on the back."

"Wow!" Addison says, thumping out "Skip to My Lou" again. "I can't believe your dad made a record."

"He sang, too," I say. "They even played his song on the radio."

"Sunny skies every morning," I sing out.

"Mom! Stop! You sing terrible," Addison says, palming his ears.

I laugh and keep singing while he grimaces.

"Seriously," he says. "Maybe someday me and your dad can play guitars together."

"Maybe," I say.

My heart hurts because I know this will never happen. I don't allow my son near my father. And Addison doesn't call him Grandpa. Because when my boy learns the truth, I don't want his identity tied to those bitter roots. I want God to fill in the blank spaces my father left behind. I want the Lord to be Addison's Papa. The thought makes me smile as I watch my boy strum his guitar. I know God is already giving Addison a legacy my earthly dad cannot. The Lord is giving Addison the beautiful, undefiled parts of Dad. The parts my father was meant to have before the world destroyed him.

God confirms this a few months later, when I sit with my eyes closed and listen to Addison play "Dust in the Wind." As my son's little fingers pick out the tune, hitting each string in perfect time, I remember Dad playing the same melody when I was a girl, remember him charming my mother with those sweet lyrics. Oh, how she loved it, how we all loved it when Dad sang us a song. That was the best part of him.

♥

The fruit of the Spirit is love, joy, peace, patience, kindness, goodness, faithfulness, gentleness, and self-control. This is how I test for God's presence. My measure for all things good. Along with courage, forgiveness, a humble heart, kind speech. The list is long, but it comes from the Bible, and it's the scale I use to measure any miniscule change I sniff out of my father. My earthly father.

After Mom died, and all those months of therapy, I kept the door of communication open with my dad. Don't ask me why. Maybe it's God. Or my sick sense of responsibility. Either way, dealing with Dad is tough. Most of the time, I regret answering the phone when he calls. He's never sober. Alcohol is his go-to, but the VA also gives him opiates. And he eats them like candy. When he's tanked, he has no filter on his mouth. He speaks hateful words about random strangers, neighbors, and family members. He talks about the past and missing Momma. He tells me about his physical woes, the majority brought on by his own poor choices. And at his lowest, he brings up molesting me and apologizes, or even better, he talks about how special we are.

"Because of Jesus," he says.

I find this revolting because the consequences of his actions still linger in my spirit. Maybe he means we are different because I've forgiven him, and so has God. But I can't be sure, so I recoil when he says we are special.

Sometimes Dad calls late at night, saying he can't sleep. These calls rattle me because he used the same excuse to molest me. When I'd try to shoo him out of my room, he'd whisper, "I can't sleep." I know he's not calling to molest me, but his voice whispering in my ear after dark triggers me. I want to hang up the phone and run. Sometimes I do. But other times, when I'm strong in the Lord, I ask him, "Dad, can I pray for you?" Because there is no better way to fight the devil.

Dad always says yes when I offer to pray.

I bow my head, close my eyes, and say, "Jesus, thank You for my dad. Thank You for hearing our prayers and loving us. Lord, Dad is afraid. There are dark memories that haunt him in the night, and he needs You to fight for him. Please drive out the enemy, remove the shadows, and show him Your light. Father God, lay Your healing hand upon Dad, release his mind from darkness and remind him who You are, the King of kings and Lord of lords. The humble and mighty Shepherd, who leaves the ninety-nine to find one lost sheep. Dad is the wandering lamb, Father. Find him tonight. Restore him so he can sleep. Lull him into peaceful rest. Fight for Your child, Lord. Fight for him."

"Amen," I say.

"Thank you, honey. I love you."

"I love you, too, Dad."

"I feel better already."

"Good night, Dad," I say.

God never fails to answer our prayers, but I often wonder why He won't just heal Dad. Why does Dad struggle when he says he loves God? I can't say for sure, but I think this mental struggle is like Paul's thorn in the flesh. A messenger from Satan to keep my dad humble and God's grace big. Also, child abuse is not okay with God. I know the Lord forgives, but He doesn't just let people off the hook for their actions. This torment may be my dad pickling in a pathetic jar of his own making. And God may just leave him there until he dies.

♥

When I pray for Dad, God answers my prayers in the moment, then He seems to drift away until I call on Him again. But when I pray for Addison, it's a different story.

One night, as I tuck my son into bed, he asks, "Mom, does your group pray for me?"

"We do."

"Can I tell you a secret?"

"Sure," I say, studying his smooth, round face.

"When we go to the mall, and I see creepy people, I also see a guy. He's just standing there. When I look away and look back, he's gone," Addison says.

Goosebumps cover my arms as I ask, "What does this guy look like?"

"He wears a black t-shirt, with blue jeans, and white tennis shoes."

"Does he have a face?" I ask.

"Yes, and blond hair," he says, fingering his blue blankie.

"Have you seen the guy anywhere else?"

"Yeah. Lots of times on the playground at school," he says.

Electricity shimmies up my spine. I pray for angels on the playground every day when I drop Addison off. The school yard butts up against an overgrown field. The kids are separated from the tall grass by a waist-high fence. Every time I drive by, I think of how easy it would be for someone to pick a kid up and carry him or her away. So I pray.

"I saw the guy on the freeway," he says.

"Where? In a car?" I ask.

"No. Sitting on the guardrail. Remember those kids with ski masks?"

I nod. We were driving home from Portland when a couple of teenage boys harassed us on the highway. When we took the exit and stopped beside them, their faces were covered.

"The guy was there, too?" I ask. Addison nods. "Just sitting on the guardrail?"

He nods again. "I see him in the grocery store," he says. "Like, when you send me down random aisles to get stuff."

"Really?" I ask.

"Remember that day I saw the creepy guy? The blond guy was there, too."

"Does the blond guy talk to you?" I ask.

"No, but I hear a voice in my head telling me not to go a certain way. Like at the grocery store."

"And you listen to the voice?"

"Yeah, I went a different direction," he says.

I study him to see if he's lying, but his story-telling face never appears.

"There is another guy, too. But he's skinny with curly, black hair. The blond guy is buff, like Dad," he says.

I nod and say, "That's interesting."

"And I see them when I'm walking in the woods behind Carter's house."

"Well, I pray for angels to guard you. Even on the playground," I say.

"I've seen lots of them on the playground, Mom, all different ones."

I stare at him and wonder what to believe.

"I feel weird seeing things other people don't see," he says.

Now I know it's true. My son sees angels.

"Addison," I say, "you aren't weird. It's a privilege when the Lord allows us to see things other people can't."

He nods, rolls his face into the pillow, and closes his eyes.

"I love you," I say in a whisper. "But Jesus loves you more. Don't ever forget that."

♥

When Addison starts middle school, the sweet boy who picked me flowers and held my hand disappears. In his place stands a kid with braces, big feet, a set of horns (just kidding), and a monstrous attitude. Gone are the days of walking him to class, getting a squeeze, and a "love you, Mom." Now I drop him at the curb, say, "I love you," and get a car door slammed in my face. As pimples spring to life, along with second glances at girls, and a continual trying of my patience, memories of my own junior high years emerge, taunting me with the possibilities awaiting my son. Drugs, alcohol, smoking, lying, stealing, cheating. Sex.

This is where God and I test each other. He tests my faith, and I test His faithfulness. I'm still waiting to see if the Lord will protect my son. In the meantime, I fight for Addison the best I can, even when he hates it. I argue with my child over what's right, teaching him God's word by telling him *no, no,* and more *no.*

It's amazing how much darkness seeps into our home through Hollywood and video games. There is a constant barrage of conflict between me and Addison over what he can watch and what games he can play. We also fight over what he can do versus what his friends do. His friends' parents are far more lenient than I am.

One night, with his buddy Tyler at his side, he asks, "Mom can we watch *The Exorcist*?"

"No."

"Why not?!"

"Because we don't allow dark things into our home."

"It's just a movie."

"It's a movie about demonic possession. It's like practicing sorcery or playing on a Ouija board," I say. "God hates it when we practice divination. So, that's a big fat *no*."

He sighs.

"The devil is not your friend, Addison."

"You don't let me do anything fun! Tyler's mom lets us watch *Goosebumps*."

This is where I feel the pinch—when Tyler is watching me. His mom is cool, and I'm rigid, overprotective, and starkly Christian (possibly even prudish). But I know the devil is real. I've seen him pop out of my father, turn his irises midnight black when Dad fell into a rage over nothing. I've felt the devil touch my flesh, violate my body, and pillage my mind. So I choose to fight, even when it means people think I'm prudish, boring, or downright crazy.

"Well, I'm not Tyler's mom. I'm yours," I say.

He responds with an exasperated sigh, an eye roll, and stomping feet.

I shake my head and let him sulk it off.

Addison's friends also play gory video games. Too many days to count, Addison asks, "Mom, can I play Grand Theft Auto?"

"No."

"But all my friends play it."

"Well, I'm not their mother. I'm your mother, and I said no."

"Why can't I just play the game?"

"Because you are not seventeen, and it contains adult subject matter."

"It's not bad, just stealing cars and shooting guns. It's not like I'm going to shoot people for real, Mom."

"There is also prostitution and rape," I say.

"I won't play that part," he says.

"No," I say. "End of conversation."

Another exasperated sigh, eye roll, and stomping feet.

These conversations pop up like thunderheads on a sunny day, unexpected and fierce. My son wants his freedom. I understand that. Part of me can't wait to cut the leash and let him run into whatever trouble finds him. Because he exhausts me.

Rather, the devil exhausts me. Always lurking in the shadows, reminding me of where I've been. Those demons of fear and control reappear; the same ones who told me to keep the secret of sexual abuse tucked in darkness, away from my mother, lest she fall ill and die. They sniff at Addison's heels and whisper lies about their plans for my child. They tell me God won't protect my son, just like He didn't protect me. Or my precious momma.

But I know the devil's a liar.

So I do what I can. I pray. Not the standard "bow your head and fold your hands" prayers. No. These are warrior prayers. Secret prayers. Written prayers. I've had enough of Satan taunting me with "what ifs." So one afternoon, I sneak into Addison's room, lift a poster off the wall, and pen this in black Sharpie:

> Lord, I pray that you would fill Addison's heart and mind with your Holy Spirit. May his life be filled with love, joy, peace, patience, kindness, goodness, gentleness, faithfulness, and self-control. Inspire Addison to live for YOU. May your purpose and will be known to him. In Christ.

I pin the poster back up, move to the next one, and write:

> A child of God lives in this room. I bind all powers of darkness and loosen the Holy Spirit's power upon Addison. In Jesus's name. Matthew 16:19

I pull a third poster down and write:

> God—make Addison a man after your own heart.

I write prayers under his desk and under the frame of his waterbed. Not out of superstition, or the expectation that God will obey me. I write them out of the passionate love I feel for God the Father and my child. I want them to know each other, love each other. I want God to be the Master of Addison's heart, not this world, or the enemy. So I call out to God. I'm His child, so I can run boldly into His throne room and make all kinds of demands. And to be honest, I think this makes Him smile.

♥

Dad moves from drinking beer and popping pills to guzzling down hard alcohol. He stayed away from whiskey, vodka, and the like when we were kids because it made him angry. He didn't want to end up a violent drunk, like his father, so beer was his go-to. Not now. Now he keeps gallon jugs stashed around his house.

As he sucks down the booze, his liver hardens. He ends up with hepatitis C and cirrhosis. His tummy swells, inflating like an exercise ball as the fluid builds up. Ascites, doctors call it. A painful condition that lands him in the emergency room to "get the fluid drawn off," he says. Doctors use a long needle, pop it through Dad's taut skin, and pull out four liters of liquid. That's two soda bottles. Like the Pepsi and 7-Up in my fridge. Yuck.

These fluid draws become old hat as Dad dumps hard liquor into his body, hoping his fibrotic, dead liver will do its thing and keep up. He's got to party, after all. It's what he does. Months pass and I don't hear from him. That's not uncommon, and I'm okay with it. One day, out of the blue, he calls up and says, "I spent a month in intensive care."

"What?" I ask. "Where?"

"Pine Bluff. My kidneys failed. They hooked me up to a blood cleaning machine."

"Dialysis?"

"Yeah, that's it," he says.

"You could have died," I say.

"They thought I was going to die," he says. I hear him pull a drag off his smoke.

"Dad," I say, "why didn't anyone call me?"

"Nothing you could do about it," he says.

"Yeah, but I'm your daughter."

"I didn't want you to worry."

"That's not up to you," I say. "Worry is my choice."

"Okay, we'll call you next time," he says.

Next time? There's going to be a next time?

Great.

17

Bruised Fruit

By the time Addison starts high school, my heart is raw from three years of his rejection. On the first day of his freshman year, I stop at the curb, look him in the eye, and say, "Son, you are a man now. Mind your own business, keep your nose clean, and be the person God created you to be. Don't follow the crowd, and don't bring home a bunch of drama. You leave all that bull crap in middle school, understand?"

He nods, gets out of the car, and says, "Love you, Mom."

"Wow," I say, "you love me again?"

He rolls his eyes and laughs before closing the car door. Middle school was rough, but Addison came through it refined like gold. He spends his time with a few trustworthy friends, plays the drums in the school band, plays guitar at home, and spends time chatting with me about life. His grades are trash, but God didn't create everyone to fit in the same box.

My son struggles to keep his mind focused on the subject at hand. Maybe he has an attention disorder? I don't know. I never asked a doctor. Instead, I say to Addison, "You are a creative person, not an academic. You play the drums, guitar, you draw and paint, you work on cars and trucks. You are amazing. You be who God made you to be."

And he cracks me up, because when I boss him, he says, "Mom, you be who God created you to be, and let me do the same. You have to trust me."

That's a tough one. But this is a time of letting go and encouraging Addison to fly on his own. So when he walks onto our patio to find me basking in the autumn sun and asks,

"Mom, can I play Grand Theft Auto?" for the umpteenth time, I say yes.

His brows shoot up.

"Really?"

"Yes, but first, let's chat," I say, gesturing for him to sit.

He plops down across from me and sits sideways on the hammock, with his long slender feet pushing him back and forth. I sigh and shake my head. Because I don't want to tell him, don't want to say any of this. Much like I didn't want to have the sex talk with him when he was twelve. But I knew Darin wouldn't, so I did. Complete with anatomy book.

I study his brown eyes and wonder how much to divulge.

"You understand what rape is?"

"Yes," he says, rocking the hammock a little faster.

"And prostitution?"

He nods.

"I'm fine with you playing the game. You are fifteen and I trust you. But I want you to know a thing or two before you open the screen and start blasting away."

He nods again.

"I don't like that game because prostitutes don't choose their line of work, it's chosen for them. And women don't ask to be raped, they are violated against their will."

He furrows his brows, crosses his arms, and keeps rocking.

"*I* was violated against *my* will," I say, holding my breath. "When I was a kid, I was molested. By a man. For a long time."

He stops rocking.

"You don't need the details, but it led me to all the wild, untoward escapades I told you about. Remember how we talked about alcohol poisoning? How I drank too much whiskey and my friends dumped me in a park?"

He nods.

"And you remember the talks we've had about the drugs and alcohol in my home? My dad's addictions?"

He nods again.

"Well, that environment made me vulnerable to abuse. And

many girls are abused in the same way. Only they don't have good mothers or Jesus. They end up on the street, owned by some pimp who feeds them drugs and sells them for sex. Those girls aren't free. They don't enjoy what they do. You remember that when you play your game."

As I say the words, I can't help but reflect on Satan's plan for my life. I could very well be trading my body for heroin or meth. Or I could be married to a guy who beats me, smokes crack, or even drinks too much. But I'm not. By God's grace, I'm not.

My son unfolds his arms, looks at me, and says, "Okay, Mom. Thanks for trusting me. And for telling me about—your stuff."

♥

While God shows up in my son, growing his heart, growing his mind, his wisdom and discernment, I wonder what He's doing with my earthly father. Dad keeps drinking. Keeps playing his guitar and popping pills and living large at the expense of his liver. And his people.

One night, I stand at the stove, browning hamburger, when my phone lights up with D-A-D.

"Crap."

I sigh and consider letting it go to voicemail. I've avoided his calls the last few weeks. My father's still a mess, calling when he's drunk. And the liver issues compound the problem, making his moods dark and ominous one minute, light and airy the next. I never know if it's Jekyll or Hyde calling.

Something deep inside tells me I should ignore this call, let it go to voicemail like all the others.

"If that's your dad, you better take it," Darin says, cutting into my thoughts.

I stare at my husband and wonder if he's right.

Darin grabs the spatula from my hands and says, "Go ahead, I've got this."

I glare at Darin, open the phone, and say, "Hey, Dad, what's up?"

"I need blarbleryou," he says, his tongue thick and slurry.

"What? I can't understand you."

In a flash, his tone turns crisp and clear.

"I put a loaded revolver in my mouth. I thought about pulling the trigger," he says.

"What?"

He raises his voice, as though yelling will help me understand his madness. "I said! I wanted to blow my brains out. But I didn't!"

My heart thuds one, two, three beats.

"I can't do this," I say in a whisper, sliding down to sit on the hardwood floor.

He slurs in my ear again.

"I cannot do this," I say again, louder this time.

"Honey, I'm sorry," he says in blurry words, "I miss your momma so much."

Tears run down my cheeks as Dad rambles on about Momma, Vietnam, his loneliness, and isolation. I love my dad, I do. I'm sorry for all the pain and loss he's had in his life. And I pray for him all the time. But I can't take another word out of his mouth.

"Dad, I need to hang up. Darin and Addison are sitting down to eat," I lie.

"I'm sorry, baby," he says, his mood shifting again.

"Yeah—," I say, pulling myself to stand.

"I didn't mean to interrupt your dinner. Forgive me."

I ignore his apology and say, "Hey, Dad. If you feel like dying, call 9-1-1."

"Okay, darlin', I will."

"Don't call me. You dial 9-1-1," I say.

"I will," he says.

"Promise?"

"I promise."

I click the phone off, slam it on the counter, and look at my husband, saying, "Do not tell me to take his calls anymore, understand?!"

Darin shakes his head and says, "I'm sorry, honey."

"You don't know him! You have no idea what those phone calls do to me!"

Tears stream down my cheeks as my husband pulls me into his arms.

"I just don't want you to have regrets," he says.

I wriggle out of his grip, wipe my face, and say, "If he dies tomorrow, I have no regrets."

Then I pull out my laptop, click open the screen and write:

> *Dear Dad,*
>
> *I cannot take your calls anymore if you are calling to tell me you are going to kill yourself. This is a form of emotional manipulation, and I cannot handle it. It is not my place to save you from your choices. I have a family to care for and my emotional health matters, too.*
>
> *If you feel you are going to harm yourself, please call 911. If you need a shoulder to cry on or an ear to listen, please call Stacy. I cannot be available for you when you are emotionally unwell. You need to seek help for the issues you are dealing with.*
>
> *Please do not call me for a time. I would like to think we can have a healthy relationship in the future. I love you and continue to pray for you. I need you to respect these boundaries. If you cannot, I will have Darin or Stacy contact you.*
>
> *Melissa*

I hit print, fold the letter, stuff it in an envelope, and seal it up. I'm done. Because my dad could choose his family over alcohol. But he never has, and we pay the price. Well, now I can choose. And I choose sanity over madness.

The next morning, I drive to the post office, toss the letter into the jaws of a big blue mailbox, and slam it shut. Then I open Dad's contact information on my phone and hit *block*.

♥

For a full year, Stacy absorbs Dad's verbal abuse, his anger, his midnight phone calls, and his madness. My brother does an amazing job of stepping up to shield me, even though it's not his place. The time away from Dad gives my heart and mind a chance to heal, so when Stacy calls to tell me Dad is back in the hospital, I have the energy to care.

"Doctors are resecting part of his large intestine," Stacy says.

"Why?" I ask.

"He's got an infection that won't heal."

I take a bite of my Popsicle and sink into the whiskey barrel rocker on our back patio.

"There is a 40 percent chance Dad will die," he says.

"I should probably unblock him," I say, swaying back and forth.

"That might be a good idea," Stacy says.

"Should we fly to Arkansas?" I ask.

"I am taking Roselyn if you want to come along. She wants to hug her papa, just in case," he says. Roselyn knows our father only by phone, but she's convinced he's amazing, and she loves him beyond measure. Stacy doesn't want to burst her bubble, so he keeps quiet and lets his daughter love her papa from a distance.

On a balmy August morning, the three of us hop a plane at the Portland International Airport, layover in sultry Dallas, then fly to Little Rock. Dad is housed at the VA hospital, just miles from our downtown hotel. We check into our room late in the day, grab a snack, and drive to the hospital. When we arrive, Aunt Shellie is there to greet us and walk us to Dad's room. Roselyn is the first one in his arms, with Stacy and me following close behind her.

"Surgery went well," Shellie says with a smile.

I survey my father's condition. His olive skin bleached

cotton white, face baggy and tired, mind foggy. My father is dying. Not today. And not with this surgery. But the devil of alcohol will devour him, and it won't be long before the bell tolls, and the consequences of his choices come to fruition. The three of us take turns resting in the chair beside his bed, holding his hand and working to understand his incoherent speech. Dad sleeps most of the time, which is great because Stacy and I can't tolerate staying too long. Something about the smell of ammonia and sickness triggers thoughts of Mom, making us dash out the door the second Dad zips his eyes shut.

Back at the hotel, Roselyn burns off her energy in the pool. For dinner, we walk across the street for a burger. Stacy and I can't be frank in front of Roselyn, so we speak in code, with him saying, "You know, I was mad at you for a long time after you made me tell Dawn."

"I know," I say. "And I understand."

"I'm not mad at you anymore," he says, taking a long sip off his beer.

"I'm glad," I say.

Roselyn glances between us. "What are you two talking about?"

"It's personal," Stacy says, winking at me.

"I'm happy it's out in the open," he says, stabbing a giant dill pickle with his fork.

"Me, too," I say.

"I've forgiven him, you know. I couldn't be here if I still hated him," Stacy says.

Roselyn furrows her brows and asks, "Forgiven Papa? For what?"

I look at her and say, "Your Papa was not a good father to your daddy and me. In fact, he was abusive."

"Yeah, Dad says Papa used to hit him," she says, stuffing a fry in her mouth.

"There is more than that, Roz," I say. "But you don't need to worry about the past. You are free to love him as the Papa you know."

She smiles at me and says, "Thank you."

Stacy glances between me and his daughter. "You're different," he says, resting his gaze on me.

"What do you mean?"

"You're nice to be around," he says.

My laughter echoes off the rafters, making Roselyn and other patrons stare as I snort and giggle. I jest, but I know he's right. I am not the twenty-something abusing him with biting words or the teenager slapping him during a drunken binge or the child welting his flesh with the palm of my hand. In this vulnerable place with him and Dad, I am peaceful and quiet. And I know it's Jesus. Plus I want a friendship with my brother. A new friendship. When Dad dies, it'll be just the two of us.

"I'm serious," he says. "When we get home, I want to spend more time with you."

"I would love that," I say.

"Your birthday is coming up," he says.

"I know! I'm pushing fifty! Holy cow I'm gettin' old."

"I'd like to buy you a tattoo for your special day."

"O, la-la," I say with a grin. "A tattoo is on my bucket list."

"Decide what you want, and I'll get one to match," he says.

"What if I want unicorns and rainbows?" I ask.

"Then . . . I'll get something else," he says.

I giggle, wink at him, and shove a fry in my mouth.

♥

Darin and I step outside to watch a fierce November windstorm bend and bow the trees dotting our property. A rainbow of earthen color flutters through the air with each mighty gust. Maple's shed their red and orange leaves, white barked birches scatter their yellow and green foliage over our grass, and fir trees dump needles and pinecones all over our manicured bark dust. The wintery sky roils in silvery blues and grays as an atmospheric river prepares to dump torrential rain onto Washington's parched ground. The Pacific Northwest has been suffering from unprecedented heat, drought, and fires, so this storm is a welcome sight.

My husband wraps me in his arms, pulling my back into his chest, as I turn my face into the wind. The warmth of his body is a welcome contrast to the breeze on my skin. I close my eyes and whisper a prayer of thanks to the God who brings the rain. Thinking of Jesus makes me smile, and for just a heartbeat, all feels right with the world. Moments like these are rare, but when they come, I remember the word penned across my arm.

"Do you like it?" I ask Darin, glancing down at the sparrow inked on my skin.

"I love a good windstorm," he says, nestling his face against my neck.

"No, silly. My tattoo."

He looks up and shakes his head.

"It's your arm," he says.

"So you don't like it?"

"I like you," he says, pulling my palm up to kiss it.

We watch the wind whip our hummingbird feeders sideways, yank petunias from the ceramic pots decorating our patio, and set our whiskey barrel chairs to rockin' like they're haunted by a couple of ghosts.

"We should probably pull our furniture under the awning," Darin says as my phone rings.

"Crap," I say, wriggling out of my husband's grip.

"Your dad?"

I nod at Darin and meander out to the field behind our house.

"Hello," I say, leaning against our white, three-rail fence.

"How are you, honey?" he asks through slurry speech.

"Fine, how are you?"

"I'm good," he says, then proceeds to ramble on about his health woes and family skirmishes. I listen quietly and watch the clouds roll over head as he jabbers on. When he turns the subject to things in our past, I grip the fence, hold my breath, and pray for patience.

"You are a good girl," he says with garbled speech.

"Thanks, Dad," I say, fighting the desire to hang up the phone.

"I am not a good person. I am a perpetrator."

I let out a sigh and listen in silence.

"Darlin', I want you to know, I'm doing my best to own what I did to you."

"What do you mean?"

"I've told a few people."

Wait . . . What?!

"Let's see . . .," I picture him squinting his eyes and counting on his fingers as he says, "My best friend, my hunting buddy, your Aunt Shellie, and my pastor."

"I'm sorry, Dad," I say, pinching my eyes shut so I can hear him better. I simply cannot believe his words. "Can you repeat what you just said?"

"You heard me, girl! I confessed! People need to know what I did to you."

"Are you telling me that you've told other people you sexually abused me?"

"Yes!"

I sit in silence and let the weight of his words melt into my soul.

"Dad," I say, "that is a really big deal."

"Well, I need to own what I did to you," he says.

"I'm proud of you," I say.

"Now it's your turn," he says.

"What do you mean?"

"You need to tell people about Jesus, and how He saved you—and me."

We sit in silence for several breaths as I gather the courage to say, "Dad, I *have* told people. I've shared my story with friends at Bible study."

"Good," he says. "Share some more! Other women need to know about the healing and freedom you've found in Jesus."

Wow!

I hesitate for a heartbeat, then say, "I was thinking of writing a book—about you, me, and Jesus."

"Yes! Write the book! Write your story, Melissa! Do it!" he says with glee.

Seriously?!

After we hang up, I stand frozen in place, slack-jawed, staring at the phone in my hand.

Did I hear him correctly? My dad told people what he did to me? And he wants me to tell other people our story? What part should I tell them? Do I tell them how confused I am that my father is on cloud nine with Jesus one minute, then scrounging in the sewer the next? Should I tell them how I still question God's goodness, even after all this redemption?

I don't know what I'd say. Authoring a book about God and abuse sounded like a great idea until I said it aloud. To my father. And he gave me permission to write it!

I pull my beanie snug around my ears and jog back toward the house as giant raindrops begin to freckle the ground around me. As I close the door against the wind and sit down at the kitchen table, I shake my head at the thought of sharing my story. I can't imagine sitting at dinner with friends and saying, "So yeah, my dad molested me, the devil tried to drown me in his punch bowl, and now here I am. Because of Jesus!" Or does God expect me to stop a stranger at the grocery store and ask, "Mind if I traumatize you with my story of abuse?"

No.

The Lord whispers in my heart . . . *Write the book.*

I stand up, push in my chair, and get busy helping Darin cook dinner. *No way. There is no way I have the strength, stamina, or will-power to write about the abuse. I don't even have the writing skills to pull off such a feat.*

When I think about it in my rational mind, I'm sure God is wrong, or I'm hearing Him wrong. I'm not the person to be telling others about Jesus. *Dude, I just flipped a guy off on the highway yesterday and will drop the F word in a heartbeat when someone frightens me or ticks me off.* God must be mistaken in choosing me to do anything Christian. Even Bible study is a stretch for this jacked-up girl.

Time passes by and I let the crazy notion of sharing my testimony roll to the back of my mind. I stay busy chasing benign activities, like keeping house, working with Darin at his business, being a mom, and studying the Bible. But Jesus won't let it go. And I know it's Him, because whenever He talks to me, He creates a theme, a rhythm, a repetitive one-sided conversation in my life. And He sends me a million messages.

My daily devotion says, *Share your story.* I read an article in a Christian magazine, and it says, *Your testimony matters.* My Bible study says, *You cannot amputate your past from your future.* An inspirational email says, *Use the pain in your life to serve others.* A podcast says, *Comfort others with the comfort God gives you.* And all I can think is *For crying in the night! Is God trying to send me a message or what?!*

I am not seeking out these phrases or these words. They just keep popping up all around me. When our pastor gives a Sunday morning sermon titled "Sharing Your Testimony," I roll my eyes toward heaven and say, "You have got to be kidding." Pastor reads from Revelation 12:11, saying, "Children in Christ conquer the devil, our accuser, *'by the blood of the Lamb'*"—Jesus's sacrifice. He is the blood of the Lamb. I have Jesus. Check. — "*'and by the word of their testimony.'*"

Seriously?! I shrug my shoulders and doodle on the church bulletin. *No. I'm not doing it, Lord.* I sigh deep, roll my eyes at God once more. *Who cares anyway, and what do I tell them?* I survey the people lining the pews. Mothers, fathers, grandmas, teenagers. *These people don't want to hear my story, Lord.*

But God's prompting is like a sliver in my heart. The peaceful mood I carried into church dissipates in God's message, leaving me deflated. When the service ends, I drag my weary bones out of the building and say to Darin, "I think God wants me to write my story."

"Then you should do it," he says without blinking.

"Do you really think so?"

"One hundred percent," he says, grabbing my hand.

I spend the rest of the day in solemn quiet. When God speaks to me, it takes time to digest the magnitude of His request. And as I reflect on all I've been through, and all He's done, my spirit grows heavy, like I'm toting around a huge balloon of tears. When I settle into a warm bath after dinner, those tears pour out of me like rain. I bow my head and let them come, fierce and hot, saying to the Lord, "I want to leave my past behind, not pull it out of the closet and shake it loose!"

I drop a mango bar under the hot water, breathe in the tangy scent, and try to clear my mind.

I know You want me to speak, Lord, but I don't have the words. What is the good news You want me to share? My story is not good news! It's broken, messed up, dirty, filthy news. I shake my head and lean back in the tub. *You are good news, Jesus. But I'm not sure how my story fits into Your pure picture.* I rub my wet hands over my face. *If I struggle to trust You, how can I minister to another person? What do I say?* Silence. *I don't want to, Lord. Please, don't make me do this.*

I slide lower in the tub and let the warm water soothe my weary bones. I close my eyes and take a deep breath. Then I hear Him whisper to my heart. *How long do you think those minutes were in the garden of Gethsemane? The slow tick of time passing as I begged My Father to remove the cup.*

I sit up straight, stop to listen, and hold my breath.

How long do you think it took Judas to leave My company, rally a mob, and climb the hill to arrest Me?

My eyes race over the bubbles in my bath, looking for understanding. I sit, slack jaw, waiting for Him to continue.

How long were those minutes when I waited to die?

My heart thunders in my ears.

I obeyed My Father, even as I sweated blood in the garden.

I don't move a muscle as He whispers, *I was innocent, too.*

I pinch my eyes, work to swallow the sobs moving up my throat.

His voice is soft, merciful, compassionate.

Every minute you suffered. Every touch, every betrayal, every wound inflicted upon you. Where was I?

I see it in my mind's eye, just as He says the words.

The cross.

Jesus knew my suffering as He hung on the cross.

The swing of a hammer slides past my ears, landing with a bang, as iron clangs against iron. Behind closed eyes, I see the point of the stake against His skin. How can this be? Time is linear. Jesus was crucified two millennia ago. Then I remember a day is like a thousand years to God. And a thousand years is like a day.

Our Lord is outside of time. And He doesn't forget.

The Holy Spirit overwhelms me. Sobs steal my breath as I see the Lord, His bloody flesh sticking to the whip flogging His back, milky white bones exposed under swollen skin. Blood covering His face, pouring from His scalp, under a crown of thorns. His body suffocating on a torture device meant for me.

Melissa, your name is written on the palms of My hands. I bear your scars to this very day. I never forget you. Every minute I hung dying, I knew your suffering.

And your father's.

18

Love On The Vine

Dad keeps sucking down the booze, shutting down his liver, and for the umpteenth time, a trip to the emergency room lands him in detox. I'm sure he's dying, but Aunt Shellie hopes for rehabilitation. I think she's dreaming, but love wins again. Miraculously, between the diet of liver wash and the absence of vodka, my father returns home after a four-month stay in rehab.

He cannot care for himself, so Shellie pays his bills, buys his groceries, and cleans his house. She hires a part-time nurse to tend to his physical needs, saying, "Oh, Miss Gina loves caring for your daddy. He sings to Jesus in the shower, prays aloud, and recites Scripture to her. He doesn't have much energy, and he gets confused. But he is peaceful."

When his energy returns, Dad calls me on three separate occasions. And each time he is stone-cold sober. The first two conversations find him somewhat muddled but focused on God. I chuckle when he spends an hour narrating stories of the Old Testament, beginning with Adam and Eve. He skews the facts, and his timeline is off, but I don't correct him. His fragmented mind stays on Jesus, where it should be. He feels safe enough to speak of the Lord as Father, and I honor his love for Christ by listening without interrupting.

The third time he calls, I pick up first ring.

"Dad!"

"Hey, hon! How are you?"

"Good!"

"How's my grandson?"

"Well, Addison graduated from high school last month. Now he's working with Darin at the company."

"Excellent! No college?"

"Addison likes to use his hands. Maybe community college or vocational school?"

"He's going to be a hard-working man, like his daddy! Does he still play guitar?"

"Mostly acoustic. He loves finger-picking, just like you," I say.

"I love that. I'm glad I contributed something positive to his life."

"Addison is such an amazing man, Dad. You'd be proud. He loves Jesus, honors me and Darin. He's honest, has integrity, good character."

"You're a good momma."

"I'm a blessed momma."

"Amen, darlin'. How's that fine husband of yours?"

"Amazing," I say with a smile.

"You married an exceptional man, Melissa."

"I sure did."

"Well, I just called to check on you. I love you very much," he says.

"I love you, too."

"May the Lord bless you and keep you," Dad says, making me smile. "May the Lord make His face shine upon you and be gracious to you. The Lord lift up His countenance upon you and give you peace."

"From the Old Testament book of Numbers," I say.

"Yes, ma'am."

When he says good-bye, I drop my phone and marvel at his words. I witness healing in my dad, the presence of the Holy Spirit giving him love, power, and a sound mind. God is warring for my earthly father, capturing him piece by broken piece. And even though I see them in blinks, like flashes of lightning on a dark horizon, they are there: God's answers to my prayers. I can't understand them yet, can't discern what

He's trying to tell me, but I know He will reveal it in His good timing.

♥

I close my eyes and let sleep work its magic at the end of a long day. Just as I fall into deep slumber, my phone rings. I pick it up and answer. It's Dad. He's drunk. And he's angry.

"Melissa! I've had it with your brother!"

Before he speaks another word, I say, "Dad, I am in bed."

When Dad yells, "You kids cannot disrespect me! I'm your father!" I hang up.

You are not my father, I think, gripping the phone tight as tears pool on the pillow around my ears. *God is my only Father.* And when my phone lights up again, I silence the call, open Dad's name in my contacts, and hit *block.*

Sighing, I recall Paul's words in Romans 7:19: "For I do not do the good I want to do, but the evil I do not want to do—this I keep on doing" (NIV). My poor dad. He is surely doing the evil he does not want to do.

♥

Seven nights later, the vibration of my cell on the nightstand pulls me awake.

"What the . . . ?"

I struggle to fix my sleepy eyes on the screen and see *Aunt Shellie* glaring back at me.

"Oh no," I say, scrambling to grab it. "Oh, no," I whisper again, tears brewing under my lids as I work to slide my finger over the phone one, two, three times.

"Damn it!"

At the fourth swipe, I say, "Hello," and click on the bedside lamp.

"He's gone," she says. "Your daddy died in the ambulance. I'm so sorry . . ."

Her words melt into my ear. I can only pick up fragments. Phrases like "hospital, Friday, transferred to the VA, fine when I left" spill into my racing mind.

Wait! What is happening? Dad is dead? I'm not ready, Lord! I'm not ready. Oh, God, I'm not ready for this! Is he in heaven, Lord? Is Your Word true?

Shellie's quiet sobs pull me to focus. "He started drinking again. I found him swollen, in pain, and rushed him to the hospital."

My mind spins faster than my pounding heart.

I'm not sure I believe God can save my dad now. I want my dad back! He can't die. He's not ready! He's too broken! How can I trust God to save Dad when my dad's a drunk?!

"You know," she whispers. "He was sober for nine months."

I nod my head, unable to tell her I blocked him last week.

"I thought . . ." a pause cuts into her words. "Can you hold on, honey? I'm getting another call," she says. "It's the VA. Why are they calling? I'll call you right back."

I drop the phone, wipe my eyes on my pajamas, look over at Darin, and say, "He's probably not dead."

He chuckles. "Wouldn't that be just like him?"

I sniffle and remember Dad's brushes with death. In Vietnam, in car wrecks, in taking too many pills. Once the hospital even toe-tagged him! He frightened a nurse when he pulled back the sheet and asked her what was going on. They thought he was dead then, too!

My phone rings. "You will not believe this," says Aunt Shellie.

I catch my breath. "He's not dead?"

"Lord, have mercy, he's not dead," she says. "The VA could not find his DNR, so they resuscitated him at the hospital! Hell, he'd been dead in the ambulance for at least twenty minutes! The paramedics knew not to resuscitate, but the VA started pumping his chest when he arrived. They just called me for permission to stop, and when I answered, they got a rhythm."

"Why in the world would they resuscitate him when he'd

been gone twenty minutes?" I ask.

It feels as if God and the world are battling over my dad. Like the devil's gripping one arm, and God's yanking the other, in a maddening game of tug-o-war. I consider all my father has been through. His pain. His struggle. His loss. As my thoughts race, God whispers to my heart, reminds me how we don't save ourselves. We can't purchase a ticket to heaven by being good, doing good, or making the right choices.

We are saved by His grace and His grace alone.

Then it dawns on me . . . *My dad was in heaven, and they brought him back?*

I glance at Darin and shake my head.

"I told them to call you, honey," Shellie says.

My phone chimes into her sentence. "I'll call you back," I say, pulling the phone away to answer the VA.

Again, I pick up word fragments like "dead on arrival, could not find the form, resuscitated, got him back just as we called your aunt." My mind wades through the doctor's thick Eastern accent. *God, help me understand this man!* "Your dad is in a coma," says the doctor. "He has only 10 percent brain activity. I've given him powerful drugs and shocked his heart into rhythm. Your aunt gave me permission to place a central line."

The image of my dad's bare chest fills my mind. His olive skin, the faded green wizard tattoo over his heart. His flesh stretched from seventy years of hard living. They want to cut him open? In my mind, I see light reflect off the scalpel, feel the slice of the blade. *No*, I think. *No more pain for this poor man. No more.*

"No central line," I say. "You can honor Shellie's request and place the line, if you must. But I am telling you, as his daughter, I do not want a central line."

The doctor sighs.

"Your dad is on a ventilator," he says.

Why didn't You just take him, God? Hasn't he been through enough pain? I don't understand. But even as I pray the words, I do understand. God is giving me an opportunity to see His grace, His mercy at work. God is telling me He is enough. God is allowing me to see the battle and surrender all my hope to Him. God is also showing me the immense power of prayer and the Holy Spirit living inside me. His word says I carry the same Holy Spirit power that raised Jesus from the dead. And He's demonstrating that with my earthly father. Didn't I just pray and beg the Lord to leave my dad here? The mystery of it all blows my mind.

"Miss? Are you there?"

"Yes, I'm here."

"I need your permission to shut off life support."

"I need to talk to my brother. Give me until five a.m.," I say.

Darin and I drive an hour up Mt. St. Helens to Lake Merwin. We find Stacy's campsite, give him the news. He agrees to unplug Dad.

By the time we get home, the sun is rising, and Dad is gone.

♥

I make a cup of tea, relax on the steps of our back patio, plop on headphones, and turn on Dad's playlist. These are some of the best songs in the world. The music I twirled to when I was five, strutted to when I was thirteen, cried to when I was twenty, thirty, and today. "Dust in the Wind" serenades my ears and tears pour down my face as I remember the good parts of my father. His musical heart, his willingness to seek truth, his fiery love for Jesus and his family. His confession, apology, and desire for restoration.

I close my eyes, imagine him in heaven. His dark hair full of body and shine, skin free of lines. Old and wise in a young man's body. His smile soft and true. No shadows lurk in his eyes, no sadness taints his countenance. His fingers pick out the last of the song. His falsetto harmonizes to the music in my ears. He sets his guitar aside and joy spills from him like light as he tells me how wonderful the Lord's paradise is, says he can't wait for me to see it.

I see Mom, too. Her skin milky white and worry free. She wears a dress the color of rainbow purple. It sits off-shoulder to reveal the curve of her neck, the graceful lines of her collar bones. A crown of lavender flowers rests atop her auburn hair. Her eyes sparkle gray, and her smile lights the space around her.

Tears cover my cheeks as I soak in the truth. My parents are alive, together, in the eternal love of Christ. There is no greater hope than in Him.

♥

Stacy and I fly to Arkansas to collect photographs and trinkets from Dad's house. "Do you think we'll find anything good?" he asks as we make the two-hour drive from Little Rock to Monticello.

His question makes me laugh because my parents never had anything of monetary value. They were quick to give it away, share it with friends, or stick it in a pipe and smoke it. What's more, Shellie removed four scruffy drug addicts from Dad's house when he went into recovery.

"The people living with him stole a bunch of his stuff, didn't they?" Stacy asks.

I nod and say, "His gun, Xbox, games, Mom's silver dollars. And his car."

Stacy shakes his head.

"We came for the pictures," I remind him.

"I sure hope Shellie told everyone to stay away until we are ready for company," he says.

We roll into Dad's cul-de-sac to find three cars and a pickup in the drive.

"Crap," Stacy says, stopping several yards back. "People are here. What should we do?"

"I really wanted to walk into his house alone," I say.

"Me, too. It's been years since we've been here."

"I know. I need a minute. Let's just park and stretch a bit," I say.

Stacy turns off the truck, and we take a stroll away from Dad's to gather our emotions before meandering back toward the house. Aunt Shellie and Dad's best friend, Tanner, meet us outside.

Tanner gives me a hug, saying, "Clint was mighty proud of you kids."

I nod, fighting the tears streaming down my face.

"Your daddy was my best friend," he says, pulling out a hanky.

"He'd come stay with me, go hunting and fishing. I miss him."

My brother embraces Aunt Shellie while I study Tanner, the blush of his cheeks and light in his eyes. Dad confessed to his best friend, and Tanner accepted him. We exchange a long look, an intimate knowledge of loving the broken. I give him another hug, walk toward Shellie, and pull her close. Awe pours over me as I hold her in my arms. Dad was unkind to her, drove her away many times, and she never gave up on him. I marvel as I consider the people who loved the man I couldn't bear to be around, and I think …

You did such a good job caring for him, Lord.

As we cross the threshold into Dad's home, I step into the time capsule of my childhood. The houses may have changed over the years, but the trinkets on the shelves, the photos on the walls, the treasures in the drawers never did. Momma packed up every gumball machine toy we ever gave her and hauled them from place to place, as though she could still see the tiny hands and shiny eyes of our childhood wrapped around each knickknack. This may have been Dad's house in the end, but it was our home from the beginning.

The smell of nicotine stains and Dad's cologne lingers in the air. My eyes traverse kitchen countertops, the bar separating the living room from the nook. Dad's hats line the windowpane, photos of Stacy and I, along with our families, pepper the fridge, the cabinets, and the walls.

My daddy's uncle sneaks up to me, wraps me in his arms, and hands me a small fabric bag. "This belonged to my sister. Jeannie Lue."

"Grandma J," I say, opening the bag to retrieve a diamond heart pendant encased in white gold.

"She never forgot her time with you. You had quite an impact on her life. I wanted you to have a piece of her."

Tears fill his eyes and mine as we gaze at each other.

"Thank you," I whisper.

I remember him telling me once, many years ago, "You are the spitting image of your grandmother," and I am honored to be a part of her DNA.

Stacy walks up to shake his hand, freeing me to wander Momma's kitchen. I open a cabinet. Her mixing bowls and casserole dishes line the shelves. I finger the thrift store plates we ate from as kids. Her measuring cups, cheese grater, cutting boards, and spoon rest remind me of Toll House cookies, cheesewiches, and sugar donuts.

I pad down the hall, touch the petite gold frames housing school and family portraits. At the spare room, I freeze at the sight of the important nothings lining the particleboard desk Mom and I built when I was in college. The old blue penny bank stares at me from the top shelf. It's not a pig, but rather a plastic money bag with a giant yellow head poking out the top. I reach for him, flip him over, knowing that his plug is missing. "Mom used to stuff a sock in that hole," I whisper to no one. Memories of dumping pennies from his base, to buy candy or play blackjack with Stacy, fill my mind.

"Aunt Kathy's record holder," I say, lifting off the fuzzy, pink cover to run my hands over her smooth forty-fives. Mom's favorite song was "Patches" by Clarence Carter. I never told Mom I accidently broke the "Patches" record and hid it away inside the cover of my Grease album.

A stained-glass jewelry box sits on the corner of the desk. Inside I find Momma's turquoise ring. Worthless to a drug addict looking to make a buck, it lay perfectly preserved for me. I free it from tangled neck chains and work it onto my finger. "I can't believe it fits."

I wander across the hall to the bedroom, drag open the chest of drawers, and giggle as I unearth sequined headbands from ballet, ticket stubs from high school plays Mom and I saw together, and a small bowling trophy marked number 1. I think Momma joined a bowling league when we first moved to Washington. Again, those years are foggy. No matter how hard I try, the memories won't come.

I kneel, open a lower drawer, pull out baby clothes, infant spoons, and cloth diapers. "These were Momma's," I whisper, fingering the ribbon and lace my grandmother stitched over each gown. In the next drawer I discover the nightshirts and cotton socks Mom wore in the nursing home. I finger the fuzzy polyester that kept Mom warm before she died, consider the contrast of life and death tucked side by side in Momma's dresser drawers.

I drag my weary bones to stand. I flip open the top of Mom's wooden jewelry case, pull out a tiny bottle of Forever Krystle, pop the plug out for a long sniff, and marinate in the musky scent of 1987. Mom teaching me to drive the VW, Christmas morning cinnamon rolls, snuggling up beside her to watch a movie. Her falling asleep in the first five minutes. Mom shoving her finger down the center of her sugar cone at Baskin Robbins, "to get the ice cream to the bottom of the cone," she'd say. I'd tell her to use a spoon, like a civilized person. She'd giggle. Every single time.

A stack of books lies on her nightstand. I free a red-letter King James Bible from the stack, open it at the bookmark, and find a note penned in Dad's scribble: *tears in a bottle.* His writing is from Psalm 56:8 which says, *God counts our tears and stores them in His bottle.* My eyes water as I recall God ministering the same verse to me during therapy.

I put the Bible aside, walk toward the closet filled with Dad's flannels, jeans, old t-shirts. His cowboy boots and tennis shoes line the floor, leather belts hang from a hook on the wall. The western cap he wore to play music rests beside them. I run my hands over the bedspread while I gaze at the photos peppering the walls, dresser, and the night stands. Family pictures aged where they rest.

I meander back to the living room, relax in Dad's worn leather recliner, pull out his Bible and thumb through the pages. My eyes wander over the space Dad spent his last days in. Random knickknacks, Mom's collection of David Winter Cottages, and Troll dolls line the shelves of his curio cabinet. The white ceramic cockatoo I painted for them so many years ago sits perched atop the television stand.

"I can't believe he kept all this stuff," I whisper under my breath.

Dad entertained more than one girlfriend over the years. One even redecorated his house after Mom was gone. I sincerely did not think any of our childhood trinkets would have survived those relationships. But they did. And my heart melts at realizing just how much our dad loved us.

As the day winds down, Aunt Shellie and her daughter make a run to the store. When they return, Aunt Shellie says, "We saw the most amazing rainbow on our way home! It was the biggest rainbow I've ever seen!"

I laugh and think, *Of course they saw a rainbow!*

I should tell them, should say something about the mystery of God and His love, but my tongue is too tired to speak.

The next morning, Stacy and I rise early and race to Walmart for boxes and packing tape. Our flight leaves in twenty-four hours, giving us precious little time to treasure hunt before our drive back to the airport in Little Rock. We box, tape, and label quick as we can, packing up old vinyl albums, Dad's army uniform and music, Mom's wedding dress and cookbooks, along with photo albums and other mementos. Just when I think we're done, I open an old metal box and pull out a stack of letters bundled with yellow twine.

"What the—?" I flip them over and inspect the script. "Oh my gosh! These are from Mom!"

"What are they?" Stacy asks, taping a box shut.

"Letters! Stacks of them! To the grandparents! And Dad!"

"Seriously?"

"Yes!" I say, working one from the stack. "May 26, 1988," I read aloud, "Dear Folks . . ." I skim to the second paragraph, "We are now an all-American family. Everyone has a job. Yes, everyone. Missy got hired at Burger Barn—she starts Monday. Only one problem: She needs a pair of brown polyester pants. Have you seen them in a size 3?" I look up at Stacy, mouth agape in wonder. "Can you believe this? Grandma saved them for her."

"Looks like there's a bunch of them," he says, shoving boxes toward the door.

Thumbing over them, I glance at the postmarks. "We have mail dating back to 1969. These are love notes they wrote when Dad was in the brig. Remember, he went AWOL to propose to Mom?"

Stacy keeps packing, far less enchanted than I.

I refold the letters, tuck them in the pile, retie the twine, and hold them close to my heart.

"These are riding on the airplane with me."

The next day, I tote those notes onto the plane, housed in one of Dad's old suitcases. Stacy and I settle into our seats, buckle up, and snooze for the better part of the flight. Every so often, I glance out the window to admire the landscape, waking Stacy when we fly over the Great Salt Lake. As Stacy settles back in his seat and I stare out the window, an odd arc appears in the sky.

"What is that?"

"Huh?" Stacy asks, pulling open his sleepy eyes.

"What the heck is that?" I ask, poking him in the shoulder.

"What's what?" he asks, glancing out the small rectangle.

"Is that—a fogbow?" I ask.

"Beats me. I don't see it," he says, reclining back in his seat.

I pull out my phone, snap a photo, and study the image. The

shape of a rainbow appears in hues of gray and white.

"That is a colorless rainbow," I say. *That would be my dad's rainbow.* I laugh. God is funny. And He's weird. Just like us. Not ten minutes later, I look out the window again. This time, a sliver of color hovers among the clouds, all bright reds and greens and blues. *And that,* I think to myself, *would be my mother's rainbow.*

19

Life Untangled

I sit at my desk and peer out the picture window of my office. Sunlight streams into the room, lighting the dust bunnies and dog dander floating in the air. Two sleeping bulldogs snore at my feet, grounding me in the present as I journey through the past. A stack of Momma's letter's rests beside me, unfolded with tender care, and placed in a three-ring binder. Her words fill in the blanks and pull memories to life from my childhood. Good memories. When I read them or touch the paper, I hear her voice, hear her laugh. She is alive to me in the script and scribbles covering her worn stationery.

God is calling me to write my story. We are currently wrestling over logistics. But I obey, best I can, by documenting the evil done to me and God's redemptive hand working in my life. As I stand at the kitchen island, tapping on the keyboard, going back over my document for edits, I arrive at age eleven. I read the words aloud and images fill my mind. Moving to Washington, unpacking my canopy bed, resting on plush brown carpet, hanging my unicorn mobile. My friendship with Jess and Kim. And just when I'm about to move on to the next chapter, without a stitch of effort, an image drops into my mind.

I drop my head and swallow rapidly. *What was that?* It happens again and I hear Dad ask, "Has your period started?"

My heart pounds in my ears as I slide down to the floor and bury my face in my hands. The memory takes on a life of its own. I cannot stop it from flooding my senses. I see the cover on Momma's bed. Thin, white, embroidered fabric with small eyelets and lace. "Oh my, Lord!" I cry out from the hardwood floor.

This is not the memory of me selling out after Dad caught me skipping school. It is not the memory of our trip to the Aqua Chutes. It is not the memory of Dad standing naked, attempting to reveal himself to my friend. This one is different. And it's graphic.

It's not rape. But it's close.

It is the lost memory I worked so hard to unbury. The escalation of abuse in living color. There are no words to describe the feelings rushing over me. I am stunned, shocked by waves of sickening grief for the little girl who knew too much. My bulldog climbs onto my lap, his stubby paws digging into my thighs. He licks at my chin, trying to distract me from the shadow of despair hovering in the room. I hug him tight and bury my face in his silky fur as tears spill over my cheeks like hot tar.

I cry until I remember Dad's cremains resting under a cabinet in my bathroom. I want to rip the lid off the plastic box and dump his ashes into my septic tank, bypass the toilet all together. He is not worthy of a flush.

I yank my phone out of my pocket and type a message to Stacy: "I unblocked a horrible memory. I want to dump Dad's ashes in my septic tank with all the other shit!"

I stare at my phone and watch the dots blink.

Stacy's text bubble lights up: "Don't do that, Mis."

My fingers fly over the phone: "I hate him!"

I sob out loud, thankful my brother can't hear the anguish in my voice.

Stacy replies: "I know. But please don't flush him."

I scream and type: "I'm not going to flush him! I'm going to dump him!"

"Don't dump him, Mis."

I stare at the text bubbles on my phone, the dot, dot, dot blinking in my face as I take one heavy breath, then another. Deep inside, I understand why God never gave me those images before. He needed me sane, to talk with my dad, to see the redemption. The Lord waited until just the right time to reveal the last ugly image stuck behind the curtains of my mind. I thank Him for protecting me, for loving me, and for redeeming me. And for the last time, after several deep breaths and a long prayer, I forgive my father.

I kiss my dog, work to stand, and blow my nose. Grabbing a soda from the fridge, I crack it open and take a long sip as my phone lights up with Stacy's words: "Just hang on a little longer."

♥

I stand on the cedar plank bridge next to Stacy. The air is always damp here, on the East Fork of the Lewis River. With tall fir trees shading the ground, soil pulpy from ancient rains, and mist evaporating off the falls, this place is a haven when the heat arrives in the Pacific Northwest. And this haven was our family's watering hole, our stomping grounds on those sweltering summer days. We'd follow the lure shining atop Dad's fishing pole, its point jutting high above the foliage, as he led us off the beaten path toward the falls.

"There's better fishing down here," he'd say. "Not so many people."

I'd dodge the spider webs strung like hammocks between the trees, careful to stay behind Mom and Stacy so I didn't walk into a sticky trap. I hated spiders, especially the backwoods variety, with their sharp points, striped legs, and fat bodies. I could just imagine the horror of stepping into a web, its silky tendrils caking my cheeks as I shrieked, "Where's the spider?!"

I giggle at the thought.

"What are you laughing at?" Stacy asks.

I shake my head and say, "Nothing."

Stacy and I journeyed up here for the day to remember and celebrate our parents. Thirteen years ago, just a quarter mile upriver, Dad and Stacy scattered their portion of Mom's ashes into the falls. Today we laid our father to rest in the same manner. I steal a glance at my baby brother. My fiercest protector. I marvel at how God has changed us, grown us, marked us. I look down at the plastic urn sitting at my brother's feet and consider how we got here. Not to the woods, not to the river, or to the bridge. I ponder the here in our hearts. How we got here. To this healthy spot in our lives. I ponder how truth splits open the heart's crevice, lets the light spill in, and scares the monsters away.

I ponder the Lord's mystery.

"I used to jump off this bridge," Stacy says, slapping the rail.

"I know," I say, glancing at the *no jumping* sign nailed in front of us.

"You and Mom sat right there and watched me," he says, pointing at the rocks below.

"Yep," I say, "we sure did."

From the river's edge, the bridge is stunning, with its wide arch spanning the narrow waterway and thick timber legs thrusting it skyward. It stands a majestic fifty-two feet above the water, high enough to break a leg or a neck, should a swimmer land the wrong way. Momma hid her eyes every time Stacy jumped. And I don't blame her. Watching my fifteen-year-old brother climb onto the rail, tuck his arms in tight, and drop like a bullet was unnerving, even for me.

"She hated it when I jumped," he says.

"It gave her gray hair," I say.

"No way I'd do it now," he says, looking down.

"You're lucky you didn't die," I say.

"I wasn't scared of anything when I was a kid."

"And I was scared of everything," I respond.

We stand in silence a moment, let the autumn breeze cool our skin, and watch Dad's thick, white cremains trickle down from the falls. Grainy remnants collect in the pools of shallow rocks and cling to the fallen red leaves dotting the placid water. But the bulk of Dad's ashes weave below us like a ribbon of smoke.

"You know, Mis, I've told lots of people what Dad did to you," Stacy says, folding his hands around the railing of the bridge. "And I swore I'd never speak those words aloud. Swore I'd never tell a soul."

"And?" I ask.

"And now the secret doesn't haunt me. It doesn't live inside me anymore," he says.

I study my brother's olive skin, the crow's feet around his eyes, the splashes of silver lighting his five o'clock shadow. Underneath his left arm a tattoo marks his skin. A tattoo matching my own. I look at the word *Free* scrolled across my arm, punctuated by a sparrow in flight. This is the only mark on my body. The only scar to tell the tales of where I've been. I smile at Stacy, weave my arm through his, and remember how we got here. Our stories are different, but they are the same. Baptized in the same pain, in the same water, in the same blood, in the same Spirit.

I resist the urge to kiss his cheeks and run my hand over his bald head. Instead, I look at the sapphire sky and think about the thief on the cross. He had to know something about Jesus. The thief certainly knew Jesus was innocent. Had Jesus invited the thief to follow Him, and the thief refused? Did the thief listen to the Lord from afar while sucking down a bottle of wine and lamenting over his sorry life? Was the thief like Dad? Wretched until the end? Incapable of saving himself—or doing even one good thing?

Hanging on a cross beside Jesus, the thief recognized his own guilt, and cried out, "Lord, remember me when you come into your kingdom." God's Word says all who call on the name of the Lord shall be saved. So Jesus said to the thief, "I tell you today you will be with me in paradise" (Luke 23:42–43 NIV).

I remember calling out to Jesus all those nights I lay barfing beside someone's toilet. Crying out to Him when Dad beat Stacy or our animals, when the sound of wailing and squealing drowned out the thumping of my heart. I remember crying out to Him when Dad screamed in my face, accusing me of things

I didn't do. I remember crying out to Him when I wanted to die.

And I remember how He saved me. Saved my brother, saved my parents. I remember Him breaking the generational curse, blessing my son with His Presence and the saving grace of Jesus. I remember Him giving me beauty for ashes and a new song in my heart. Best of all, I remember Him giving me the sacred, glorious, holy grace of Jesus Christ, our Lord.

I smile at the thought. And in my heart, I whisper the words only God can hear, *Thank You, Father. Thank you for setting us free.*

EPILOGUE

Then you will know the truth, and the truth will set you free.
—John 8:32 (NIV)

Addison playing guitar . . . age twenty.

ACKNOWLEDGMENTS

Jesus: Thank You for writing my story and allowing me to be Your coauthor. There is no more blessed gift than me knowing You and You knowing me!

Darin: For always offering all of yourself to the world, for inspiring me to be my best, for prompting me to get my lazy butt out of bed and get to work, and for loving me in my broken. You are my hero among heroes, my man among men, and the greatest husband a girl could ask for. I love you more. Always and forever.

Addison: For forgiving all my failings, loving me unconditionally, letting me be me, even as your crazy mom. For all the late-night trips to the grocery store, for playing "Dust in the Wind" on your guitar, for wrestling on the trampoline, rides in the Gator, and rides in your truck. For sticky floors and stickier faces. God knew I needed a boy to love. You are stitched into the fabric of my heart for all of eternity. I love you, child.

Stacy: A girl could not ask for a better brother. When I see how you are loved, how your personality touches this world, I am honored to have shared my childhood with you. I hold a slot in your life no other can claim—sister. I am honored to share your DNA, your blood, your history. There are no words for how much I love you. We are the last two of four.

Brian: Thank you for having the heart and the courage to find us, invite us into your life, and invest in discovering your roots. Knowing you now is a blessing, even as I wish I had known you before. Oh, so many days I needed an older brother. But I'll take what I can get and be ever so grateful. May God bless us with time to know each other more. I love you.

Lana: May God bless you for filling my shoes in the tumultuous job only you could handle. For your faithfulness to listen to God, even when he carried you back to a house of madness. For your friendship in a place where friendship felt impossible. For reading this book in the earliest stage of creation and then reading it again. You are a champion, Girl, and I love you.

My Prayer Warriors: Mary Ann, Marilyn, Vikki, Katherine, Reenie, and the many others I cannot name. Your prayers carried me through this process. God gave me the strength to reenter the past, type it on the page, and give it away, because of you. Truly, you have taught me what a difference prayer makes in each of our lives. I love you as Jesus does—my sisters in Christ.

Pastor Trish: For having the strength to enter my darkness, for viewing my story through the lens of Scripture, for taking the time to read it thoroughly, and for the excellent notes you gave me! You changed this book for the better. Thank you for blessing me and my readers.

Kathy: Thank you for always protecting my heart, for giving me tools for my toolbox, for making me feel welcome and normal, and for loving my broken. You changed my life. May God bless you for the unconditional love you pour into fractured souls.

Christi Krug: Thank you for teaching me to show, show, show, my story, rather than to tell it; thank you for your kind, encouraging words and for giving me the courage to add the hard parts.

My Beta-Readers – Lana, Jocelyn, Belinda, Nancy, Kate, Amy, Trish, and Kathy. Your willingness to dive into my story inspired me to keep writing. Thank you for spending your time investing in me and the people reading this book. The value of your feedback cannot be measured. May God bless each of you for loving Him and loving me.

Margot Starbuck: I love your style. Thank you for handling these words with kindness and humility, for allowing me to discover my own errors through your gentle prompting, and for your honesty. I love your spirit, your humor, and the fun emails. You are a diamond among treasures.

Erin Healy: You were my first reader. From the first ten thousand words, your tact and gentle spirit allowed me the courage to move about the garden, scatter my ashes, then harvest the roses from the soil of this writing. I found the courage to pen my pain because you treated me with such kindness during my excursion through *The Creative Way*. May God bless you richly for your faithfulness.

Evelyn Bence: Thank you for your wise and thorough review. Your experience and insight led to the final completion of this book. Your notation of my silly mistakes humbled me and made me laugh. Guess I'm not such a grammar goodie after all.

Mike and Denise: Thank you for always being there, for the super-fun photo shoot, the enchiladas and margaritas, the pictures for my wall, and for loving Darin and me. Best Friends Forever.

Mary Ann: "Your friendship is where I hang my heart." Thank you for creating the beautiful bee intended to grace the cover of this book. Your work of art inspired my own. And thank you for all the car prayers. I learned to call God Father because of you. I love you.

Marilyn: For the thousands of prayers, for knowing the real me and still loving me, for treating me better than a sister ever could, for feeding my tummy when my soul was hungry. You helped heal me when neither of us knew I needed it, not once, not twice, but three times. I love you.

JOT Staff: Without your hard work and support, I could not have stayed home to write this book. You are a blessing to our family, our business, and our community. May God's favor rest upon each of you.

Olson Family: Y'all are a tough bunch! Thank you for sharpening my iron. I sure hope I sharpened yours, too. All my love.

ABOUT THE AUTHOR

Melissa Kay Olson

Melissa survived fifteen years of sexual abuse. Unable to fully trust God, she spent decades reading, researching, and wrestling with Him to find the narrow path to freedom. Today she uses the voice God gave her to write the messy stories of her life, beginning with her debut memoir Broken Girl Fly. Melissa lives in the Pacific Northwest with her husband, her son, and her favorite creature in this world - Yogi - her snoring, farting, obnoxiously stubborn English bulldog. You can connect with Melissa at www.brokengirlfly.com.

Made in the USA
Coppell, TX
26 May 2023